go getter 4

Students' Book

Jayne Croxford • Graham Fruen

Contents

▶ Grammar/Communication video   ▶ Grammar animation   ▶ Culture video

Unit	Vocabulary	Grammar	Skills	Revision
0 **Get started!** p.4	• Free-time activities • Adjectives • Weather	• Present Simple and Present Continuous, stative verbs [Exam] ▶ • Present Continuous for future arrangements • Comparative and superlative adjectives • Articles: *a/an*, *the*, 0 article • *was*, *were* [Exam]	**Communication:** Introducing oneself, talking about arrangements, opinions, holidays	
1 **Who we are** p.10	• Clothes and accessories • Describing clothes [Exam] • Hairstyles • Personality adjectives • Negative adjectives	• Past Simple [Exam] ▶▶ • Past Continuous and Past Simple [Exam] ▶	**Communication:** Telling a story and reacting [Exam] **Reading:** Teenage fashions [Exam] **Listening:** First impressions **Writing:** Describing a friend	Language Revision [Exam] Pronunciation: /s/ and /ʃ/
p.22	**BBC Get Culture!** Clothes for special occasions [Exam] ▶ The history of tweed **Project:** Clothes for a special occasion (a video or a poster)			
2 **Working hard** p.24	• Jobs • Describing jobs [Exam] • *make* and *do* • Learning and exams • Expressions with *take*	• *have to*, *must*, *mustn't* [Exam] ▶▶ • *had to*, *could* ▶	**Communication:** Asking for and giving advice [Exam] **Reading:** Weird and wonderful jobs [Exam] **Listening:** Learning and exams [Exam] **Writing:** Describing a school [Exam]	Language Revision [Exam] Pronunciation: /h/
p.36	Skills Revision 1&2 [Exam]			
3 **That's exciting!** p.38	• Experiences [Exam] • Sports verbs • Sports equipment • Compound nouns	• Present Perfect, *ever* and *never* ▶▶ • Present Perfect with *just*, *already* and *yet* ▶	**Communication:** Instructions [Exam] **Reading:** Girl power [Exam] **Listening:** Skydiving [Exam] **Writing:** A holiday email	Language Revision [Exam] Pronunciation: /ʊ/ and /uː/
p.50	**BBC Get Culture!** Extreme sports ▶ Sports in the Lake District **Project:** A popular or extreme sport (a digital presentation)			
4 **A good story** p.52	• Types of films and books [Exam] • Life stages • Film jobs • Verbs followed by a preposition	• Present Perfect with *for* and *since* [Exam] ▶▶ • Present Perfect and Past Simple ▶	**Communication:** Making and accepting apologies [Exam] **Reading:** Don't forget to be awesome! [Exam] **Listening:** An extra [Exam] **Writing:** A review	Language Revision [Exam] Pronunciation: /ɔː/
p.64	Skills Revision 3&4 [Exam]			

Contents

Unit	Vocabulary	Grammar	Skills	Revision
5 **Don't stop the music!** p.66	• Music styles and instruments • Music collocations Exam • Crime • Personal qualities • Adjectives from nouns	• *going to* and *will* Exam • Defining relative clauses with *who, which, that, where*	**Communication:** Talking about plans Exam **Reading:** Alma Deutscher – the new Mozart? **Listening:** A talent show **Writing:** An email asking for information	Language Revision Exam Pronunciation: /w/ and /v/
p.78	**BBC Get Culture!** **Festivals** ▶ The Notting Hill Carnival **Project:** A school festival (a video invitation)			
6 **Protect the planet** p.80	• Wild animals • Environment verbs Exam • Natural events • Big numbers	• First conditional • Verbs followed by infinitive or *-ing*	**Communication:** Persuading Exam **Reading:** Message in a bottle Exam **Listening:** Natural events Exam **Writing:** A leaflet with tips or instructions	Language Revision Exam Pronunciation: /θ/ and /f/
p.92	Skills Revision 5&6 Exam			
7 **Material world** p.94	• Materials • Adjectives to describe objects • Verbs of discovery and creativity • Technology verbs • Phrasal verbs with *up* and *down*	• Present Simple passive • Past Simple passive	**Communication:** Asking for clarification and checking understanding Exam **Reading:** What's it made of? Exam **Listening:** Your favourite gadgets Exam **Writing:** Describing a popular product	Language Revision Exam Pronunciation: voiced or voiceless endings
p.106	**BBC Get Culture!** **American cities** Exam ▶ New York City **Project:** A famous landmark (a digital presentation)			
8 **That's life** p.108	• Relationships and conflicts Exam • Feelings • Extreme adjectives	• *be allowed to* and *let* Exam • Revision of tenses Exam	**Communication:** Sympathising and encouraging Exam **Reading:** Bedroom battles Exam **Listening:** Bullying Exam **Writing:** Replying to a problem page letter	Language Revision Exam Pronunciation: /aʊ/ and /əʊ/
p.120	Skills Revision 7&8 Exam			
p.122	Extra reference: Student A activities			
p.123	Wordlist			
p.127	Irregular verbs			
p.128	Extra reference: Student B activities			

0 Get started!

What are they doing? I can use the present tenses.

In this unit

Vocabulary
- Free-time activities
- Adjectives
- Weather

Grammar
- Present Simple, Present Continuous, stative verbs
- Present Continuous for future arrangements
- Comparative and superlative adjectives
- Articles: *a*, *an*, *the* and 0 article
- *was*, *were*

0.1 Intro Video

Hello!

Adam: Hi, I'm Adam. I'm fourteen and I love animals and nature. I want to become a vet when I'm older. At the weekend, I often hang out with my friends, and we sometimes play basketball. At the moment, I'm waiting for my friend Josh. Where is he? He's always late!

Josh: Hi, I'm Josh and I'm fifteen. I live with my mum, dad and sister. This is my bedroom. I love Saturday mornings. I get up late, have a big breakfast, and then I … oh, that's my phone. What? Really? OK, give me ten minutes … Sorry, my friend Adam is waiting for me. I need to hurry!

Bella: Hi, I'm Bella. I'm fourteen years old and I live with my mum. My mum's from Italy, and this is her café. She's making a chocolate cake at the moment. Mmm, that looks good! Mum works really hard, so at the weekend I sometimes help her. I'm working right now, so I can't talk. See you later!

Zadie: Hi, I'm Zadie and I'm fifteen. I play the guitar and I sing. At the weekend I often practise with my band. At the moment I'm trying to learn a new song. I'm watching an online video to help me. I know the words, but the music is hard. I need to practise a little bit more … so bye for now!

1 ▶ 1 🔊 1.2 Watch or listen and read. Who:
1 likes music?
2 wants to work with animals?
3 is half Italian?
4 has got a sister?

2 Exam Spot Introduce yourself and say what you usually do at the weekend.

Hi. I'm … and I'm fifteen years old. At the weekend, I usually …

Grammar Present Simple and Present Continuous

	Present Simple		Present Continuous	
+	I **work** hard.	My mum **works** hard.	I**'m working** now.	He**'s working** now.
−	I **don't work** hard.	My mum **doesn't work** hard.	I**'m not working** now.	He **isn't working** now.
?	**Do** you **work** hard?	**Does** she **work** hard?	**Are** you **working** now?	**Is** he **working** now?
	Yes, I **do**. / No, I **don't**.	Yes, she **does**. / No, she **doesn't**.	Yes, I **am**. / No, I**'m not**.	Yes, he **is**. / No, he **isn't**.
	Where **do** you **work**?		What **are** you **doing**?	
Time expressions				
	always, usually, often, sometimes, never		now, right now, at the moment	

3 Circle the correct answer.

1 On school days, Bella (doesn't help) / isn't helping at her mum's café, but today is Saturday, so Bella helps / is helping at the café.
2 Right now, Zadie learns / is learning a new song. She learns / is learning a new song every month.
3 Adam often plays / is playing basketball with his friends, but he doesn't play / isn't playing at the moment.
4 Usually, Josh doesn't get up / isn't getting up early at the weekend, but he gets up / is getting up now because Adam is waiting for him!

4 Complete the dialogue with the correct form of the verbs.

Zadie: Hi, Adam. What ¹ _are you doing_ (you / do)? Do you want to meet?

Adam: Sorry, Zadie. I can't right now. I'm with Adam. We ² _____ (play) basketball.

Zadie: Oh, that's a pity … ³ _____ (you / always / play) basketball on Saturday mornings?

Adam: No, not every week, but I ⁴ _____ (often / do) sport. What ⁵ _____ (you / do) at the moment?

Zadie: I'm by the river. I ⁶ _____ (take) my dog for a walk. He ⁷ _____ (sometimes / go) for a swim, but he ⁸ _____ (not swim) at the moment. Oh, yes, he is! Speak to you later!

Adam: Bye for now!

Grammar Stative verbs

We don't usually use the Present Continuous with these verbs:
believe, hate, know, like, love, need, understand, want
I like animals. ✔ NOT ~~I'm liking animals.~~ ✘

5 Complete the sentences with the correct form of the verbs in the Present Simple or the Present Continuous.

1 Josh and Adam _are practising_ (practise) basketball now. They _____ (want) to do well in the match!

2 Bella's mum _____ (hate) cleaning tables, so Bella _____ (help) her at the moment.

3 Josh's sister _____ (believe) studying is important. She _____ (do) her online French homework right now.

4 Josh's parents are in the kitchen. They _____ (plan) a family meal. They _____ (need) to plan a meal for ten people!

6 **Exam Spot** In pairs, talk about your best friend, brother or sister and parents. What are they doing now? What do they like and hate doing?

0.2 I'm working on Sunday
I can use the Present Continuous for future arrangements.

See you on Sunday!

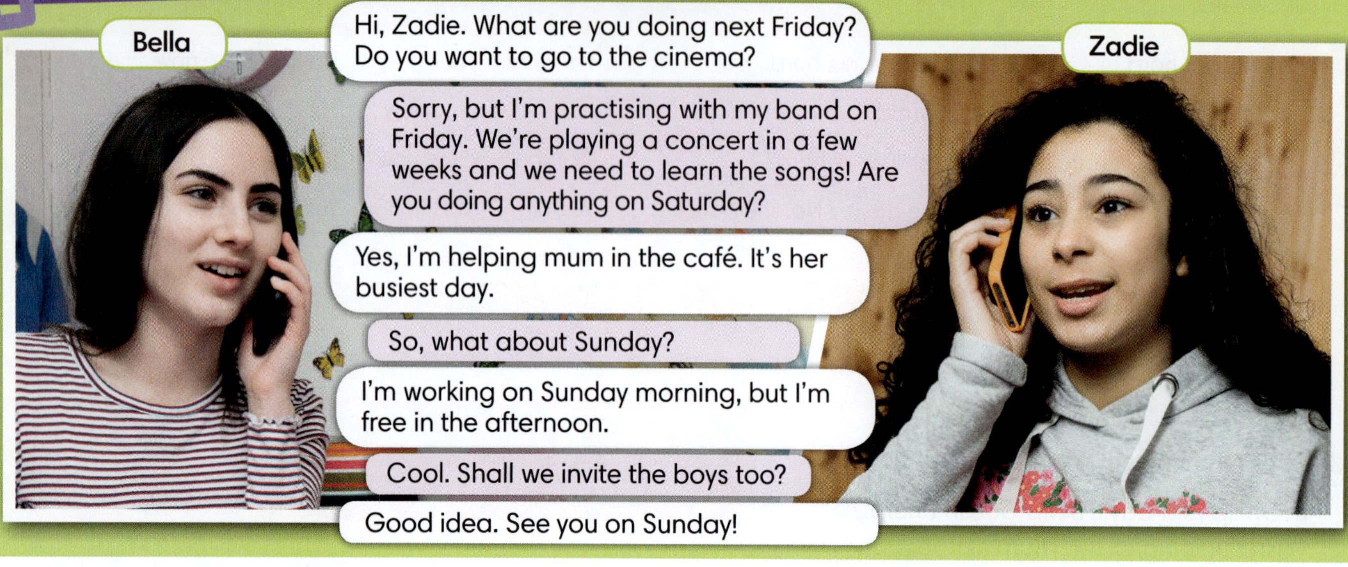

Bella: Hi, Zadie. What are you doing next Friday? Do you want to go to the cinema?

Zadie: Sorry, but I'm practising with my band on Friday. We're playing a concert in a few weeks and we need to learn the songs! Are you doing anything on Saturday?

Bella: Yes, I'm helping mum in the café. It's her busiest day.

Zadie: So, what about Sunday?

Bella: I'm working on Sunday morning, but I'm free in the afternoon.

Zadie: Cool. Shall we invite the boys too?

Bella: Good idea. See you on Sunday!

1 Read the dialogue and complete the sentences.
1. Bella invites Zadie to the _cinema_.
2. Zadie is busy on _____.
3. Bella is busy on _____ and Sunday _____.
4. They agree to meet on Sunday _____.
5. They decide to invite the _____.

Grammar Present Continuous for future arrangements

I**'m practising** with my band on Saturday.
He**'s seeing** the doctor tomorrow.
We**'re playing** a concert in a few weeks.
What **are** you **doing** next Friday?

Time expressions

tomorrow, on Saturday, next Friday, in a few weeks

2 Look at Adam's planner and complete the dialogue.

Zadie: Hi, Adam. Can you come to the cinema on Sunday afternoon?
Adam: Sorry, but I ¹ *'m playing* tennis.
Zadie: Are you free on Monday then?
Adam: No, I ² _____ my grandma.
Zadie: What about Tuesday?
Adam: Sorry, but Josh and I ³ _____ to London.
Zadie: And Wednesday?
Adam: I ⁴ _____ my school project. Sorry, Zadie, this week is really difficult! Why don't you go without me?
Zadie: OK. See you soon, Adam.

Sun 4
3.00 p.m. play tennis
Mon 5
visit Grandma
Tues 6
go to London with Josh
Wed 7
do school project

3 🔊 1.3 Listen and repeat. Which activities do you do at the weekend?

Vocabulary Free-time activities

go   cycling / ice-skating / shopping
go to a concert / a museum / the cinema
help your parents   play sport
stay at home   visit your grandparents

I often go cycling. I sometimes …

4 Plan your week. Write five activities in the agenda. In pairs, try to find a day when you can go ice-skating together.

Monday
Tuesday
Wednesday
Thursday
Friday
Saturday
Sunday

A: *Let's go ice-skating next week. Are you free on Tuesday?*
B: *Sorry, but I'm … on Tuesday.*

I can use comparative and superlative adjectives.

Pizza is better 0.3

I think it's cool!

Josh: Hey, what do you think of the new PX10 games console?
Adam: I think it's cool. The games are more exciting than games on the PX9. It's easier to use and it's faster too. It's the fastest of all the PX consoles!
Josh: True, but it's more expensive than the PX9.
Adam: It's the most expensive because it's the best! And you can play good games, like *Sky Burger*.
Josh: Hmm … burgers, I'm hungry. Have you got anything to eat?
Adam: We've got sausages and pizza in the fridge.
Josh: Great! Pizza is better than sausages.
Adam: But it's from last night and it's cold.
Josh: We can heat it up in the microwave.

Two minutes later …

Adam: It's ready.
Josh: Ouch, it's hot! … and it isn't as good as sausages. It's awful!

1 Read the dialogue. Who:
 1 really likes the PX10 games console? *Adam*
 2 thinks *Sky Burger* is a good game?
 3 wants something to eat?
 4 prefers pizza to sausages?

2 🔊 **1.4** Listen and repeat. Which adjectives do the boys use to describe the PX10 games console and which to describe the pizza?

Vocabulary Adjectives

awful boring cheap cold delicious difficult
easy exciting expensive fast hot slow

3 Use the adjectives in the Vocabulary box to describe 1–6.
 1 a Ferrari car
   It's fast and expensive.
 2 an old bicycle
 3 Maths homework
 4 a roller coaster
 5 the Sahara desert
 6 strawberry ice cream

Grammar Comparative and superlative adjectives

Comparative adjectives

The PX10 games console is **faster** than the PX9.
It's **more exciting** than the PX9.
Pizza is **better** than sausages.
Sausages are **worse** than pizza.

Superlative adjectives

The PX10 game console is **the fastest** of all.
The PX10 games console is **the most expensive**.
The PX10 games console is **the best** / **the worst**.

(not) as … as

The pizza isn't **as** good **as** the sausages.

4 Compare the two things. Use the comparative form of the adjective. Which sentences do you agree with?
 1 Burgers / good / sausages.
   Burgers are better than sausages.
 2 Maths / difficult / English.
 3 Computers / expensive / smartphones.
 4 Motorbikes / fast / cars.
 5 Sandwiches / good / school meals.
 6 Football / easy / tennis.

5 In your notebook, write the sentences in Exercise 4. Use *not as … as*.
 Sausages aren't as good as burgers.

6 Complete the questions with the superlative form of the adjectives. Then ask and answer in pairs.

QUIZ What's your opinion?

1 What's *the best* (good) computer game?
2 What's _____ (bad) phone app?
3 What's _____ (exciting) programme on TV?
4 What are _____ (cheap) trainers you can buy?
5 Which is _____ (expensive) smartphone?
6 Which is _____ (difficult) school subject?

0.4 She wants to be an archaeologist | I can use articles.

Meet the Explorers

Meet the Explorers: Pops, Mac and Eva. They love adventure and they often travel around the world! They visit places in Africa, Asia and South America but at the moment they're at Pops's house in London, in England.

Pops is Eva and Mac's grandfather. Pops's wife, their grandmother, isn't an explorer, but she loves listening to their stories. In their house there is a big map on the wall. When they go to a new place, they mark the place on the map!

At the moment, Eva is reading a book. The book is about the pyramids. Eva wants to be an archaeologist and find Egyptian treasure. Mac wants to be a mountain climber and meet the Yeti! Pops wants to explore the rainforest in Brazil. He also wants to visit Australia!

1 🔊 **1.5 Read and listen. Circle true (T) or false (F). Correct the false sentences.**

1 Pops often goes to different places. (T)/ F
2 Pops's house is in Australia. T / F
3 Eva is interested in history. T / F
4 Mac is reading about the pyramids. T / F
5 Eva is interested in mountains. T / F
6 Pops, Mac and Eva are very adventurous. T / F

Grammar Articles: *a/an*, *the*, 0 article

a/an and plural form

It's **a** book.	They are books.
It's **an** apple.	They are apples.
It's **a** big book.	They are big books.
It's **an** interesting book.	They are interesting books.

a/an with jobs

Pops is **an** explorer.
Mac wants to be **a** mountain climber.

a/an, the

Pops has got **a** map. **The** map is on the wall.
Eva is reading books. **The** books are interesting.

0 article with geographical names

Continents, e.g. Africa, Asia, South America
They visit places in Africa.
Cities, e.g. London, New York, Paris
Pops's house is in London.
Countries, e.g. England, Egypt, Brazil
Pops wants to go to Brazil.
But: **the** UK, **the** United States

2 Complete the sentences about Pops's house with *a/an* or *the*.

1 Pops lives in _a_ big house. There are ten rooms in ___ house!
2 Pops's house has ___ big living room and ___ garden. Pops likes spending his free time in ___ living room. Gran likes relaxing in ___ garden.
3 There are old apple trees in ___ garden. The Explorers like eating apples from ___ apple trees.

3 🔊 **1.6 Circle the correct answer. Listen and check.**

Inside Pops's backpack there's ¹(a)/ an map, an archaeology book and ² a / an jungle hat. Pops often wears ³ a / the jungle hat. There's also ⁴ a / an old camera and a diary. Pops writes in ⁵ a / the diary every day. It's full of exciting stories. One story is about an adventure in ⁶ the / 0 Brazil. Another is about a trip to ⁷ the / 0 United States!

4 Write down what you have got in your school bag today. Use *a/an* and *the*.

In my school bag I've got a book, an old school tie, and a pencil case …
I got the pencil case for my birthday …

I can use *was*, *were*, and talk about the weather. **It was snowy**

The pyramids were closed!

Last week, Pops was on a trip to Egypt, Antarctica and Brazil. Eva and Mac weren't with him. They were at school. The trip was a disaster.

Pops: Hi, kids, I'm back! Here are some photos. Look!
Mac: How was your trip?
Pops: It was terrible!
Eva: Oh, no! Why?
Pops: On Monday, I was in Egypt. It was nice and sunny, but the pyramids were closed! They are always closed on Mondays!
Eva: Oh dear!
Pops: On Wednesday, I was in Antarctica. It was windy and snowy, and I was lost.
Mac: Were you scared, Pops?
Pops: Yes, I was. There were some penguins, but they weren't very helpful.
Eva: Maybe they were lost too!
Pops: On Friday, I was in Brazil, in the jungle. It was rainy and I was hungry. There were some bananas in a tree, but there was a big monkey too!
Mac: Was it friendly?
Pops: No, it wasn't!
Eva: Oh, poor Pops! Here, have a cup of tea.
Pops: Thanks, kids. It's good to be back home!

1 🔊 **1.7 Read and listen. What places can you see in Pops's photos? Why was Pops's trip terrible?**

2 🔊 **1.8 Listen and repeat. What's the weather like in Pops's photos?**

Vocabulary Weather

cloudy   cold   hot   rainy   snowy   sunny   warm   windy

A *It's sunny …*

3 Look at the pictures. What's the weather like?

1 2 3 4 5 6

1 *It's hot.*

Grammar *was, were*

+	I **was** in Egypt.	−	I **wasn't** in Egypt.
	They **were** helpful.		They **weren't** helpful.
?	**Was** the monkey friendly?		Yes, it **was**. / No, it **wasn't**.
	Were the penguins lost?		Yes, they **were**. No, they **weren't**.

there was / there were

+	There **was** a monkey.	−	There **wasn't** a monkey.
	There **were** some trees.		There **weren't** any trees.
?	**Was** there a monkey?		Yes, there **was**. No, there **wasn't**.
	Were there any penguins?		Yes, there **were**. No, there **weren't**.

4 Read the dialogue again. Complete the sentences with *was*, *wasn't*, *were* or *weren't*.

1 Pops __wasn't__ in Egypt on Wednesday.
2 The pyramids _____ open.
3 The weather _____ good in Antarctica.
4 The penguins _____ unhelpful.
5 There _____ some food in the jungle.
6 The monkey _____ nice to Pops.

5 🔊 **1.9 Complete the dialogues with *was*, *wasn't*, *were* or *weren't*. Then listen and check.**

1 **Mac:** __Were__ the pyramids open later?
  Pops: No, they _____ .
2 **Mac:** _____ it cold in Antarctica?
  Pops: Yes, it _____ !
3 **Eva:** _____ there polar bears in Antarctica?
  Pops: No, there _____ .
4 **Mac:** _____ the monkey friendly?
  Pops: No, it _____ !

6 Exam Spot **In pairs, ask and answer about your last holiday. Use the ideas below.**

1 Where / you / last summer?   3 people / friendly?
2 weather / nice?   4 food / good?

A: *Where were you last summer?*
B: *We were in the Lake District.*

9

1 Who we are

Vocabulary   I can talk about clothes and accessories.

In this unit
Vocabulary
- Clothes and accessories
- Describing clothes
- Hairstyles
- Personality adjectives
- Negative adjectives

Grammar
- Past Simple
- Past Continuous and Past Simple

1 How many names of clothes do you know?
T-shirt, jeans …
a Which clothes are you wearing now?
b Which clothes do you wear in the summer and in winter?

I know that!

Street Style
Let's have fun with fashion!

Hi there! I'm Hannah and I'm interested in fashion. This is my Street Style blog :) Every week, I take photos of people wearing interesting clothes and of cool accessories! You can check out my photos here. I also talk to people about their style. Listen to the interviews here. And I make my own designs. See them here.

A B C D E F G H

2–3
1.2 Grammar video

4
1.2 Grammar animation

5
1.3 Grammar animation

6
1.4 Communication video

7
BBC Culture video

1.1

2 🔊 **1.10** Read and listen to Hannah's blog on page 10. What's her hobby? What can you find in her blog?

3 🔊 **1.11** Listen and repeat. Which items can you see in the photos on page 10?

Vocabulary Clothes and accessories

belt boots bracelet cardigan coat dress
earrings handbag hat hoodie jacket
leggings ring sandals scarf shirt shorts
skirt socks tie tights top trainers

4 In your notebook, match the clothes in the Vocabulary box to the body parts.

1 Head: *earrings*
2 Neck: _____
3 Body: _____
4 Hands: _____
5 Legs: _____
6 Feet: _____

5 🔊 **1.12** Listen and repeat. Look at photos A–H in the blog and answer the questions below.

Vocabulary Describing clothes

Patterns: checked floral plain spotted striped
Style: baggy casual smart tight

Who is wearing:
1 a blue checked shirt?
   the boy in photo H
2 a baggy striped top?
3 a spotted dress?

4 a plain skirt?
5 a floral top?
6 tight jeans?
7 smart clothes?
8 casual clothes?

6 🟥 **Exam Spot** 🔊 **1.13** Listen to Hannah's interviews. Complete her notes.

Jake

Usually wears: ¹ *smart clothes* :
² _____ , ³ _____ ,
⁴ _____
Never wears: ⁵ _____
Favourite clothes: ⁶ _____

Usually wears: ⁷ *comfortable, casual clothes* : ⁸ _____ ,
⁹ _____ , ¹⁰ _____
Never wears: ¹¹ _____
Favourite clothes: ¹² _____

Amy

7 In pairs, ask and answer questions to complete the form. Then tell the class about your friend.

Name: _____
Usually wears: _____
Never wears: _____
Favourite clothes: _____

A: *What kind of clothes do you usually wear?*
B: *I usually wear hoodies and jeans.*
A: *Max usually wears hoodies and jeans. He …*

8 🟥 **Exam Spot** 🔊 **1.14** Look at Hannah's design. Circle a, b or c. Then listen and check.

My designs

Hi and welcome to my design page! I use lots of different styles and patterns for my clothes. Some of the ideas are from magazines, but the best ideas are from the people I meet! This is one of my favourite designs.

The model is wearing a ¹ _c_ white T-shirt with a red checked ² _____ . She's also wearing red ³ _____ and ⁴ _____ socks! She's got a checked ⁵ _____ too. Her clothes look comfortable and ⁶ _____ .

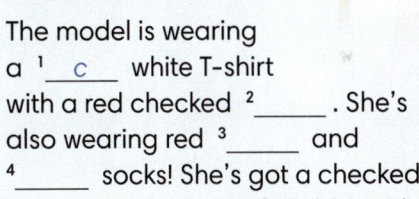

1 a striped	b checked	(c) plain
2 a shirt	b skirt	c dress
3 a trainers	b shoes	c boots
4 a plain	b checked	c striped
5 a scarf	b a tie	c belt
6 a smart	b casual	c tight

9 Imagine you have some money to spend on clothes. Make a list of five items you would like to buy. Include colours and patterns. Compare your ideas in pairs.

I'd like to buy a striped T-shirt, some plain, black jeans …

💭 **I remember that!**

1.2 Grammar — I can use the Past Simple.

Where did I put my jumper?

Josh had a great summer. Yesterday was the first day back at school. Things didn't start well. First, he forgot to set his alarm.

1

Mum: Get up, Josh! It's eight o'clock.

Then, he got dressed … well, he tried to get dressed.

2

Josh: Where did I put my school jumper?
Mum: Did you put it in the washing machine?
Kate: No, he didn't, Mum. He never puts anything in the washing machine.
Dad: I saw a jumper on that chair five minutes ago.
Kate: That was mine, Dad.

He finished breakfast, then he looked everywhere. Finally, he found it … in his school bag!

3

Dad: Did you leave it in your bag all summer, Josh?
Josh: Yes, I did.
Mum: Oh dear, you left your dirty sports socks in your bag too!
Kate: That's gross!
Mum: Well, you can't wear this jumper.

He also lost his summer writing project …

4

Josh: And where is my summer writing project?
Mum: Your summer writing project?
Josh: I wrote it yesterday and I left it here. I put it on the table …
Kate: Oh, here it is, under the teapot! And it's wet.
Josh: Oh, no! This is the worst day of my life! I don't have a jumper and I don't have my homework! I can't go to school!

---

1 ▶ 2 🔊 **1.15 Watch or listen and read. What day is it? What's the problem?**

2 ▶ 2 🔊 **1.15 Watch or listen again. Read the sentences. Circle true (T) or false (F). Correct the false sentences.**

1 Josh hasn't got an alarm clock.
Josh forgot to set his alarm clock.   T / **F**
2 Kate's jumper was on the kitchen chair.   T / F
3 Josh's jumper was the only thing in his bag.   T / F
4 Josh's writing project is in the bathroom.   T / F

3 🔊 **1.16 Listen and repeat. Find these expressions in the story.**

> That's gross!
> This is the worst day of my life!

Say it!

4 ▶ **Guess!** Does Josh go to school? Have a class vote.

5 ▶ 3 🔊 **1.17 Now watch or listen and check.**

Grammar Past Simple

	Regular verbs	Irregular verbs
+	I **finished** breakfast.	I **found** it in my bag.
–	I **didn't finish** breakfast.	I **didn't find** it in my bag.
?	**Did** you **finish** breakfast?	**Did** you **find** it in your bag?
	Yes, I **did**. / No, I **didn't**.	Yes, I **did**. / No, I **didn't**.
	When **did** he **finish** breakfast?	Where **did** he **find** it?

Time expressions

yesterday, the day before yesterday
last week, last month, last year
a minute ago, an hour ago, two days ago

▶ 4 **Get Grammar!**

Fluffy **had** a great holiday.
She **went** camping.

6 Find the Past Simple forms of these verbs in the story. Which are regular and which irregular?

> find   finish   forget   get   have   leave
> look   lose   put   see   try   write

find – found – irregular verb

7 I know that! Choose a verb below and play irregular verb tennis!

make, drink, go, sleep, take, buy

make → *made!*

feel, come, eat, know, meet, read

8 Complete Josh's summer writing project with the Past Simple form of the verbs. Which three verbs are regular?

My holiday by Josh

This summer we ¹ *had* (have) a family holiday in Cornwall. We ² ____ (stay) with my cousins in a hostel near the beach. The weather is always great there. There's lots to do in Cornwall. In the morning, we ³ ____ (go) swimming in the sea and I ⁴ ____ (try) surfing. In the afternoon, I ⁵ ____ (read) my book. I also ⁶ ____ (make) some new friends. One day, we ⁷ ____ (visit) Newquay and I ⁸ ____ (get) my own surfboard. I also ⁹ ____ (eat) a tasty Cornish pasty (a traditional meat pie). Yum! What a great holiday!

9 Read Adam's notes. Write about his holiday in your notebook.

ADAM'S HOLIDAY
1 not go to Cornwall – go to Scotland
2 not stay with family – stay in a hotel
3 not visit Newquay – visit Edinburgh
4 not eat a pasty – eat pancakes
5 not buy a surfboard – buy a kilt

1 *Adam didn't go to Cornwall. He went to Scotland.*

10 🔊 **1.18** In your notebook, put the words in the correct order. Then listen about Bella and Zadie's holiday and write down the answers.

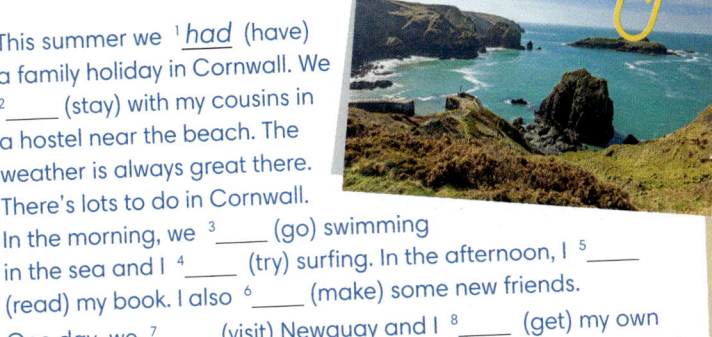

1 did | Where | Bella and Zadie | go | ?
Where did Bella and Zadie go?
2 stay with | they | did | Who | ?
3 they | What | did | do | ?
4 a museum | Did | they | visit | ?
5 they | anything | buy | Did | ?
6 they | What | eat | did | ?

11 Exam Spot In pairs, ask and answer about your last summer holiday. Use the questions in Exercise 10.

A: *Where did you go?*
B: *I went to France.*

1.3 Grammar — I can use the Past Continuous and the Past Simple.

The Explorers — Princess Zara

Pops, Mac and Eva are in Egypt. They want to find the lost tomb of Princess Zara.

1 Pops's Diary
Monday 1st September, Egypt

What a day! At 9 a.m. we left home to look for the tomb. At 5 p.m. we were still looking for it! Then we had some luck. We were cycling through the desert when we finally saw it!

2
Eva: Look at these shoes … and this necklace!
Pops: Yes, Princess Zara loved clothes.
Mac: What happened to her?
Pops: It's a sad story.

3
Pops: The princess lived in Egypt 3,000 years ago. On the night of her 18th birthday, she had a big party. It was fantastic!

4
Eva: Was she wearing this necklace?
Pops: Yes, she was! The princess wasn't wearing casual clothes, of course! She was wearing a very special dress. It was really long and that's why something terrible happened. While Princess Zara was dancing, she tripped on her dress and fell into the river!
Eva: Oh, no!

5
Pops: A crocodile was waiting nearby.
Mac: Oh, no! What happened, Pops?
Pops: Well, no one could save the princess. She disappeared.

6
Eva: How awful! But the necklace is beautiful. Help me put it on, Mac. Ooh, your hands are cold!
Mac: Those aren't my hands – it's Princess Zara! RUN!

1 Look at the cartoon. Where are the Explorers? Which clothes and accessories can you see?

> boots   bracelet   coat   dress
> necklace   sandals   scarf   tie

2 🔊 1.19 Read and listen. Then answer the questions.
1 What did Princess Zara love?
2 When did Princess Zara live in Egypt?
3 Why did she have a party?
4 What happened to the princess?
5 Who is helping Eva with the necklace?

Grammar Past Continuous and Past Simple

Past Continuous

+	I **was** waiting. They **were** waiting.	−	I **wasn't** waiting. They **weren't** waiting.
?	**Was** she **waiting**? **Were** they **waiting**? What **was** she **wearing**?		Yes, she **was**. / No, she **wasn't**. Yes, they **were**. / No, they **weren't**.

Time expressions

(yesterday) at five o'clock, yesterday morning, yesterday evening

Past Continuous and Past Simple

We **were cycling** when we **saw** the lost tomb of Princess Zara.
While Princess Zara **was dancing**, she **fell** into the river.

▶ 5 Get Grammar!

At four o'clock Fluffy **was having** a party. Max and Anna **were dancing**. Hammy **was eating** a cake.

3 Say what Pops, Eva and Mac were and weren't doing yesterday morning at 8.30.

1 Pops, Eva and Mac / have / breakfast. ✗
   Pops, Eva and Mac weren't having breakfast.
2 Pops / clean / his boots. ✔
3 Eva / ride / her bike. ✗
4 Eva and Mac / play cards. ✗
5 Mac / pack / his backpack. ✔
6 Eva / read / a book about Egypt. ✔

4 Look at the pictures. Then ask and answer in pairs.

8 a.m.

1 Princess Zara / talking on the phone?
   A: *Was Princess Zara talking on the phone at 8 a.m.?*
   B: *No, she wasn't.*
2 she / have breakfast?

12 p.m.

3 Princess Zara and her pet scorpion / play / football?
4 they / play chess?

5 p.m.

5 Princess Zara / read / a book?
6 she / sleep?

5 Circle the correct answer. Then circle true (T) or false (F).

1 Pops, Mac and Eva *cycled* /(*were cycling*) through the desert when they saw the tomb. (T)/ F
2 While Eva *looked* / *was looking* at clothes, Pops started to tell a story. T / F
3 The princess *had* / *was having* an accident while she was dancing. T / F
4 A snake was watching them when the princess *fell* / *was falling* into the river. T / F
5 Eva *was putting* / *put* on the necklace when Princess Zara appeared. T / F

6 Exam Spot 🔊 1.20 Complete Princess Zara's diary. Use one word in each gap. Then listen and check.

Yesterday ¹*was* an interesting day! I had visitors. I was sleeping ²___ they arrived. While they ³___ exploring my tomb, I woke up. An old man and a boy were ⁴___ hieroglyphics and a girl ⁵___ putting on my necklace. I was trying to help her ⁶___ the boy saw me and screamed! It was strange because I ⁷___ trying to scare them! I wanted to help.

7 Break the code to find out Princess Zara's question. Then answer the question.

What
 erwe
het strangers
alkitgn about
wneh ythe erwe
 ni ym tomb?

1.4 Communication — I can tell a story and react to a story.

What happened next?

Bella: Guess what happened on Saturday!
Adam: What?
Bella: I went shopping with Zadie for some new trainers. First, we went to *Lacey's*, but it was closed. Then, we went to *Bramley's*. Zadie tried on ten pairs before she finally found a pair she liked.
Adam: No way! So what happened next?
Bella: She paid, and we were leaving the shop when the alarm went off.
Adam: Oh, no! Why?
Bella: Well, she was still wearing one of the pairs of shoes that she tried on.
Adam: Did the security guard stop her?
Bella: Yes, but luckily he laughed when we showed him Zadie's old trainers on the floor!
Adam: Poor Zadie! How embarrassing!

1 ▶ 6 🔊 **1.21** Watch or listen and read. Answer the questions.
  1 What did Bella and Zadie do on Saturday?
  2 What happened in the shop?
  3 What did the security guard do?

2 🔊 **1.22** Listen and repeat.

Communication
Telling a story and reacting

Telling a story
Guess what happened *on Saturday*!
First, *we went to Lacey's*.
Then, *we went to Bramley's*.
Finally, *she found a pair she liked*.

Reacting
No way!
Then what? / So what happened next?
So what did he do?
Poor *Zadie*!
Lucky *him*!
How *funny / embarrassing / strange*!

3 🔊 **1.23** Complete the dialogue with sentences a–f. There are two extra sentences. Then listen and check.

  a How funny! Poor you!
  b No way! What did you do?
  c What was he wearing?
  d No, it was on Monday.
  e What?
  f So what happened next?

Boy: Guess what happened last week!
Girl: ¹ _e_
Boy: I washed my football kit. My red hoodie was dirty, so I put that in too.
Girl: ² _____
Boy: Well, when I took the washing out, my white football shorts were pink!
Girl: ³ _____
Boy: Well, they're my only pair, so I wore them in a match yesterday. Everyone was laughing!
Girl: ⁴ _____

4 **Exam Spot** In pairs, act out the two dialogues. Use the Communication box to help you.

  1 **Student A:** You were at a friend's party when you dropped some cake on the sofa and your friend sat on it. Tell the story to Student B.
     Student B: React to Student A's story.
  2 **Student B:** You were playing football. Your friend kicked the ball to you, but it hit you on the head and you fell over. Tell the story to Student A.
     Student A: React to Student B's story.

Teenage fashions

Reading 1.5

I can understand a text about fashions from the past.

What did young people wear thirty years ago? What about sixty years ago? Let's look at fashions from the past.

In the 1960s, a lot of young people were **hippies**. Women wore long dresses and sandals, and had long wavy hair. Men wore colourful shirts with floral patterns, and also had long hair and beards. Hippies wanted peace and freedom, and often painted their faces with flowers and peace signs.

Punk rock was popular in the 1970s and 1980s. The music was loud and angry. **Punks** wanted to look different and shock people. They wore tight trousers with holes in them, old T-shirts and leather jackets. They had dyed spiky hair – blue, pink and green were popular colours – and they wore safety pins as earrings.

In the 1990s and 2000s, skateboarding became cool. **Skaters** wanted to be comfortable, so they wore casual T-shirts and old baggy jeans or shorts, often with colourful trainers. Their hair was usually long and messy, and they wore baseball caps or hoodies. A lot of people wore skateboarding fashion, even if they didn't have a skateboard!

A

B

C

Comments

Suzie Yesterday, I was looking at some old photos. I found one of my grandma when she was young. She was wearing a red leather jacket and had green hair. My grandma was a punk!

Leo My uncle was a skater. He was showing me some of his old tricks last weekend when he fell off the skateboard! He wasn't hurt – just embarrassed!

1 🔊 **1.24** Listen and repeat. Which of the features can you see in pictures A–C?

Vocabulary Hairstyles

curly hair   dyed hair   shaved hair   spiky hair
straight hair   wavy hair   bald   beard   moustache

2 I know that! What words describe people's:
1 look? *pretty, …*
2 height? *tall, …*
3 build? *slim, …*
4 face? *blue eyes, …*

3 Describe your best friend.
Pavel is tall. He's got short blond hair.

4 🔊 **1.25** Read and listen to the text. What fashions can you see in the pictures? What are the people wearing? When were these fashions popular?

5 **Exam Spot** 🔊 **1.25** Read and listen to the text again. Read the questions and circle H (hippies), P (punks) or S (skaters).
1 Which fashion was popular in the 1990s? H / P /(S)
2 In which fashion did people wear casual, sporty clothes?   H / P / S
3 Which fashion is connected with music?   H / P / S
4 Which fashion is the oldest?   H / P / S
5 In which fashion did people dye their hair different colours?   H / P / S

6 Which fashion style in the text do you like the most? Why?

7 Read the comments to the text. What do you think your relatives wore when they were young and what was their hair like? In your notebook, write a few sentences.
My mum wore pink baggy T-shirts and a lot of plastic jewellery.

1.6 Listening and Vocabulary

I can understand a listening text about personality.

1 🔊 1.26 Listen and repeat. Which adjectives describe you, your best friend, your mum and dad?

Vocabulary
Personality adjectives

friendly   generous   hard-working   honest
kind   lazy   organised   patient   polite   rude
selfish   serious   shy   talkative

I'm talkative, friendly …

2 I know that! Work in pairs. What other personality adjectives do you know? Make a list.
funny, …

3 Complete the sentences with the adjectives in the Vocabulary box.

1 Sam only thinks about himself. He's *selfish*.
2 Leah never does any work. She's _____.
3 Frank never laughs. He's _____.
4 Tina talks a lot. She's _____.
5 Shaun is nervous and quiet when he meets new people. He's _____.
6 Gina likes giving presents to people. She's _____.

4 Read the text about first impressions. In pairs, talk about your first impressions of Liam and Molly.

A: *I think Liam looks serious.*
B: *I agree. / I don't agree. I think he looks shy.*

5 🔊 1.27 Listen to Matt and Elsa talking about Liam and Molly. Were their first impressions about them right?

6 🔊 1.27 Listen again and answer the questions.
1 What was Matt's first impression of Liam?
2 What did he think about Liam later?
3 What was Elsa's first impression of Molly?
4 What did she realise about Molly later?

7 Read the Vocabulary Builder. Match the negative adjectives in the Vocabulary Builder to quotes 1–6.

Vocabulary Builder   Negative adjectives

friendly ≠ **un**friendly, kind ≠ **un**kind
organised ≠ **dis**organised, honest ≠ **dis**honest
polite ≠ **im**polite, patient ≠ **im**patient

1 'I'm not always nice to people.'   *unkind*
2 'I'm not good at organising things.'
3 'I'm angry when I have to wait for something.'
4 'I don't always tell the truth.'
5 'I sometimes talk to people in a rude way.'
6 'I'm not always friendly.'

8 Complete the sentences with a personality adjective. Then discuss as a class.

1 A good friend is someone who is _____.
2 I don't usually like people who are _____.
3 I admire people who are _____.

First impressions

When we meet someone for the first time, we often look at them and form a 'first impression'. We decide if they are polite or rude, funny or serious, and we decide if we like them or not. Scientists say we do all of this in seven seconds!

Liam

Molly

I can write a text about my best friend. **Writing**

My best friend by Jonah

1 My best friend is called Sam. He's tall and slim, with long blond hair and big blue eyes. He's not really interested in fashion, but he always looks cool. He likes wearing big old T-shirts and shorts or jeans.

2 Sam and I met on our first day at secondary school. I was playing football with some friends when he asked if he could join in. We got on well straight away, and now we often play football together!

3 Sam looks quite serious in this photo, but he's actually really funny. He's very talkative and loves telling stories. He plays the guitar too! He's also very generous, and is a great friend.

1 Read Jonah's description of his best friend, Sam. What does Jonah like about Sam?

2 Read the text again. Circle true (T) or false (F). Correct the false sentences.
  1 Sam is quite short. *Sam is tall.*   T /(F)
  2 Sam and Jonah met during the holidays.   T / F
  3 They both like playing football.   T / F
  4 Sam is serious and quite shy.   T / F
  5 Sam is selfish.   T / F

3 Read the Writing box. Which expressions can you find in Jonah's description?

Writing Describing a friend

1 Appearance
He's *tall / slim / well-built*.
He's got *straight hair / blue eyes*.
He likes wearing *casual clothes / jeans*.

2 How you met
I met … *at school / in a theatre club*.
We got on well straight away.
At the beginning, I thought … , but then …

3 Personality
He's *kind / friendly*. He looks *serious / shy* but actually he's *very funny / really talkative*.

4 Read the box. Find another example of a noun with more than one adjective before it in Jonah's description.

Adjective order

1 size	2 age	3 colour	4 noun
short	new	red	dress
long		blond	hair
big	old		T-shirts

5 In your notebook, complete the sentences with the words in the correct order.
  1 My friend Sophie has got *short dark hair* (hair / dark / short).
  2 She usually wears jeans and an _____ (hoodie / grey / old).
  3 Today she's wearing a _____ (red / dress / new).
  4 Her dad has got a _____ (black / beard / big).
  5 He often wears a _____ (scarf / green / long).

6  Write about your best friend.

** Find ideas**
Make notes about his/her appearance, how you met, and his/her personality.

Draft
Organise your ideas into paragraphs. Use the ideas in the Writing box to help you.

Check and write
Check the order of adjectives and write the final version of your text.

1.8 Language Revision

Vocabulary

1 Look at the pictures and circle the correct answer.

Mac is wearing a ¹(checked)/ striped shirt with ²tight / baggy shorts. He's got ³tights / socks and ⁴sandals / boots on.

Princess Zara is wearing a ⁵smart / casual white ⁶coat / dress, with a ⁷spotted / striped scarf. She's got a ⁸bracelet / necklace on.

2 Complete the text. What hairstyles have people got in your family?

That's me in the photo with my family!

I've got long ¹straight hair and brown eyes. My mum's got ²w_____y hair and it's ³d_____d . Right now it's blond, but it was pink last summer! My dad has got a ⁴b_____d but he hasn't got a ⁵m_____e .

3 Complete the table with the words in the box.

> dishonest ~~friendly~~ generous hard-working
> honest lazy selfish shy talkative ~~unfriendly~~

Definition	Adjective	Opposite
1 A person who is kind and nice	friendly	unfriendly
2 A person who does a lot of work		
3 A person who likes giving presents		
4 A person who talks a lot		
5 A person who always tells the truth		

Grammar

4 Complete the story with the verbs in the Past Simple.

> Yesterday Pops ¹ _had_ (have) a bad day. He ² _____ (not find) any treasure. He ³ _____ (not take) any photos because he didn't have his camera. He ⁴ _____ (leave) his map in the tent, so he ⁵ _____ (get) completely lost! He ⁶ _____ (forget) to wear his hat and the sun was really hot!

5 In your notebook, put the words in the correct order. Then ask and answer about Exercise 4.

1 find Did Pops any treasure ?   *Did Pops find any treasure?*
2 any photos Did take he ?
3 in the tent What Pops leave did ?
4 forget What he to wear did ?
5 he Did a good day have ?

6 Write sentences in the Past Continuous. Then, in pairs, ask and answer about what you were doing last Saturday.

1 9 a.m / Zadie / talk to Bella
   At 9 a.m. Zadie was talking to Bella.
2 11 a.m. / Adam / clean his room
3 1 p.m. / Josh and Adam / play basketball
4 4 p.m. / Bella / help at the café
5 6 p.m. / Zadie and Bella / watch a video

A: *What were you doing at 9 a.m. last Saturday?*
B: *I was reading in bed.*

7 Circle the correct answer.

1 Adam was playing in a match when he (scored)/ was scoring a goal.
2 While Josh *did / was doing* his homework, Adam fell asleep!
3 Zadie *listened / was listening* to music when she got a text message.
4 While Josh and Zadie *argued / were arguing*, Bella made some sandwiches.

Round up 1.8

Communication

8 🔊 **1.28** Complete the dialogue with the words in the box. Then listen and check. Act out the dialogue in pairs.

> do ~~guess~~ happened how poor way what when

Boy: ¹ _Guess_ what happened last weekend?
Girl: ² _____ ?
Boy: It was my grandma's seventieth birthday, so we went to a restaurant. We were all wearing smart clothes.
Girl: So what ³ _____ next?
Boy: Well, the waiter was bringing the food to the table ⁴ _____ he dropped a bowl of soup on my dad's shirt.
Girl: No ⁵ _____ ! What did your dad ⁶ _____ ?
Boy: He ran to the bathroom and took his shirt off. When he came back to the table, he was wearing a jacket and tie, but no shirt!
Girl: Oh, no! ⁷ _____ embarrassing! Your ⁸ _____ dad!
Boy: No, actually he looked great! We had a lot of fun!

Dictation

9 **Exam Spot** 🔊 **1.29** Listen to a short text. Then listen again and write down what you hear. Make sure you spell the words correctly.

Pronunciation

10 🔊 **1.30** Listen and repeat: /s/ or /ʃ/?

Serious **S**imon wore **s**andals and **s**ocks.
Shy **Sh**eila wore a T-**sh**irt and **sh**orts.

Check yourself! ✓

- I can talk about clothes, accessories, hairstyles and personality. ☐
- I can use the Past Simple and the Past Continuous. ☐
- I can tell a story and react to a story. ☐

11 Read the sentences. Circle the correct answer a, b or c.

1 These jeans are too big. I need a _____ .
  a scarf   ⓑ belt   c top
2 It was a very expensive restaurant, so he wore a _____ jacket and a tie.
  a smart   b spotted   c tight
3 My mum has long _____ hair.
  a bald   b baggy   c wavy
4 Her dad is usually quite _____ , but he was laughing too.
  a serious   b selfish   c generous
5 I love my aunt Sheila. She's very talkative and _____ .
  a shy   b lazy   c friendly
6 Does your uncle have a _____ or just a moustache?
  a beard   b ring   c coat
7 I _____ sleep well last night.
  a didn't   b don't   c wasn't
8 Where _____ my earrings, Mum?
  a you put   b did you put
  c you did put
9 What _____ yesterday at five o'clock?
  a you were doing   b you doing
  c were you doing
10 We _____ in the park when suddenly it started to rain.
  a walked   b were walking
  c walking
11 They _____ looking when the boy crossed the road.
  a didn't   b wasn't   c weren't
12 While Jess was walking to school, she _____ a famous singer.
  a was seeing   b saw   c sees
13 Guess what _____ yesterday – I put my phone in the washing machine!
  a happened   b left   c saw
14 I fell over in P.E. this morning. It was so _____ .
  a embarrass   b embarrassing
  c embarrassed
15 We're both wearing the same T-shirts! _____ funny!
  a What   b Who   c How

21

Get Culture!

Clothes for special occasions

Clothes for special occasions

We all sometimes dress up for special occasions. When do British people dress up, and what do they wear? We talk to three teenagers.

**Saskia Taylor, 16
from Oxford**

**Ewan Campbell, 17
from Edinburgh**

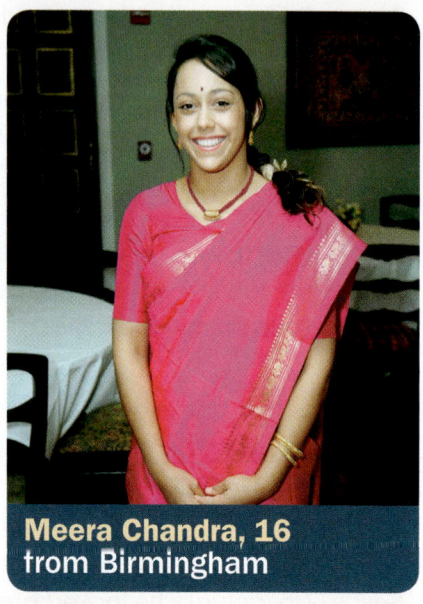

**Meera Chandra, 16
from Birmingham**

Last June we had our school prom – a big party to celebrate the end of exams. Everybody dressed up in special clothes. The girls wore evening dresses, earrings and high-heeled shoes, and the boys wore smart suits and ties. When we arrived, everyone was smiling and taking photos. We had a meal and then everyone danced. It was a great party!

Last week, I went to a Burns Night dinner. Burns Night is a Scottish celebration that happens every year on 25 January. We celebrate the life and poetry of Scotland's national poet, Robert Burns. I wore a kilt with a white shirt and a tie. All the men were wearing kilts – a traditional Scottish skirt for men. There was a special meal of haggis and vegetables, and I played the bagpipes!

My sister got married in the summer. My grandparents are from India, and a lot of my family still lives there, but everyone came over for the wedding – there were about 300 guests! I wore a bright pink sari – a traditional Indian dress – with a gold bracelet and a necklace. All of my cousins wore different coloured saris, so it was a very colourful wedding!

1 🔊 **1.31** Read and listen to the text. What occasions do the teenagers talk about? What clothes did they wear?

2 **Exam Spot** Read the text again and answer the questions.
  1 What does the school prom celebrate?
  2 What did Saskia and her friends do at the school prom?
  3 What does Burns Night celebrate?
  4 What did Ewan do at the Burns Night dinner?
  5 How many people went to Meera's sister's wedding?
  6 Why was it a 'colourful' wedding?

3 🔊 **1.32** Listen to Joe. Where is he from? Tick (✔) the occasion he talks about.
  ☐ Halloween   ☐ Mother's Day
  ☐ New Year's Eve ☐ Saint Patrick's Day

4 🔊 **1.32** Listen again and answer the questions.
  1 When is Saint Patrick's Day?
  2 Who can you watch in a big parade?
  3 What does Joe wear?
  4 What does Joe's family do in the evening?

5 Which of the occasions would you like to go to? Why?
  I'd like to go to … because …

The history of tweed

A ▶ 7 Watch the video and answer the presenter's questions. Name three things that people make from tweed.

B ▶ 7 Watch the video again and circle the correct answer.

1 The Isle of Harris is an island in *Wales / Scotland* .
2 People started to make tweed there *200 / 300* years ago.
3 In the past, the different colours came from *insects / plants*.
4 There are some colourful *suits / skirts* in the shop.
5 Doctor Who is wearing a tweed *hat / jacket*.

C Which of the clothes from the video are your favourite? Why?

PROJECT

- Work in groups. Make a video or a poster presenting the clothes people wear in your country on a special occasion.

- Choose an occasion. Use these ideas to help you.

  > weddings   parties   family events
  > school events   festivals   other celebrations

- Prepare clothes for a boy and a girl. Take a photo or make a video of one of you wearing these clothes and prepare a description of the occasion and the clothes. Use these questions to help you.

  What is the occasion? When and where is it?
  What do people wear? What do people do?

- Share your videos or posters with the class. Which is your favourite presentation? Why?

Clothes for a special occasion

> The occasion we want to talk about is …
> It happens every year in …
> People usually wear …
> Traditionally boys wear …
> and girls wear …
> People usually dance / eat … / have a lot of fun!

2 Working hard

Vocabulary I can talk about jobs and work.

In this unit
Vocabulary
- Jobs
- Describing jobs
- *make* and *do*
- Learning and exams
- Expressions with *take*

Grammar
- *have to, must, mustn't*
- *had to, could*

8–9
2.2 Grammar video

10
2.2 Grammar animation

11
2.3 Grammar animation

12
2.4 Communication video

1 Work in groups. Think of a job for each letter of the alphabet. Here are some jobs to get you started:
astronaut   **b**us *driver*   **c**hef   **d**og *walker*   **E**nglish *teacher*

I know that!

52 jobs in 52 weeks!

When Jack Miller left school, he was worried. He didn't know what he wanted to do. Then Jack saw a TV show called *52 jobs in 52 weeks*. He decided to take part and try different jobs! This is what he did in his first five weeks.

1 In week one, Jack was a ¹_____ . He worked in a toy factory. The toys were cool, but the job was `boring`!

2 After that, he was a ²_____ . Jack didn't like it – and his customers hated their hairstyles!

3 In week three, he was a ³_____ . It was `exciting`, but it was `dangerous` too.

4 How many windows are there?

Next, he was a ⁴_____ in London. He liked his uniform, but the job was `challenging`. Tourists asked him difficult questions!

5 How many windows are there?

This week Jack is a ⁵_____ . It's interesting and `well-paid` and he meets famous people. Now Jack asks the difficult questions!

2.1

2 🔊 **1.33** Listen and repeat. Which jobs would you like to try?

Vocabulary Jobs

architect   cleaner   computer programmer   dentist
engineer   factory worker   firefighter   hairdresser
journalist   secretary   tour guide

3 🔊 **1.34** Read the cartoon on page 24 and complete it with the names of the jobs. Then listen and check.

4 Write the names of the jobs. Who:
1 looks after your teeth? *dentist*
2 cleans offices and schools?
3 designs or builds machines?
4 writes programmes for computers?
5 designs new buildings?
6 makes phone calls and organises meetings?

5 🔊 **1.35** Listen and repeat. Find the opposites of adjectives 1–4 in the Vocabulary box.

Vocabulary Describing jobs

badly paid   boring   challenging   dangerous
easy   exciting   safe   well-paid

1 exciting ≠ *boring*   3 badly paid ≠ _____
2 easy   ≠ _____   4 safe   ≠ _____

6 🔊 **1.36** Read about Jack's other jobs. Complete the sentences with the correct adjectives. Then listen and check.

7 Which of Jack's jobs do you think is the most and the least interesting? Why?

8 🔊 **1.37** Listen to three people. What jobs do they do? How do they describe them?

	Speaker 1	Speaker 2	Speaker 3
Job			
Description			

9 **Exam Spot** Which jobs do people in your family do? What are their jobs like?

My aunt is a teacher. It's a challenging job, but she loves it.

10 Complete the sentences. Choose jobs from this page or use your own ideas. Compare your answers in pairs.

1 The most exciting job is _____ .
2 The most boring job is _____ .
3 The easiest job is _____ .
4 The most challenging job is _____ .
5 The strangest job is _____ .
6 The most dangerous job is _____ .
7 The best job for me is _____ !

I remember that!

My other jobs

The police officer's job was ¹e*xciting* . It was never boring. We caught a famous criminal, so it was ²d_____ too!

I enjoyed working as a computer programmer. I played a lot of computer games. This job wasn't dangerous, it was ³s_____ .

My week as a cleaner was not bad, but I didn't earn much money. It was a ⁴b_____ job.

Was my job as an engineer ⁵e_____ ? No, it wasn't! Building roads and bridges is difficult! It's really ⁶c_____ ! What job's next? Who knows …

2.2 Grammar — I can use *have to*, *must*, *mustn't*.

I have to help mum

Saturday, 2 October

My mum has her own café and we live in the flat above it. The café is a dream come true for mum, but she sometimes gets tired. Mum's the chef, the waitress and the cleaner, so she has to work very hard! Yesterday, Zadie came round …

Zadie: Hi, Bella. Do you want to come to the park?
Bella: I'd love to, but I have to help mum. She's super busy today.
Zadie: What do you have to do?
Bella: I have to make some sandwiches.
Zadie: No problem. I can help.
Bella: Hmm, I don't know. Mum?
Mum: Sure, Zadie. You can help Bella with the salami sandwiches. But you must wash your hands before you start, and you must put on an apron and gloves.

Bella: Oh, Zadie, you're making a mess!
Zadie: Oops … sorry. I'm doing my best.
Bella: Yes, but be careful! You mustn't mix up the chillies and the peppers.
Zadie: Oh, are they chillies?
Mum: Can you take a salami and pepper sandwich to table two, please, Bella?
Bella: OK, Mum. Do I have to do the dishes next?
Mum: No, you don't. You don't have to do anything else, Bella. I can manage. Thanks for your help, girls.

Five minutes later …

Customer: Er … excuse me. Can I have some water, please? It's a bit … spicy.
Mum: Bella, Bella! What did you give this gentleman?
Bella: A salami sandwich, Mum.
Zadie: Oops! I think I put some chillies in that sandwich.

---

1 Read the extract from Bella's diary. Where do Bella and her mum live? What jobs does Bella's mum do?

2 ▶ 8 🔊 **1.38** Watch or listen and read. Answer the questions.

1 Where does Zadie want to go?
2 Why can't Bella go?
3 What does Zadie offer to do?
4 What food does the customer order?
5 What did Zadie put in the sandwich?

3 🔊 **1.39** Listen and repeat. Find these expressions in the story.

> She's super busy.   I can manage.

Say it!

4 ▶ **Guess!** What happens next? Have a class vote.

a The customer complains about the sandwich.
b The customer loves the sandwich.

5 ▶ 9 🔊 **1.40** Now watch or listen and check.

Grammar have to, must, mustn't

have to

+	I **have to** help.	–	I **don't have to** help.
	He **has to** help.		He **doesn't have to** help.
?	**Do** you **have to** help?		Yes, I **do**. / No, I **don't**.
	Does she **have to** help?		Yes, she **does**. / No, she **doesn't**.
	What **do** you **have to** do?		

must, mustn't

+	I **must** clean up.	–	They **mustn't** clean up.

I **have to** help mum. = I **must** help mum. (= It's necessary.)
You **don't have to** help mum. (= It isn't necessary.)
You **mustn't** mix up the chillies and peppers. (= Don't do it!)

▶ 10 Get Grammar!

Fluffy is ill. She **has to** stay in bed.
Max and Anna **have to** take care of her.

9 Circle the correct answer.

1 You (mustn't) / don't have to stay up late. You've got an exam tomorrow.
2 We mustn't go / don't have to go to school today. It's Sunday!
3 You mustn't / don't have to touch the cooker. It's hot!
4 We mustn't / don't have to help this morning. There aren't many customers.

6 Complete Bella's diary with *have to, has to, don't have to* or *doesn't have to*.

Sunday, 3 October
My mum ¹ has to wake up very early! She ² _____ make cakes in the morning, and she ³ _____ do the shopping too, but she ⁴ _____ make the sandwiches. She does that when the café opens. I sometimes help her when she's busy, but I ⁵ _____ help on weekdays. I ⁶ _____ do my homework then! I usually help at the weekend – I ⁷ _____ clean the tables, make sandwiches or salads and serve customers. Luckily, we ⁸ _____ do the dishes – there's a dishwasher in the kitchen!

7 In pairs, ask and answer questions about the expressions highlighted in Exercise 6.

A: *Does Bella's mum have to wake up early?*
B: *Yes, she does.*

LOOK!
You **must** wash your hands.
NOT You must ~~to~~ wash your hands.

You **mustn't** mix up the chillies.
NOT You mustn't ~~to~~ mix up the chillies.

8 The next day Bella is making a salad. What are her mum's instructions? Use *must* or *mustn't*.

1 wash the cucumbers ✔
   You must wash the cucumbers.
2 cut up the tomatoes ✔
3 use the chillies – they're too hot! ✘
4 add a lot of salt ✘
5 add some olive oil ✔
6 sneeze in the salad ✘

10 🔊 1.41 Listen and repeat. Then complete the questions with *make* and *do*.

Vocabulary Make and do

make	make a mess	make your bed
	make breakfast / lunch / dinner	
do	do my homework	do the dishes
	do the shopping	do your best

1 Who usually has to do the shopping in your family?
2 Do you often have to _____ breakfast or lunch?
3 Do you have to _____ homework at the weekend?
4 Do you have to _____ your bed in the morning?
5 Who has to _____ the dishes after meals?
6 Do you always have to tidy up when you _____ a mess?

11 **Exam Spot** In pairs, ask and answer the questions in Exercise 10.

2.3 Grammar — I can use *had to* and *could*.

The Explorers — Amazon adventure

The Explorers are in the Amazon. They're looking for the lost tribe of Anamata.

1
Eva: We have to go down the river. Look, there's a motorboat.
Pops: When I started exploring, there weren't any motorboats. We had to use a canoe, but I could paddle really well!
Mac: We know, Pops!

2
Pops: Look! A monkey! Where's my camera?
Eva: Use my phone, Pops.
Pops: When I was a travel journalist, we had to use a camera!
Mac: Did you have to use that one, Pops?
Pops: Yes, I did. It's old but it still works!

3
Eva: Which way now?
Pops: Let's look at my map.
Mac: Don't worry, Pops. The GPS says 'turn right'.
Pops: When I was a jungle guide, I could get to places without GPS! And I could read a map really well!

Finally, the Explorers find the tribe.

4
MATINATI XIAO KAPIGA XAI HI GO

It's OK, Pops. Look! He's got a mobile phone!

A Smartphone 100? Cool!

… I give up!

Mac: What are they saying? Use the translate app!
Eva: I can't! The phone is out of battery.
Pops: In my day, we didn't have to worry about phones or batteries. When I couldn't speak a language, I used my dictionary. Here!

1 I know that! Look at the cartoon. What travel equipment can you see?

> backpack   camera   map   guidebook
> sleeping bag   suitcase   tent   torch

2 🔊 **1.42** Read and listen. Answer the questions.
1 Which boat did Pops use in the past?
2 What does he want to take a picture of?
3 Which jobs did Pops do in the past?
4 What didn't Pops have in the past?
5 Why does Pops 'give up'?

Grammar *had to, could*

had to

+	We **had to** use canoes.	–	We **didn't have to** use canoes.
?	**Did** you **have to** use canoes?		Yes, I **did**. / No, I **didn't**.
?	What **did** you **have to** use?		

could

+	She **could** use a phone.	–	She **couldn't** use a phone.
?	**Could** she use a phone?		Yes, she **could**. / No, she **couldn't**.
?	What **could** she use?		

▶ 11 **Get Grammar!**

Prehistoric cats **had to** find their own food. They **could** hunt really well!

We **had to** use canoes. (= It was necessary.)
We **didn't have to** use a phone. (= It wasn't necessary.)
I **could** read a map. (= I was able to do it.)
I **couldn't** speak a language. (= I wasn't able to do it.)

3 Complete the sentences with *had to* or *didn't have to*.
1. When Pops was young, he <u>had to</u> use canoes.
2. When the Explorers were in the Amazon, they _____ use canoes – they used a motorboat.
3. When Pops was young, he _____ take photos with a camera.
4. When the Explorers were in the Amazon, they _____ take photos with a camera – they used a phone.
5. When Pops was young, he _____ use a map.
6. When the Explorers were in the Amazon, they _____ use a map – they used GPS.

4 What did Pops have to do last weekend? Ask and answer in pairs.

1. get up early ✔   4. wash his socks ✘
2. cook breakfast ✘ 5. write his diary ✔
3. wake up Mac ✔   6. read a guidebook ✘

A: *Did Pops have to get up early last weekend?*
B: *Yes, he did.*

5 In pairs, ask and answer about what you had to do last weekend.
1. get up early?   3. do homework?
2. tidy your room? 4. go shopping?

A: *Did you have to get up early?*
B: *Yes, I did. / No, I didn't.*

6 In pairs, ask and answer questions about what Pops *could* or *couldn't* do when he was a young explorer.

1. ride a bike ✘   ride a camel ✔
2. climb mountains ✔   climb trees ✘
3. speak Chinese ✘   speak French ✔
4. play chess ✔   play football ✘

A: *Could Pops ride a bike?*
B: *No, he couldn't. But he could ride a camel.*

7 Ask and answer about what you *could* or *couldn't* do when you were ten years old.

A: *Could you play chess?*   B: *No, I couldn't!*

8 🔊 1.43 Complete the dialogue between Pops and his friend Albert. Use one word in each gap. Then listen and check.

Albert: Did you find the lost tribe of Anamata?
Pops: Yes, we did.
Albert: Were they friendly?
Pops: Yes, they were. But we ¹<u>couldn't</u> speak their language.
Albert: Did you ²_____ to use your dictionary?
Pops: No, we ³_____. We used a translate app.
Albert: ⁴_____ they understand you?
Pops: Yes, they could. They invited us to a party!
Albert: Did you have ⁵_____ eat jungle food?
Pops: Yes, we ⁶_____. We ate fried snake.

2.4 Communication — I can ask for and give advice.

What should I wear?

Adam: I need your advice, Josh. I've got a Saturday job and tomorrow's my first day. What should I wear?
Josh: I think you should look smart on your first day. What about wearing a white shirt and black trousers?
Adam: OK, wait a minute.

Adam: What do you think?
Josh: Hmm, not bad, but in my opinion, you shouldn't wear trainers. They don't look very smart. And why don't you put on a tie?
Adam: What about this?
Josh: Oh, yes, that's much better. By the way, what's the job?
Adam: Well, it's not a job really. I'm a volunteer. At the animal rescue centre in town.
Josh: Animal rescue centre? What do you have to do?
Adam: I have to clean the cages and feed the dogs!
Josh: In a white shirt and a tie?

1 ▶12 🔊 1.44 Watch or listen and read. What advice does Adam need? What's Josh's advice?

2 🔊 1.45 Listen and repeat.

Communication
Asking for and giving advice

Asking for advice
I need your advice. / Can I ask your advice?
What should I *wear*?

Giving advice
You should *look smart*.
You shouldn't *wear trainers*.
In my opinion, you shouldn't *wear trainers*.
What about *wearing a white shirt*?
Why don't you *put on a tie*?

---

4 Exam Spot In pairs, act out the two dialogues. Use the Communication box to help you.
  1 **Student A:** You want to go to the cinema, but you've got an exam tomorrow. Ask Student B for advice.
    Student B: Give advice to Student A.
  2 **Student B:** You'd like to earn some extra money, but you don't know how. Ask Student A for advice.
    Student A: Give advice to Student B.

5 In pairs, act out dialogues for these unusual situations. Then think of your own ideas.
  1 There's a giant owl in my bed!
    A: *There's a giant owl in my bed! What should I do?*
    B: *You should give it a sausage!*
  2 My mum's coming to teach English at my school!
  3 Help! I think I'm an alien.
  4 I can't stop watching videos of cats on the Internet.

3 🔊 1.46 Put the dialogue in the correct order. Listen and check. Act out the dialogue in pairs.
  ☐ **Anna:** You shouldn't go to bed so late.
  ☐ **Kate:** But I've already set three alarms on my phone!
  ☐ **Kate:** You're right. I should go to bed earlier.
  ☐ **Anna:** You should set another one then!
  ☐ **Anna:** And why don't you set an alarm on your phone?
  [1] **Kate:** I need your advice, Anna. I was late again for school this morning. What should I do?

I can understand a text about unusual jobs. **Reading** 2.5

Weird and wonderful jobs!

What do you want to be when you grow up? A footballer, a doctor, an engineer? Before you decide, take a look at these unusual jobs!

Circus performer — Dan Thomas

I work as a circus performer. I have to travel a lot and practise hard, but I love performing! How did I get the job? I could juggle when I was six. Then, when I was eighteen, I went to a circus school. There aren't any animals in my circus – so I don't have to train lions … But it can still be dangerous when you're juggling with knives or with fire!

Chocolate taster — Megan Lester

I work for a chocolate company. My job is to taste new types of chocolate. I have to give them a score out of ten. I also write down the taste, for example: sweet, creamy, or bitter. You don't have to have any special training to do the job, but you have to love chocolate! It's a great job, but last year I had to visit the dentist six times!

Games tester — Robbie Jackson

I work as a games tester. I test the different levels of each game, and I have to write down any problems. It's fun, but it can be boring. Last week I had to test a really easy kids game again and again! You don't have to be an expert to do the job but you have to be good at computer games. I'm studying computing in the evening because I'd like to become a programmer.

1 🔊 1.47 Look at the photos. What do you think the people do? Read and listen to the text and check.

2 Find words 1–6 in the text. Match definitions a–f to words 1–6.

1 [f] practise
2 [ ] juggle
3 [ ] score
4 [ ] bitter
5 [ ] train
6 [ ] expert

a teach an animal to do something
b a person who knows a lot about something
c opposite of 'sweet'
d throw objects into the air and catch them
e the number of points
f do something again and again, so that you get better

3 **Exam Spot** Read the text again and complete the sentences with one, two or three words in each gap.

1 Dan loves his job but he has to practise hard and <u>travel a lot</u>.
2 Before he got his job, Dan was at _____ .
3 To be a chocolate taster, you don't need any _____ .
4 The bad thing about Megan's job is that she often has to go _____ .
5 Robbie's job is sometimes boring because he has to test the same game _____ .
6 Robbie is studying in the evening because he wants to _____ .

4 Which of the jobs in the text would or wouldn't you like to do? Why? / Why not?

Fun Spot

5 Play *What's my job?* Think of an unusual job and do a short mime. The class must ask questions to guess the job. You can only answer *Yes* or *No*.

A: *Do you work with animals?* B: *Yes.*
C: *Do you have to wear a uniform?* B: *No.*
D: *Are you an elephant trainer?* B: *Yes!*

2.6 Listening and Vocabulary

I can understand a listening text about learning.

1 **I know that!** How many school subjects can you name in one minute? Which subjects do you like and dislike?

2 🔊 1.48 Listen and repeat. Which expressions go with Perfect Patricia, and which go with Lazy Lenny?

Vocabulary Learning and exams

copy someone's work   do well / badly   take notes
get a good / bad mark   hand in your homework
pass / fail an exam   revise for a test   take an exam

Perfect Patricia — *do well*

Lazy Lenny — *copy someone's work*

3 Complete the quiz with the verbs in the box. There are two extra verbs.

> copy do fail get hand
> miss ~~pass~~ revise take

QUIZ — What kind of student are you?

1 You've got an important exam next Friday. What do you do?
 a I start revising now. I want to ¹ _pass_ the exam.
 b I ² _____ for half an hour the night before the exam.

2 You forget to do your English homework.
 a I ask my teacher if I can ³ _____ in the homework tomorrow.
 b I ask a friend if I can ⁴ _____ their homework.

3 You ⁵ _____ an exam. What do you do before the next one?
 a I try to ⁶ _____ better notes in class.
 b Nothing. Some people ⁷ _____ badly at school, but they're still successful.

Your score: a = 2 points, b = 0 points

4 🔊 1.49 Do the quiz and add up your score. Then listen to find out what kind of student you are. Do you agree?

5 🔊 1.50 Listen to Alice talking to Oscar. Answer the questions.
 1 What did Oscar have to give up last month because of exams?
 2 Who's more hard-working: Oscar or Alice?

6 **Exam Spot** 🔊 1.50 Listen to Alice and Oscar again. Circle the correct answer a, b or c.
 1 What exam did Oscar take today?
  a History ⓑ Science c Maths
 2 What did he have to do in the exam?
  a do an experiment b write an essay
  c answer questions
 3 What does he think about the exam?
  a He thinks he failed.
  b He thinks he did quite well.
  c He thinks he did really well.
 4 What does he have to do tonight?
  a go to the cinema b help his mum
  c revise for his next exam
 5 What is Alice going to do about her English homework?
  a hand it in late b do it at the cinema
  c copy her friend's work

7 Read the Vocabulary Builder. Then complete the sentences.

Vocabulary Builder
Expressions with *take*

take a photo   take an exam   take medicine
take notes   take the bus

 1 Can I take a _photo_ of you with my new camera?
 2 I'm taking an English _____ next week.
 3 Did you take any _____ in today's history lesson?
 4 I usually walk to school, but when it rains I take the _____ .
 5 A: I've got a headache.
    B: You should take some _____ .

8 **Exam Spot** Discuss the questions as a class.
 1 Do you have to take a lot of exams? Do you think it's a good idea to take a lot of exams? Why? / Why not?
 2 How much homework do you get a week? Is it too much or not enough?

I can write a text about my ideal school. **Writing**

My ideal school
by Susie Marshall

1. My ideal school is a large sunny building in the countryside. There are comfortable sofas in every classroom and there aren't any desks. Outside, there's a big playground with trampolines and a funfair!

2. Lessons start at ten o'clock, so that students don't have to get up early. Students don't have to take tests or exams and they don't have to wear a uniform. They can wear casual clothes, such as T-shirts and jeans.

3. After school, there are lots of school clubs, including drama, sports and music. There's a school trip every month, for example a visit to an IMAX cinema, or a trip to the beach. The atmosphere is very good and the teachers are friendly. It's a great school!

1 Exam Spot What do you like best about your school? What don't you like?

2 Read Susie's essay. Tick (✔) the things she writes about.
- ✔ the school building
- ☐ classrooms
- ☐ clothes
- ☐ food
- ☐ school trips
- ☐ exams
- ☐ a typical day
- ☐ homework
- ☐ after-school clubs
- ☐ school holidays

3 Read the Writing box. Which expressions can you find in Susie's essay?

Writing Describing a school

① The building
It's a *big / small* building *in the countryside*.
There's *a playground / a swimming pool*.
There are *computers / sofas* in every classroom.

② The school routine, rules, clothes
Lessons start at … and finish at …
You can *wear casual clothes*.
You have to / don't have to *wear a uniform / take exams*.

③ After-school activities, the atmosphere and conclusion
There are *school clubs / trips*.
The atmosphere is *good / great / amazing*.
It's a great place. I love going there.

4 Read the box. Then complete the sentences with *such as*, *for example* or *including* and your own ideas.

Giving examples
There is a school trip every month, *for example* a visit to an IMAX cinema, or a trip to the beach.
They can wear casual clothes, *such as* T-shirts and jeans.
There are lots of school clubs, *including* drama, sports and music.

1 In my school there are lots of sports to choose from, *for example basketball and football*.
2 The school shop sells great food, _____.
3 You can wear the clothes that you like, _____.
4 There are some really good clubs, _____.

5 Writing Time Write about your ideal school.

 Find ideas
Make notes about your ideal school. Use Exercise 2 to help you and add your own ideas.

 Draft
Organise your ideas into paragraphs. Use the ideas in the Writing box.

 Check and write
Check you have included examples and write the final version of your text.

2.8 Language Revision

Vocabulary

1 Who needs these things? Label photos A–F with the names of jobs.

A _cleaner_
B _____
C _____
D _____
E _____
F _____

2 Match the word halves. Match each adjective to one job in Exercise 1. More than one answer is possible.

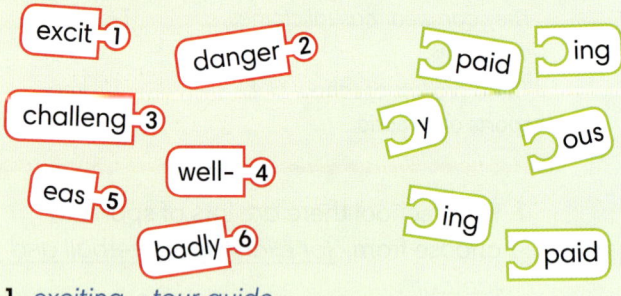

excit 1
danger 2
challeng 3
well- 4
eas 5
badly 6

paid
ing
y
ous
ing
paid

1 _exciting – tour guide_

3 Match sentence halves a–e to 1–5.

1 [e] The dishwasher isn't working. Can you do
2 [ ] On Saturday morning I always do
3 [ ] Don't worry about your exams. Do
4 [ ] Tidy your room and make
5 [ ] I have to make

a the shopping with my dad.
b your best and you'll be fine!
c my packed lunch before I go to school.
d your bed, please!
e the dishes, please?

4 Complete the questions. Then ask and answer in pairs.

> copy   do   ~~hand~~   pass   take

1 Do you usually _hand_ in your homework on time?
2 Do you always _____ notes in your English class?
3 Do you ever _____ other people's work?
4 Did you _____ all of your exams last year?
5 Do you usually _____ well or badly in Maths tests?

Grammar

5 Complete the dialogue with the correct form of *have to*.

Adam: ¹ _Do_ you _have to_ go to football practice this afternoon?
Josh: No, I ² _____ . We ³ _____ play today. Why?
Adam: I've got four free tickets for the cinema.
Josh: Cool! Are Bella and Zadie free?
Adam: Zadie's free – she ⁴ _____ go to band practice.
Josh: ⁵ _____ Bella _____ help her mum?
Adam: No, she ⁶ _____ .
Josh: Great – we can all go!

6 Complete the sentences with *must*, *mustn't* or the correct form of *have to*.

1 You _must_ put on some sun cream. It's very hot today.
2 We _____ get up early. It's the summer holidays!
3 You _____ touch the dog. It can bite!
4 Mark _____ wash his school uniform. It's already clean.
5 Sheila _____ take her medicine. It's important!

7 Complete the text about Pops with *had to*, *didn't have to*, *could* or *couldn't*.

Pops wasn't very good at school. He was good at sports: he ¹ _could_ run very quickly. He ² _____ also read very well, but he ³ _____ spell words correctly. He made lots of mistakes! He often ⁴ _____ write his essays again because his teachers ⁵ _____ read them! However, he loved the Geography lessons: he ⁶ _____ revise for Geography tests because he knew more than his teacher!

Round up 2.8

8 Complete the sentences with *had to, didn't have to, could, couldn't* and the correct verbs.

1. I can ride a bike now. ✔
   I *couldn't ride* a bike when I was five. ✘
2. We don't have to help mum today. ✘
   We _____ mum yesterday. ✔
3. She can't ride a horse now. ✘
   She _____ a horse when she was a child. ✔
4. You can play basketball well. ✔
   You _____ basketball well when you were a child. ✘
5. He has to finish his homework today. ✔
   He _____ his homework last night. ✘

Communication

9 🔊 1.51 Complete the dialogue with one word in each gap. Listen and check.

Girl: I need your ¹ *advice* . I've got an English exam next month and I want to do well. What should I ² _____ ?

Boy: You ³ _____ start revising now. You ⁴ _____ wait.

Girl: You're right.

Boy: What ⁵ _____ taking notes when you revise?

Girl: That's a good idea. Thanks.

Boy: And ⁶ _____ don't we revise together sometimes?

Girl: Great idea! Let's start tomorrow.

Dictation

10 **Exam Spot** 🔊 1.52 Listen to a short text. Then listen again and write down what you hear. Make sure you spell the words correctly.

Pronunciation

11 🔊 1.53 Listen and repeat: /h/.

Harry isn't very happy.
His hair is messy!
He has to have a haircut with
Hannibal the hairdresser.

Check yourself! ✓
- I can talk about jobs and learning.
- I can use *have to, must* and *mustn't*.
- I can use *had to* and *could*.
- I can ask for and give advice.

12 Read the sentences. Circle the correct answer a, b, or c.

1. My dad's job is dangerous, but he loves it. He's a/an _____ .
   a architect   **b firefighter**   c tour guide
2. Hannah did well in her exams. She _____ good marks for everything!
   a got   b did   c made
3. Who _____ breakfast in your family?
   a does   b helps   c makes
4. Did you _____ notes in Maths today? Can I copy them?
   a do   b take   c revise
5. Teaching isn't an easy job, it's very _____ .
   a challenging   b boring   c well-paid
6. I have to hand _____ my homework tomorrow.
   a in   b on   c of
7. Do you _____ finish your science project today?
   a have to   b has to   c have
8. Be careful! You _____ touch the cooker. It's very hot!
   a must   b mustn't   c don't have to
9. You _____ start revising soon – you've got exams next week!
   a don't have to   b must   c mustn't
10. She didn't go out last night. She _____ look after her little brother.
    a has to   b didn't have to   c had to
11. I _____ skateboard when I was a teenager, but I can't now!
    a couldn't   b could   c had to
12. A: My sister missed the school bus yesterday.
    B: Did she _____ walk to school?
    a have to   b has to   c had to
13. You _____ copy your friend's homework. It isn't a good idea!
    a should   b shouldn't   c need to
14. A: I haven't got anything to wear tonight!
    B: What about _____ this T-shirt?
    a wear   b to wear   c wearing
15. In my opinion, this dress is not smart enough. _____ you wear the red one?
    a Why   b Why don't   c Why not

35

1 & 2 Skills Revision

Reading and Writing

An unusual job!

Susie Little has an unusual job – she's a wing walker! Every weekend, Susie stands on a plane and does acrobatics in air shows. It's exciting and it's well-paid, but it isn't easy! 'You must be fit and strong,' says Susie. 'You also have to be small.' Susie is 1.60 metres tall and very strong, but she still finds it difficult. 'The first time I was on a plane, I had to wave and smile. The plane was going at 160 kilometres per hour so it was really hard!' she says. 'After the show, I felt tired. I couldn't move my arms!'

Susie has to wear a special flying suit, and she mustn't eat before a show. 'Before the last air show I was really hungry,' she says, 'but I couldn't eat even a packet of crisps!' However, she loves performing in the air. Does she sometimes worry about the danger? 'Not really', she says. 'I don't think my job is dangerous. When I see police officers or firefighters then I think 'Wow, that's a dangerous job! Wing walking is fun – it's my dream job!' she adds.

1 Look at the photo. What's the woman's job? What adjectives would you use to describe it?

2 **Exam Spot** Read the text and complete the notes with one, two or three words in each gap.

1 Susie is a _wing walker_ .
2 She works every _____ .
3 When Susie is on the plane, she has to wave, smile and do _____ .
4 Susie has to wear a special _____ .
5 Susie is small: she's only 1.60 _____ .
6 She can't eat anything before the show so she's often _____ .
7 Susie thinks her job is difficult, but it isn't _____ .

3 **Exam Spot** Write about your ideal job. Say:
- What is your ideal job? How would you describe it?
- Where do these people work?
- What do they have to do? What don't they have to do?

My ideal job is an astronaut. I think it's an exciting job! Astronauts work in … They have to …

Use of English

4 **Exam Spot** Read the texts and circle the correct answer a, b or c.

1

Second-hand clothes sale!

Is your wardrobe full of clothes you never wear? Do you have smart, formal clothes or _____ , comfortable clothes that you don't like?

Come and make some money from your old ties, trousers, shirts and skirts.

Recommended price: £5 per item
Wednesday 6 p.m., school hall

(a) casual   b tight   c favourite

2

HOW TO _____

You should:
- find a quiet place to study,
- take regular breaks and go for a walk sometimes,
- drink water and eat healthy snacks.

a get bad marks   b take tests
c revise for exams

3

Moments Café
Opening hours: 9 a.m. – 6 p.m.

Special lunch time offer: a sandwich & a tea or coffee for only £5!

We're _____ our best to make you happy!

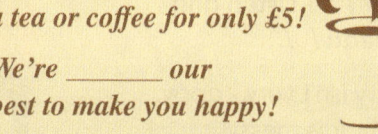

a doing   b making   c taking

4

Dear Lily, I'm really sorry, but I can't find your Maths book. I think I left it in the library when I was revising. Sorry! I'm so _____ ! I can buy you a new one this weekend.

a lazy   b disorganised   c impolite

Skills Revision 1 & 2

Listening

5 **Exam Spot** 🔊 **1.54** Listen to Holly and Emma talking about a concert and circle the correct answer a, b or c.

1 How much did Holly pay for the tickets?
   a ☐ £5   b ☐ £10   c ☑ £15

2 What is Luke's hairstyle?
   a ☐   b ☐   c ☐

3 What did Holly wear for the concert?
   a ☐   b ☐   c ☐

4 What time did the concert finish?
   a ☐ 8:00   b ☐ 8:30   c ☐ 9:00

Communication

6 Read the dialogues and circle the correct answer a, b or c.

1 A: Guess what happened yesterday! I won a camera!
   B: a Poor you!   **ⓑ Lucky you!**
      c How embarrassing!

2 A: I need your advice. It's Irene's birthday on Sunday. What should I buy her?
   A: a Why don't you wear a smart dress?
      b What about buying some nice earrings?
      c No, you shouldn't.

3 A: Why don't you change your hairstyle? You'd look good with shorter hair.
   B: a Lucky you!   b You shouldn't do it.
      c OK, I think it's a good idea.

7 **Exam Spot** Ask and answer the questions in pairs.

1 What are your favourite clothes?
2 What is your best friend like?
3 What jobs are the most exciting?
4 How do you revise for exams?

Exam Language Bank

Clothes and accessories
belt	earrings	ring	socks
boots	handbag	sandals	tie
bracelet	hat	scarf	tights
cardigan	hoodie	shirt	top
coat	jacket	shorts	trainers
dress	leggings	skirt	

Describing clothes
checked, baggy
floral, casual
plain, smart
spotted, tight
striped

Hairstyles
curly hair, wavy hair
dyed hair, bald
shaved hair, beard
spiky hair, moustache
straight hair

Personality adjectives
friendly
generous, polite
hard-working, rude
honest, selfish
kind, serious
lazy, shy
organised, talkative
patient

Negative adjectives
disorganised
dishonest
impatient
impolite
unfriendly
unkind

Jobs
architect
cleaner
computer programmer
dentist
engineer
factory worker
firefighter
hairdresser
journalist
secretary
tour guide

Describing jobs
badly paid, dangerous, safe
boring, easy, well-paid
challenging, exciting

Make* and *do
make a mess, make your bed, do the shopping
make breakfast / lunch / dinner, do my homework, do your best
do the dishes

Learning and exams
copy someone's work, revise for a test
do well / badly, take an exam
get a good / bad mark, take notes
hand in your homework
pass / fail an exam

Expressions with *take*
take the bus
take a photo
take medicine
take an exam
take notes

Telling a story
Guess what happened *on Saturday!*
First, *we went to Lacey's.*
Then, *we went to Bramley's.*
Finally, *she found a pair she liked.*

Reacting
No way!
Then what? / So what happened next?
So what did *he* do?
Poor *Zadie!*
Lucky *him!*
How *funny / embarrassing / strange!*

Asking for advice
I need your advice. /
Can I ask your advice?
What should I *wear*?

Giving advice
You should *look smart*.
You shouldn't *wear trainers*.
In my opinion, you shouldn't *wear trainers*.
What about *wearing a white shirt*?
Why don't you *put on a tie*?

3 That's exciting!

Vocabulary I can talk about things I'd like to do.

In this unit
Vocabulary
- Experiences
- Sports verbs
- Sports equipment
- Compound nouns

Grammar
- Present Perfect, *ever* and *never*
- Present Perfect with *just*, *already* and *yet*

▶ 13-14
3.2 Grammar video

▶ 15
3.2 Grammar animation

▶ 16
3.3 Grammar animation

▶ 17
3.4 Communication video

▶ 18
BBC Culture video

I know that!

1 Match the verbs to the nouns. Think of more nouns that go with each verb.

Verbs	Nouns
~~climb~~ play write take catch	a big fish a selfie with a pop star the guitar a blog about fashion ~~a very high mountain~~

climb a very high mountain
climb a tree, climb the stairs, climb a ladder

Hi, my name's Scarlett and I was fourteen last week. On my birthday, I made **a Dream Map**. It's a collage of all the things I want to do before I'm eighteen. I probably can't do all of them, but it's fun to try!

My Dreams

A B C D E F G H

Be Happy

Think Big

38

2 🔊 **2.1** Look at the photos on page 38. Listen and read what Scarlett says. What is Scarlett's dream map?

3 🔊 **2.2** Listen and repeat. Match the activities to photos A–H.

Vocabulary Experiences

do a parachute jump   go scuba diving   have a party
learn to ski   meet a famous person   ride a camel
stay in a castle   win a competition

4 Match the phrase halves.

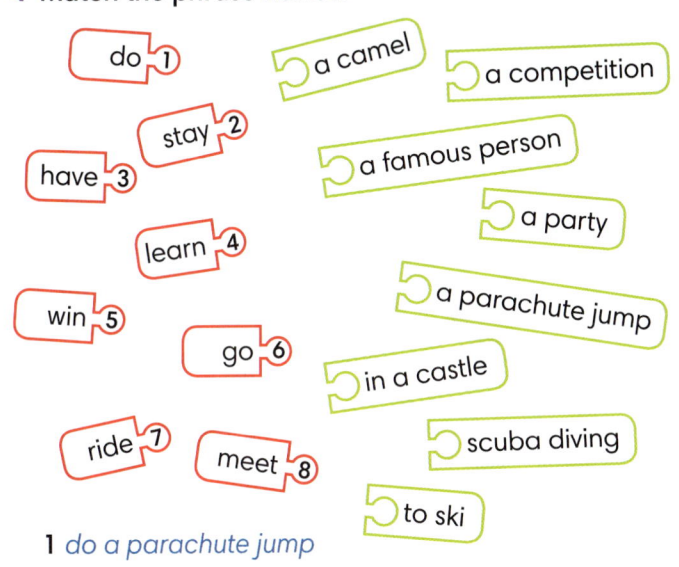

- do 1 — a camel
- stay 2 — a competition
- have 3 — a famous person
- learn 4 — a party
- win 5 — a parachute jump
- go 6 — in a castle
- ride 7 — scuba diving
- meet 8 — to ski

1 do a parachute jump

5 🔊 **2.3** Complete what Scarlett says with the phrases in the Vocabulary box. Then listen and check.

> I'd like to ¹ *go scuba diving*. It looks amazing and I'd love to swim with fish and other creatures.

> For my 18th birthday, I want to ² _____ at my house with all my friends.

> One of my dreams is to ³ _____. I love the idea of flying up high and looking down at the Earth.

> I'd love to ⁴ _____, especially Ed Sheeran. I think he's a really talented musician.

> I'd like to ⁵ _____ in the desert. I don't know why, but it sounds fun!

6 Complete the phrases with a verb in the Vocabulary box.

- a horse, a roller coaster, bungee jumping, ice-skating
- 1 *ride*
- 2 _____
- in a hot-air balloon, snowboarding
- a language, to play the guitar
- a prize, a race
- 3 _____
- 4 _____
- to surf, a football match

7 **Exam Spot** 🔊 **2.4** Listen and match dreams a–g to people 1–5. There are two extra dreams.

Person		Dream
1	e Scarlett's dad	a win a football match
2	☐ Lily	b learn to surf
3	☐ Leo	c go bungee jumping
4	☐ Maria	d learn to ski
5	☐ Thomas	e ride in a hot-air balloon
		f go scuba diving
		g ride a roller coaster

8 In pairs, talk about the experiences in Exercise 3 and Exercise 6.

1 Which of the experiences sounds exciting? Why?

I think winning a competition sounds exciting because you can win a really good prize.

2 Which sounds boring? Why?
3 Which sounds the most dangerous? Why?
4 Which sounds the scariest? Why?

9 Make a list of eight things you'd like to do before you're eighteen. Is your list similar to Scarlett's? Tell the class.

I'd like to …

I remember that!

3.2 Grammar — I can use the Present Perfect, *ever* and *never*.

We've won!

Have you ever done any extreme sports? For example, have you skied down a mountain, or been scuba diving? Bella and Zadie haven't done any extreme sports, but Josh has tried lots of them! Today he's invited Bella and Zadie to go to a go-karting track.

Josh: Have you ever driven a go-kart, Zadie?
Zadie: No, I haven't.
Josh: Well, don't worry. I've done it lots of times. Just follow me …
Zadie: Erm, it's OK, thanks, Josh. Bella hasn't driven before, just like me, so we're going to go slowly. We don't want to crash.

Bella: Have you ever crashed, Josh?
Josh: No, I haven't. I've never had an accident. Right, it's time for our race. Ten laps and the loser buys lunch!
Bella: Hey, that's not fair!

Zadie: We've won!
Bella: You've won! Well done! High five!
Zadie: I've never been so terrified … or excited! But where's Josh?

---

1 Look at the photos. Where are Josh, Zadie and Bella?

2 ▶13 🔊 2.5 Watch or listen and read. Answer the questions.
  1 Do Zadie and Bella know how to drive a go-kart?
  2 Does Josh know how to drive?
  3 Why does Zadie say 'Erm, it's OK, thanks Josh'?
  4 What does the loser of the race have to do?

3 🔊 2.6 Listen and repeat. Find these expressions in the story.

> Follow me!   That's not fair.   High five!

Say it!

4 ▶ **Guess!** What has happened to Josh? Have a class vote.
  a He's crashed his car.   b He's still racing.

5 ▶14 🔊 2.7 Now watch or listen and check.

40

3.2

Grammar Present Perfect, ever and never

+	I've won.	−	I haven't won.
	He's won.		He hasn't won.
?	Have they won?		Yes, they have. / No, they haven't.
	Has he won?		Yes, he has. / No, he hasn't.
	What has he won?		

Have you ever driven a go-kart? (ever = in your life).
I've never driven a go-kart.

▶ 15 **Get Grammar!**

Has Fluffy ever done a parachute jump?
No, she hasn't.
Fluffy has never done a parachute jump.

6 Match the infinitives to the past participles.

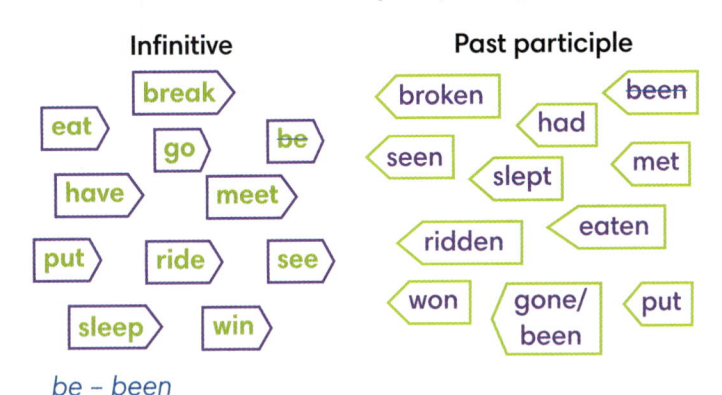

Infinitive: break, eat, go, be, have, meet, put, ride, see, sleep, win

Past participle: broken, been, had, seen, met, slept, ridden, eaten, won, gone/been, put

be – been

LOOK! I never go scuba diving.
I would like to go to Paris.
BUT:
I've never been scuba diving.
I've never been to Paris.

7 Complete the sentences with the Present Perfect form of the verbs.
1 Today, Josh _has invited_ (invite) the girls to a go-karting track.
2 The kids _____ (put) helmets on.
3 Josh _____ (crash) his car.
4 Luckily, he _____ (not break) an arm or a leg!
5 He _____ (not win) the race.

8 In your notebook, write sentences in the Present Perfect.
1 Bella and Zadie / see a dolphin ✔ a shark ✘
Bella and Zadie have seen a dolphin, but they haven't seen a shark.
2 Zadie / ride a horse ✔ a camel ✘
3 Bella / meet Emma Watson ✔ Taylor Swift ✘
4 Josh / climb a mountain ✔ a volcano ✘
5 Josh and Bella / go surfing ✔ skydiving ✘

9 In pairs, ask and answer about the activities in the photos. Use the Present Perfect and ever. Take notes. Then tell the class about your friend.
1 **A:** *Have you ever been surfing?*
   B: *No, I haven't.*
Lila has never been surfing.

1 go surfing
2 climb a mountain 
3 win a competition  
4 ride a roller coaster 
5 break your arm 
6 try sushi 

Fun Spot

10 Write five questions with *Have you ever* about crazy or funny experiences. Then ask your friends.
Have you ever eaten a chocolate pizza?
Have you ever touched a spider?

3.3 Grammar — I can use the Present Perfect with *just*, *already* and *yet*.

The Explorers — The Golden Boomerang

The Explorers are in Australia.

1

Mac: What are you reading, Pops?
Pops: It's a book about the Golden Boomerang of Woolawarra. I've just finished it.
Eva: The Golden Boomerang?
Pops: Yes. It's an ancient treasure. No one has ever found it, so … what are we waiting for?! Let's get ready!

Later …

2

Pops: So … is everything ready? Have you packed the tent yet, Mac?
Mac: Yes, I have. I haven't checked the weather forecast yet, but I've already made the sandwiches.
Pops: Good work, Mac!

3

Pops: Have you filled the jeep with petrol, Eva? It's a long drive.
Eva: Yes, I have. I've already done that.
Pops: Good work, Eva! I've just filled the water bottles, so we're ready to go! Now, where's the map?
Eva: It's in the jeep, Pops, but I don't think we need it. There's only one road through the desert. Look!

Two hours later …

4

Pops: It's getting really hot! Can you pass me some water? I'm thirsty.
Eva: Sure, erm, where is it, Pops?
Mac: Oh, no! We've forgotten the water!

To be continued …

1 Look at the cartoon and answer the questions.
1. Where are the Explorers?
2. Where do they want to go?
3. How are they travelling?
4. What's the weather like?

2 🔊 2.8 Listen and read. Answer the questions.
1. What is the Golden Boomerang of Woolawarra?
2. Is Woolawarra far?
3. Are there lots of roads in the desert?
4. What have the Explorers forgotten to take?

3.3

Grammar Present Perfect with *just*, *already* and *yet*

+	I've just finished my book.
	Eva's already filled the jeep with petrol.
−	I haven't looked at the map yet.
?	Have you packed the tent yet?
	Yes, I have. / No, I haven't.

▶ 16 **Get Grammar!**

Hammy has already packed his suitcase. He's just left the house.

3 Read the cartoon again. Circle true (T) or false (F). Correct the false sentences.

1 Mac hasn't packed the tent yet.   T / **F**
   Mac has already packed the tent.
2 Mac has already checked the weather forecast.   T / F
3 Mac has already made the sandwiches.   T / F
4 Eva hasn't filled the jeep with petrol yet.   T / F
5 Pops hasn't filled the water bottles yet.   T / F

4 🔊 2.9 Look at the next part of the story. What has just happened? Write sentences with *just*. Then listen and check.

1 The Explorers / arrive / in Woolawarra.
   The Explorers have just arrived in Woolawarra.
2 Pops / buy / some water / from a shop.
3 Eva and Mac / see / a kangaroo.
4 Mac / put up / the tent near the Woolawarra mountain. 
5 Eva / discover / a small cave.
6 Hooray! She / find / the Golden Boomerang!

5 🔊 2.10 Complete Pops's diary with the Present Perfect form of the verbs. Then listen and check.

16 November, 4 p.m.
We ¹have just driven (just / drive) to Woolawarra Museum and we ² _____ (already / give) the Golden Boomerang to the museum director. He is really happy! Where is he going to put it? He ³ _____ (not decide / yet)! He ⁴ _____ (already / tell) the newspapers and a journalist ⁵ _____ (just / take) our photo!

6 In your notebook, write true sentences about what you've done today. Use *yet* or *already*.

1 do my homework
   I haven't done my homework yet.
   I've already done my homework.
2 chat with my friends
3 take a selfie
4 buy a snack
5 send a text message
6 have lunch

7 In pairs, ask and answer about Exercise 6.

A: *Have you done your homework yet?*
B: *Yes, I have. I've already done my homework.*
   No, I haven't. I haven't done my homework yet.

43

3.4 Communication I can ask for and give instructions.

Something's not right

Bella: Hi, Josh. What's that?
Josh: Oh, hi, Bella. It's my new goal. I've just put it up, but something's not right.
Bella: Yes, I can see. Where are the instructions?
Josh: Instructions?
Bella: Ah, here they are. Now what's the first step?

Ten minutes later …

Bella: Then, put this post here.
Josh: OK … and what do I have to do next?
Bella: Put the goal upright. And … it's finished.
Josh: How do I put the net on?
Bella: That's easy. Like this …
Josh: Great! It's ready!
Bella: Be careful, Josh. Don't kick the ball too hard.
Josh, Bella: Oh, no!

1 ▶ 17 🔊 2.11 Watch or listen and read. Where are Josh and Bella? What is Josh doing?

2 🔊 2.12 Listen and repeat.

Communication Instructions

Asking for instructions
How do I *put the net on*?
What's the first step?
What do I have to do next?

Ordering instructions
Before you begin, …
First, … Then, … Next, … Finally, …

Giving instructions
Put this post here.
Next, *put the goal upright*.
Be careful.
Don't / Try not to *kick the ball too hard*.

3 🔊 2.13 Complete the dialogue with one word in each gap. Then listen and check.

Girl: Hey, what are you doing?
Boy: Playing football on my games console.
Girl: It looks fun! ¹*How* do I play?
Boy: Well, ² _____ , choose a player. ³ _____ , you start the game. Next, move your player … like this.
Girl: OK.
Boy: But ⁴ _____ careful – ⁵ _____ press the red button. That turns off the game.
Girl: Right. So I've chosen my player. Erm, what do I ⁶ _____ to do now? Oops!
Boy: I don't believe it! You've pressed the red button!

4 **Exam Spot** 🔊 2.14 Listen to four people giving instructions and circle the correct answer a, b or c.

1 Helen is talking about how to make pancakes. Which ingredients do you need to make them?
  a eggs, flour and milk
  b milk and flour
  c eggs, flour and water

2 What is Karl giving instructions about?
  a how to play a computer game
  b how to watch a DVD
  c how to download a film

3 Lewis is giving instructions about how to start practising a sport. Which sport is he talking about?
  a tennis
  b ice hockey
  c football

4 Freya is talking about how to take a good selfie. When are selfies more interesting?
  a When you take them in dark places.
  b When you do something interesting.
  c When you eat something.

5 **Exam Spot** Work in pairs. Take turns to give instructions.
Student A: Go to page 122.
Student B: Go to page 128.

I can understand a text about a sports person. **Reading** 3.5

Girl power

Profile: Rene Gangarosa
School: Brighton, USA
Age: 16

It's 7 a.m. and most teenagers are still in bed. But not Rene Gangarosa. She's already got up and she's had her breakfast. She's training with her lacrosse* team, and she's just scored a goal!

16-year-old Rene lives for sport: when she was three years old, she started judo. Then, when she was five, she competed in tennis matches. She won lots of tennis competitions. But Rene's favourite sport isn't lacrosse, judo or tennis. It's a sport that she plays with the boys … Rene loves ice hockey!

Rene is really interested in ice hockey – she supports her local team and her favourite player is Jaromir Jagr. However, ice hockey is a difficult game for a girl. The boys are stronger than Rene. When Rene joined the team, they were worried – they didn't want to lose matches. But Rene has worked hard and today she's one of their best players!

Rene can compete in so many sports because her family help her. Her parents take her to lacrosse practice before school and to hockey practice after school. She's so busy that she hasn't got much time for homework! Rene does most of it at break times in school.

It's 10 p.m. now, and Rene has just finished an ice hockey match. She's very tired! Has she ever wanted to stop playing? No, she hasn't! This is the price of success and she wants to be the best!

* lacrosse – a sport that you play with a stick and a small ball

1 I know that! Work in pairs. What sports words do you know? Which sports do you do?

2 🔊 **2.15** Look at the photos. Which sports can you see in the photos? Read and listen. Which photo shows Rene's favourite sport?

3 Exam Spot Read the text again and answer the questions.
1 Which sports does Rene do?
2 How did the hockey team players feel about Rene?
3 How do Rene's family help her?
4 When does Rene usually do her homework?
5 Why does she train so hard?

4 🔊 **2.16** Listen and repeat. Then find the verbs in the text. Match them to their definitions 1–6.

Vocabulary Sports verbs

| compete | lose | score | support | train | win |

1 practise _train_
2 want a team to play well _____
3 not come first in a competition _____
4 be in a competition _____
5 come first in a competition _____
6 get a point in a game _____

5 Match the sentence halves a–d to 1–4.
1 [b] Rene sometimes trains
2 [ ] Rene supports
3 [ ] Rene scored a goal
4 [ ] Rene competes in

a her local ice hockey team.
b at the weekend.
c lots of different sports.
d in her last hockey match.

6 Exam Spot Ask and answer in pairs.
1 Have you ever competed in a sports event?
2 Which team do you support? Do your friends support the same team?

3.6 Listening and Vocabulary

I can understand a listening text about an extreme sport.

1 🔊 **2.17** Listen and repeat. Then label photos A–L with the words in the Vocabulary box.

Vocabulary Sports equipment

boots   gloves   goggles   helmet
hockey stick   ice skates   rollerblades
skateboard   skis   snorkel mask
swimsuit   tennis racket

A *tennis racket*

2 Put the equipment in the Vocabulary box into the correct category. Which equipment is for your:

1 head/face? *goggles, …*
2 body? _____
3 feet? _____
4 hands? _____

3 🔊 **2.18** Listen to a radio interview. Which sport is Rufus talking about? Tick (✔) the equipment Rufus uses.

☐ helmet   ☐ gloves   ☐ racket
☐ goggles   ☐ parachute ☐ skis

4 **Exam Spot** 🔊 **2.18** Listen to the interview again. Read the questions and circle the correct answer a, b or c.

1 What sports doesn't Rufus mention?
  a school sports b extreme sports **c** water sports
2 Rufus's friends think the sport is _____ .
  a dangerous   b safe   c cool
3 Before Rufus jumps he feels _____ .
  a worried   b excited   c scared
4 Rufus travels at the speed of _____ .
  a 200 km/h   b 300 km/h   c 1300 km/h
5 What's the most dangerous part?
  a landing   b jumping
  c opening the parachute
6 How old do you have to be to skydive?
  a seventeen   b eighteen   c sixteen

5 **Exam Spot** Ask and answer in pairs.

1 Have you ever tried an extreme sport?
2 Would you like to try skydiving? Why? / Why not?

6 Read the Vocabulary Builder. Can you think of more compound nouns?

Vocabulary Builder Compound nouns

In English we often use a noun to describe another noun.
tennis racket   hockey stick   ice skates   skateboard

7 Match a–f to 1–6.

1 [f] tennis   a stop / ticket
2 [ ] summer   b bus / playground
3 [ ] bus   c pool / competition
4 [ ] swimming   d skates / rink
5 [ ] school   e holidays / sports
6 [ ] ice   f racket / player / match / ball

8 Cover Exercise 7. Read the definitions and write the correct compound nouns.

Compound nouns quiz

1 We wait here for the bus. *bus stop*
2 We can swim here.
3 We don't go to school at this time of year!
4 We need these things to play tennis!
5 We can play football here at break time.
6 We can ice-skate here.

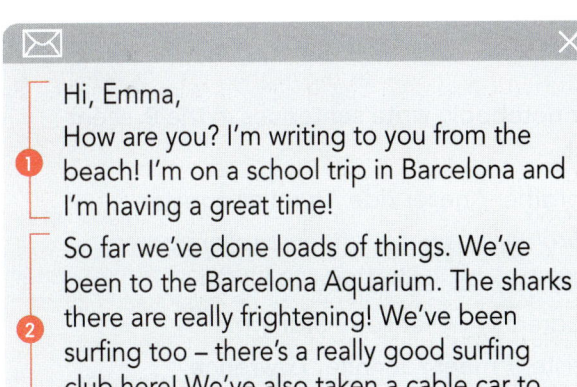

I can write a holiday email. **Writing**

3.7

Hi, Emma,

① How are you? I'm writing to you from the beach! I'm on a school trip in Barcelona and I'm having a great time!

② So far we've done loads of things. We've been to the Barcelona Aquarium. The sharks there are really frightening! We've been surfing too – there's a really good surfing club here! We've also taken a cable car to the castle on Montjuic hill. It's really cool!

③ Tomorrow we're going to the Camp Nou football stadium, so I can meet a famous FC Barcelona player! Then we're off to Tibidabo theme park. I'm looking forward to the roller coaster rides!

④ Hope you're having a good summer too. Write and tell me your news.
Bye for now!
Paul

1 Read Paul's email to Emma. What can you see in the photos?

2 Read the email again and complete the table.

What Paul has already done	What Paul hasn't done yet
He's already been to the Barcelona Aquarium.	

3 Read the Writing box. Which expressions can you find in Paul's email?

Writing A holiday email

❶ Beginning
How are you?   Thanks for your email.
I'm writing this email in *Barcelona*.
The weather is *great*.

❷ What you have done
So far we've done loads of things.
We've been to …
We've seen …

❸ What you are doing tomorrow
Tomorrow we're *going / visiting* …
Then we're off to …
I'm looking forward to …

❹ Ending
Write and tell me your news.
Bye for now.   See you soon.

4 Read the information in the box. Can you add more examples of informal language?

Informal language
When you write to a friend, use informal language, e.g.
- **short forms:** *I'm writing … We've done …*
- **informal expressions:** *We're off to … It's really cool!*
- **informal beginnings and endings:** *Hi! Bye for now!*

5 Look at the things you can see and do in London. Tick (✔) the activities you would like to do.
- ☐ take a boat ride on the river
- ☐ see the Globe Theatre
- ☐ go shopping in Oxford Street
- ☐ ride on the London Eye
- ☐ visit the Natural History Museum

6 Writing Time Imagine you are on a trip in London or in another city or town you know. Write an email to your friend.

? Find ideas
Decide what you have already done and what you haven't done yet. Put the activities in a table, as in Exercise 2.

✎ Draft
Organise your ideas into paragraphs. Use the Writing box to help you.

👍 Check and write
Remember you are writing to a friend, so use informal language.

3.8 Language Revision

Vocabulary

1 Complete the sentences with the verbs in the box.

| ~~do~~ | go | have | learn | stay | win |

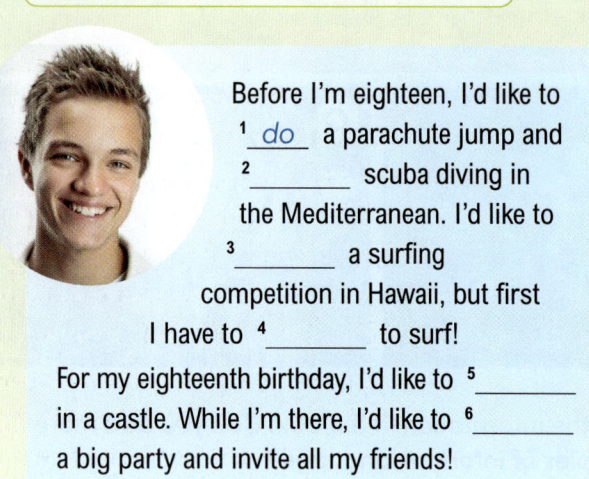

Before I'm eighteen, I'd like to ¹ *do* a parachute jump and ² _____ scuba diving in the Mediterranean. I'd like to ³ _____ a surfing competition in Hawaii, but first I have to ⁴ _____ to surf! For my eighteenth birthday, I'd like to ⁵ _____ in a castle. While I'm there, I'd like to ⁶ _____ a big party and invite all my friends!

2 Complete the sentences with the correct form of the verbs in the box.

| compete | score | ~~train~~ | win | support |

1 Our school basketball team *trains* twice a week.
2 I've always _____ my local football team.
3 Ryan often _____ goals for his hockey team.
4 Jess has never _____ a chess competition.
5 My dream is to _____ in the Olympics.

3 What sports equipment do they need?

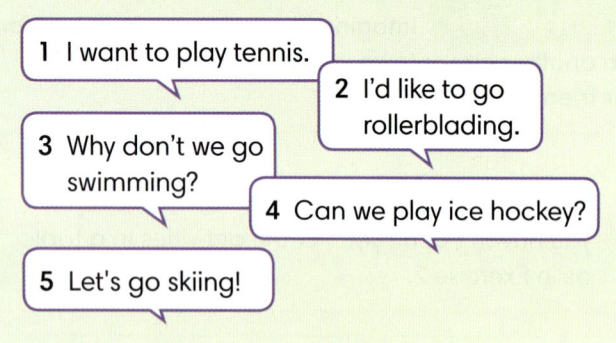

1 I want to play tennis.
2 I'd like to go rollerblading.
3 Why don't we go swimming?
4 Can we play ice hockey?
5 Let's go skiing!

1 *a tennis racket, a tennis ball*

4 Match the noun halves a–f to 1–6.

1 [e] tennis   a uniform
2 [ ] snorkel   b player
3 [ ] school   c mask
4 [ ] swimming e match
5 [ ] football f pool

Grammar

5 In your notebook, write sentences in the Present Perfect.

1 My brother / never **ride** / a roller coaster.
   My brother has never ridden a roller coaster.
2 Sheila / **try** / a really hot curry.
3 My parents / never **see** / *Star Wars*.
4 My sister / **meet** / Jennifer Lawrence.
5 Jacob / never **go** / bungee jumping.
6 My friends / **stay** / in a castle.

6 In pairs, ask and answer questions with *Have you ever* about the experiences in Exercise 5.

A: *Have you ever ridden a roller coaster?*
B: *Yes, I have. / No, I haven't.*

7 In your notebook, put the words in the correct order. Cross out the extra word in each sentence.

1 homework ~~haven't~~ we've done already our .
   We've already done our homework.
2 just my have tennis played has parents .
3 cleaned he bedroom yet hasn't they his .
4 scored yet they have a goal he ?
5 have she seen yet this film you ?
6 already read ever she's that book .

8 The Explorers are getting ready to leave Australia. Look at the list of things to do. Ask and answer the questions in pairs. Use *(not) yet* and *already*.

Things to do
• find the passports ✗
• pack the bags ✓
• print the tickets (Eva) ✓
• phone a taxi (Pops) ✗
• make sandwiches for the journey (Mac) ✗
• buy a present for Gran ✓

A: *Have the Explorers found the passports yet?*
B: *No, they haven't. They haven't found the passwords yet.*

B: *Have they packed the bags yet?*
A: *Yes, they have. They've already packed the bags.*

Round up 3.8

Communication

9 🔊 **2.19** Complete the dialogue with sentences a–d. Then listen and check. Act out the dialogue in pairs.

a Don't go too fast!
b and how do I stop?
c before you begin,
d What's the first step?

Girl: Have you tried rollerblading before?
Boy: No, I haven't. ¹ _d_
Girl: Well, ² ____ put the rollerblades on.
Boy: OK. What do I have to do now?
Girl: Go forward and use your arms to balance. ³ ____ Go slowly!
Boy: OK … ⁴ ____
Girl: Use the back of the rollerblade to stop. That's it. Now try it on your own. Be careful!
Boy: Help!

Dictation

10 **Exam Spot** 🔊 **2.20** Listen to a short text. Then listen again and write down what you hear. Make sure you spell the words correctly.

Pronunciation

11 🔊 **2.21** Listen and repeat /ʊ/ or /uː/?

L**oo**k! J**u**de's p**u**t on his n**ew** bl**ue** b**oo**ts.
He's got a n**ew** f**oo**tball t**oo**!

Check yourself! ✓
- I can talk about experiences and sports. ☐
- I can use the Present Perfect, *ever* and *never*. ☐
- I can use the Present Perfect with *just*, *already* and *yet*. ☐
- I can ask for and give instructions. ☐

12 Read the sentences. Circle the correct answer a, b, or c.

1 My sister _____ a singing competition last weekend.
  a scored   b got   **(c) won**

2 I'd really like to learn _____ a motorbike.
  a to ride   b ride   c riding

3 Katie _____ ten points in the gymnastics competition.
  a made   b scored   c trained

4 When you go cycling, you should always wear a _____ .
  a goggles   b helmet   c mask

5 I need to buy a new _____ before the match on Saturday.
  a hockey stick   b snorkel mask   c rollerblades

6 When he plays in goal, he always wears _____ to protect his hands.
  a skates   b boots   c gloves

7 A: _____ ever slept in an ice hotel?
  B: Yes, I have, and it was amazing.
  a Do you   b Have you   c You have

8 I've never _____ Polish food.
  a ate   b eat   c eaten

9 She's _____ broken her hockey stick.
  a yet   b just   c ever

10 It's the beginning of the competition and he's _____ fallen off his skateboard.
  a already   b ever   c yet

11 Wait! I _____ packed my bags yet.
  a don't have   b haven't   c haven't got

12 Have you had lunch _____ ?
  a yet   b ever   c just

13 How _____ the TV off?
  a you turn   b do you turn   c turns

14 Be _____ ! Try not to fall over on the ice.
  a careful   b carefully   c care

15 What's the first _____ in finding a good teacher?
  a pass   b step   c way

Get Culture!

Extreme sports

1 🔊 **2.22** Read and listen to the text about New Zealand. Complete the information.

1 a famous climber: _____
2 an extreme sport: _____
3 a famous team: _____

2 Read the text again. Choose the correct answer a or b.

1 The first people to arrive in New Zealand were
  ⓐ the Polynesians.
  b the British.
2 Sir Edmund Hillary climbed Mount Everest in
  a 1840.
  b 1953.
3 New Zealand is a perfect place for
  a indoor sports.
  b outdoor sports.
4 The first bungee jump for tourists was at
  a Kawarau Bridge.
  b the Eiffel Tower.
5 New Zealand has a very famous
  a rowing team.
  b rugby team.
6 Before matches, the All Blacks perform a special
  a dance.
  b song.

3 🔊 **2.23** Kristel is travelling around New Zealand. Listen to a phone conversation with her dad. Where is she? What is special about the place?

4 🔊 **2.23** Listen again and tick (✔) the activities that Kristel has already done.
- [ ] bungee jumping
- [ ] snowboarding
- [ ] mountain biking
- [ ] paragliding
- [ ] climbing
- [ ] skiing

5 Are extreme sports popular in your country? Which ones?

The Land of the Long White Cloud

What's the connection between bungee jumping, the world's best rugby team and the first man to climb Mount Everest? The answer is: they're all from New Zealand!

New Zealand is an island country in the South Pacific Ocean. The Maori people first arrived there nearly 800 years ago. They travelled across the ocean from Polynesia in small canoes! Then, in 1840, the first British people arrived.

New Zealanders have always been strong and adventurous. It's not surprising that Sir Edmund Hillary, the first man to climb Mount Everest, in 1953, came from New Zealand!

Today New Zealand is still a great place for adventure. In fact, it's the number one extreme sports destination in the world! People visit it to go climbing, snowboarding, skydiving and more.

Have you ever wanted to try bungee jumping? Did you know that a New Zealander, A.J. Hackett, made it popular? In 1987, he bungee jumped from the Eiffel Tower in Paris! Then, in 1988, he opened the world's first bungee jump for tourists at Kawarau Bridge in New Zealand. Over 35,000 people go there every year.

New Zealand is famous for less extreme sports too. It has top athletes in rowing and sailing, and a world champion rugby team called the All Blacks. The team perform a New Zealand 'haka' (a Maori war dance) before every match they play. Perhaps that's why they've won the World Cup three times!

Paragliding in New Zealand

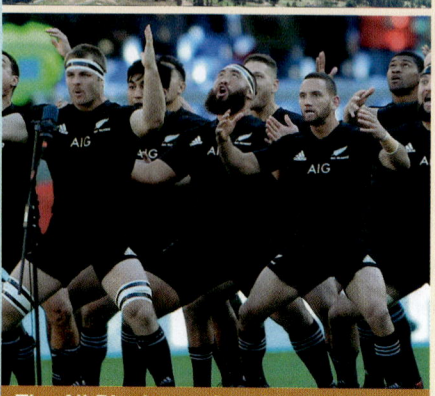

Kawarau Bridge

The All Blacks performing 'haka'

Did you know?
▶ New Zealand is about the same size as the UK, but only 4.7 million people live there!
▶ Polynesians call New Zealand *Aotearoa* or 'The Land of the Long White Cloud'.

Sports in the Lake District

A ▶18 Watch the video and answer the presenter's question. Can you name four sports you can do in the Lake District?

B ▶18 Watch the video again. Complete the sentences.
1 The Lake District is in the _____ of England.
2 There are lots of hills and quiet roads for _____ .
3 The mountain, Scafell Pike, is _____ metres high.
4 You should never go _____ on your own.
5 People wear wetsuits to keep _____ .
6 The most extreme sport you can do is _____ .

C Have you ever been on an extreme sports holiday? Which extreme sports would you like to try? Discuss your ideas as a class.

PROJECT

- Work in groups. Make a digital presentation about a popular or extreme sport in your country.

- Do research on the Internet. Use these questions to help you.
    - When did people start to do the sport?
    - What sports equipment do you need?
    - Why do you think it's popular?
    - Have you ever tried this sport? Did you like it? If not, would you like to try it?

- Plan your presentation. Write the texts. Find photographs to illustrate each part. Try to include one surprising fact.

- ... has been a popular sport for a long time.
- In order to do it, you need ...
- It's popular because ...
- I would / wouldn't like to try it because ...

- Share your presentations with the class. Which is the most interesting sport? Why?

51

4 A good story

Vocabulary I can talk about films and books.

In this unit
Vocabulary
- Types of films and books
- Life stages
- Film jobs
- Verbs followed by a preposition

Grammar
- Present Perfect with *for* and *since*
- Present Perfect and Past Simple

1 Put the cinema words into the correct category.

> ~~3D glasses~~   actor   director   film star
> ice cream   popcorn   seat   sweets   ticket

People	Food	Objects
		3D glasses

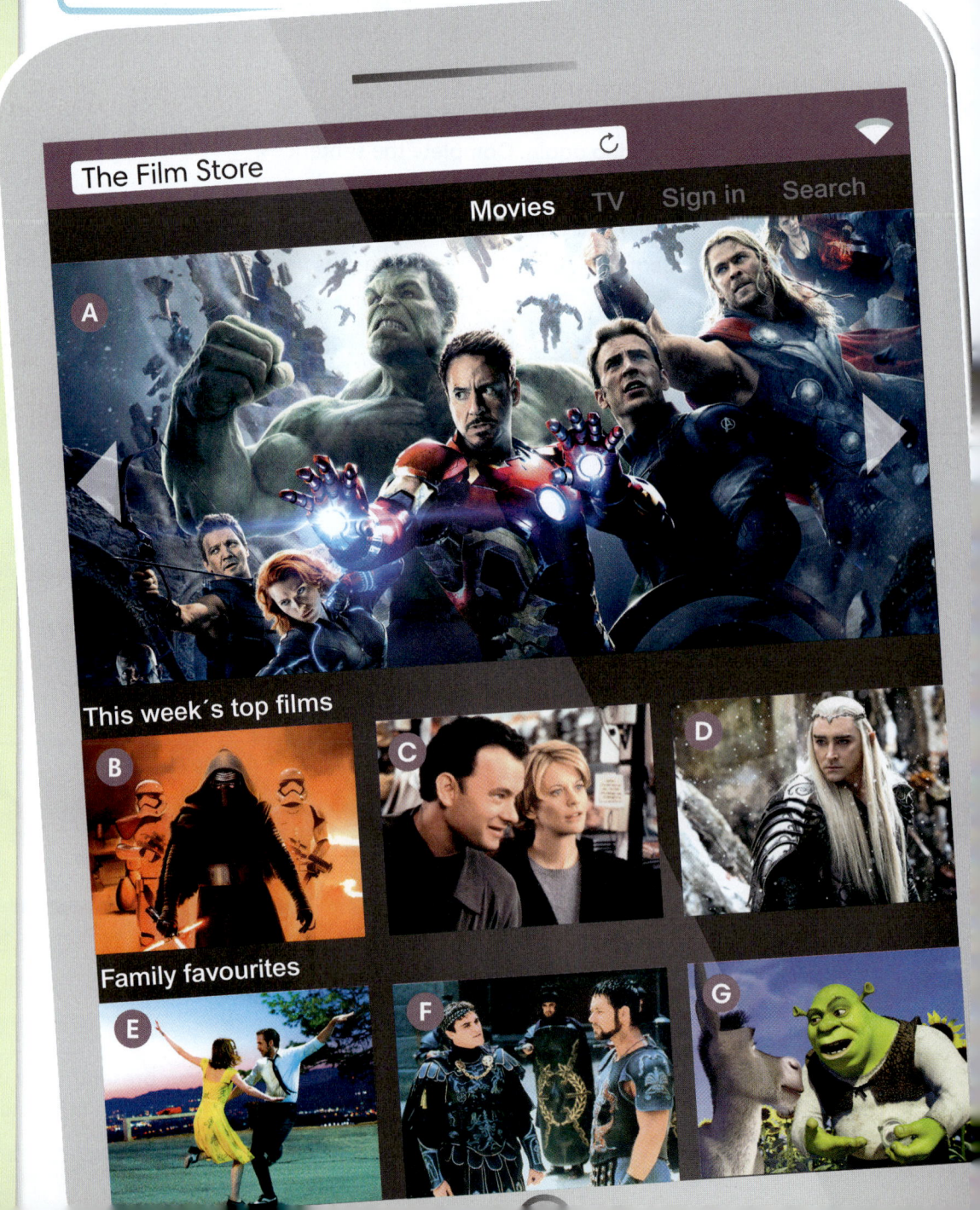

I know that!

▶ 19–20
4.2 Grammar video

▶ 21
4.2 Grammar animation

▶ 22
4.3 Grammar animation

▶ 23
4.4 Communication video

The Film Store

Movies   TV   Sign in   Search

A

This week's top films

B   C   D

Family favourites

E   F   G

52

2 🔊 **2.24** Listen and repeat. Which types of films can you see in the photos on page 52? Do you know these films?

Vocabulary Types of films

action film   adventure film   animation
comedy   fantasy film   historical film
horror film   musical   romantic comedy
science fiction film

A – *action film, 'Avengers'*

3 Match the types of films in the Vocabulary box to descriptions 1–6.
1 It has a lot of magic. *fantasy film*
2 People often sing in this type of film.
3 It's about love, but it's also funny.
4 You laugh a lot when you watch this type of film.
5 It has a lot of scary moments.
6 It doesn't use real actors. It uses drawings.

4 How many titles of the types of films in the Vocabulary box can you name?
1 Action film: *'Wonder Woman', …*
2 Adventure film: *'Indiana Jones', …*
3 Animation: _____

5 Read the reviews and match them to the films on page 52.

Your review

1 Mia wants to become an actress. Sebastian dreams of being a jazz musician. They meet and fall in love. The music and dancing are great. more

2 It is the year AD 180 and a Roman soldier must fight for his life in the Colosseum. The costumes are amazing! more

3 In a galaxy far away the Jedi fight against evil. The story is very exciting and the special effects are really good. more

4 A giant green monster and his friend, a talking donkey, must rescue a beautiful princess. It's very funny. more

6 🔊 **2.25** Listen and repeat. Match the types of films and books into pairs, where possible.

Vocabulary Types of books

adventure novel   autobiography   cookbook
fantasy novel   historical novel   horror story   romance
science fiction novel

fantasy film – fantasy novel

7 In which type of book can you find:
1 dragons and monsters? *fantasy novel*
2 a recipe for pancakes? _____
3 a king and a queen? _____
4 spaceships and aliens? _____
5 the story of a famous person's life? _____

8 **Exam Spot** 🔊 **2.26** Listen to the conversation with Harriet and complete the questionnaire.

Film and book questionnaire
1 What type of films do you like watching?
   Action films and _____ films
2 What films don't you like? _____
3 What's the best film you've seen recently? _____
4 What type of books do you enjoy reading? _____
5 What books don't you enjoy? _____
6 What's the best book you've ever read? _____

9 **Exam Spot** In pairs, ask and answer the questions in Exercise 8.
A: *What type of films do you like watching?*
B: *I like watching horror and fantasy films.*

10 Think about films you know. Decide on five film and book awards. Tell the class.
The funniest animation is Minions.
The scariest horror story is …

I remember that!

	funniest	animation
	scariest	fantasy film/novel
The	most exciting	horror film/story
	most boring	science fiction film/novel
	…	…

4.2 Grammar — I can use the Present Perfect with *for* and *since*.

A present for Bella

It's Bella's birthday on Saturday and she's invited Adam and Josh to a party, so they need to buy her a present …

1

Adam: What shall we get for Bella?
Josh: Don't ask me! You've been friends with Bella for a long time. You should know.
Adam: Well, I've known her since primary school, but it's tricky!
Josh: What about some tennis balls? She likes tennis.
Adam: Really? She hasn't played tennis for about two years!
Josh: What about a book then?
Adam: Good idea. Let's go to the bookshop.

2

Josh: Does she like horror stories? This one looks scary.
Adam: *Screams after Dark*. No, I don't think so.
Josh: What about a cookbook? Here's one – *Easy Chicken Recipes*.
Adam: Josh, Bella has been a vegetarian since she was ten.
Josh: So what do you suggest?
Adam: This one. *100 Cake Recipes* … She doesn't eat meat, but she likes making cakes.
Josh: OK. Let's go and pay.

3

Bella: Oh, hi, boys. What are you doing here?
Adam: Erm … just looking. In fact, we're going. We've been here for ages. And you?
Bella: I've found a nice book about making cakes.
Adam: Erm … it's lovely but … do you really need a book to make cakes? There are lots of good recipes on the Internet.
Bella: Yes, but this book looks so nice.

1 Look at the photos. Where are Josh and Adam? What are they buying?

2 ▶19 ◆) 2.27 Watch or listen and read. Match the sentence halves a–e to 1–5.

1 [d] The friends   a suggests that they buy a horror story.
2 [ ] Adam   b is a vegetarian.
3 [ ] Josh   c isn't at the bookshop.
4 [ ] Bella   d are going to celebrate Bella's birthday.
5 [ ] Zadie   e was at primary school with Bella.

3 ◆) 2.28 Listen and repeat. Find these expressions in the story.

Say it!
What shall we get?   It's tricky!
I don't think so.   Just looking.

4 ▶ Guess! Does Bella buy the cookbook? Have a class vote.

5 ▶20 ◆) 2.29 Now watch or listen and check.

4.2

Grammar Present Perfect with *for* and *since*

+	We've been here for ages.	−	We haven't seen him since twelve o'clock.
	Adam has known Bella since primary school.		She hasn't played tennis for two years.
?	Have you been here long?		Yes, we have. / No, we haven't.
	Has she been a vegetarian for a long time?		Yes, she has. / No, she hasn't.
	How long have you known her?		

for three years, *for* two months, *for* a long time, *for* ages (= period of time)
since 2018, *since* February, *since* she was ten (= point in time)

▶ 21 **Get Grammar!**
Hammy has a new job.
He's had this job since Thursday.
He's had this job for a week.

---

6 Put the expressions in the box into the correct column.

~~Monday~~ ~~two weeks~~ last weekend July
an hour three years one o'clock ages
I was five years old

for	since
two weeks	Monday

7 Complete the sentences with *for* or *since*.

1 Adam has known Bella ___for___ eight years.
2 Josh has known Adam _____ he was twelve.
3 Bella hasn't played tennis _____ two years.
4 Adam and Josh have been in the bookshop _____ ages.
5 Bella has been in the bookshop _____ three o'clock.

8 Complete the text with the Present Perfect form of the verbs. Circle *for* or *since*.

I ¹*have known* (know) Zadie ²*for / since* I was ten. We ³_____ (be) friends ⁴*for / since* almost two years. We both like cooking, reading and watching films. We sometimes disagree about what films to watch, but luckily we ⁵_____ (not have) an argument ⁶*for / since* a long time! I like science fiction films but Zadie prefers animations – she ⁷_____ (love) them ⁸*for / since* she was little! Tonight we're going to watch *Mulan* – it's an old film, but we both love it!

9 In your notebook, write sentences using the Present Perfect form of the verbs and *for* or *since*.

1 Josh started playing basketball six years ago. (play basketball)
Josh has played basketball for six years.
2 Adam bought these headphones in November. (have these headphones)
3 Bella and her mum moved to this house in 2017. (live in this house)
4 Bella stopped eating meat four years ago. (be a vegetarian)

10 Write questions with *How long*. Use the Present Perfect.

1 you / study / English?
How long have you studied English?
2 your best friend / know / you?
3 you / have / your phone?
4 your English teacher / teach / you?
5 you / live / in your house?

11 **Exam Spot** In pairs, ask and answer the questions in Exercise 10.

A: *How long have you studied English?*
B: *I've studied English for … / since …*

4.3 Grammar — I can use the Present Perfect and the Past Simple.

The Explorers — Pops's autobiography

1

Mac: What are you doing, Pops?
Pops: I'm writing my autobiography. I started yesterday.
Eva: Really? How many pages have you written?
Pops: I've written a hundred pages. I wrote fifty pages last night. I want to write about all my famous discoveries and adventures!

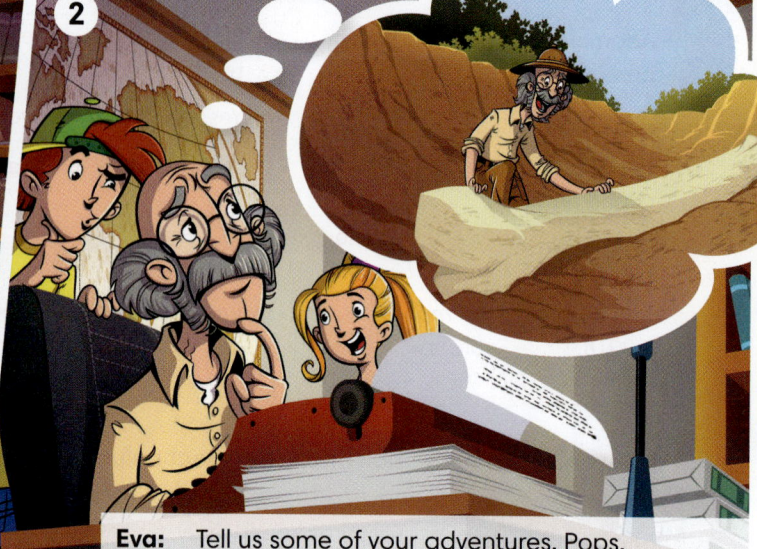

2

Eva: Tell us some of your adventures, Pops.
Pops: Well, I've made a lot of exciting discoveries. I found a dinosaur bone in 2015.
Mac: Are you sure, Pops? I don't think you've ever found a dinosaur bone, but you've found some prehistoric skeletons.
Pops: Oh, yes, you're right. I discovered one last summer. It was 10,000 years old.

3

Pops: I've also climbed Mount Everest.
Mac: Erm … when did you climb Everest, Pops?
Pops: I'm not sure now. It was a few years ago.
Eva: You haven't climbed Everest, Pops, but you have climbed K2. You climbed it in winter 1999. You were on the front page of all the newspapers!

4

Pops: Oh dear! My memory isn't very good these days. This is a terrible autobiography.
Eva: Don't worry, Pops. Mac and I can help you.
Mac: Yes, it's going to be amazing!

---

1 Look at the cartoon. What is Pops doing? What is he thinking about?

2 🔊 2.30 Read and listen. Tick (✓) the things Pops has done.
1. ✓ He's started his autobiography.
2. ☐ He's found a dinosaur bone.
3. ☐ He's found a 10,000-year-old skeleton.
4. ☐ He's climbed Mount Everest.
5. ☐ He's been in the newspapers.

4.3

Grammar Present Perfect and Past Simple

	Present Perfect	Past Simple
+	I've made a lot of discoveries.	I made a discovery last summer.
–	You haven't climbed Everest.	You didn't climb Everest in 1999.
?	Have you ever climbed Everest?	When did you climb Everest?
	Yes, I have. / No, I haven't.	I climbed it last year.
Time expressions	ever, never, in my life, just, yet, already, for, since	last night, on Sunday, in 1992, three weeks ago, when he was young

▶ 22 Get Grammar!

Fluffy's been to Japan.
She went there last year.

---

3 Circle the correct answer.
1 Pops *made / has made* a lot of discoveries.
2 He *climbed / 's climbed* K2 in 1999.
3 He *didn't find / 's never found* a dinosaur bone.
4 He *found / has found* a skeleton last summer.
5 Mac and Eva *started / have started* travelling with Pops when they were little.
6 Pops, Eva and Mac *all travelled / have all travelled* a lot.

4 🔊 **2.31** Complete the dialogue with the Present Perfect or the Past Simple form of the verbs. Then listen and check.

Eva: How long ¹*have you been* (you / be) an explorer, Pops?

Pops: ²_____ (I / have) this job since I was eighteen. When I was a boy, ³_____ (I / read) a lot of adventure stories. That's when ⁴_____ (I / decide) to travel the world, looking for treasure.

Eva: ⁵_____ (you / ever / find) any treasure, Pops?

Pops: Yes, I have. ⁶_____ (I / find) a silver bracelet yesterday.

Eva: Wow! Really? Where ⁷_____ (you / find) it?

Pops: ⁸_____ (I / find) it under the sofa. Gran lost it two weeks ago!

Eva: Ha-ha! Very funny, Pops.

5 Look at the job advert. Write questions for the interview about activities 1–4. Use the Present Perfect and Past Simple.

Wanted!
EXPLORER FOR JUNGLE ADVENTURE
You will need to …
1 drive a jeep
2 build a fire
3 paddle a canoe
4 eat insects

1 *Have you ever driven a jeep?*
  When and where did you drive a jeep?

6 Work in pairs. Student A: You are the interviewer. Use the questions in Exercise 5. Student B: You are the explorer (Horatio or Florida). Use the information below. Then swap roles.

A: *Have you ever driven a jeep, Horatio?*
B: *Yes, I have.*
A: *When and where did you drive a jeep?*
B: *I drove a jeep in the Sahara Desert in 2016.*

Horatio McHugh
- drive a jeep ✔ – in the Sahara Desert in 2016
- build a fire ✘
- paddle a canoe ✔ – in the Congo River – last year
- eat insects ✘

Florida Drake
- drive a jeep ✔ – in Australia in 2017
- build a fire ✔ – in my garden last night
- paddle a canoe ✘
- eat insects ✔ – ants in the jungle three weeks ago

4.4 Communication — I can make and accept apologies.

It was an accident!

Bella: Here are your drinks …
Zadie: Thanks.
Bella: … my ice cream and your burger, Josh. Josh? Here's your burger and there's your drink.
Josh: Oh, thanks, Bella. I'm just doing a puzzle.
Bella: Josh, be careful! Your drink!
Zadie: Oh, no! My book! It's completely wet!
Josh: Oops - sorry, Zadie!
Zadie: Oh, no! And it's my favourite book! What a mess!
Josh: Don't be mad. I didn't mean to …
Bella: Calm down, you two. It was an accident.
Zadie: You're right, Bella. It doesn't matter, Josh. Forget about it.
Josh: I'm sorry, Zadie. Really I am … but can you help me with this puzzle? Thanks.
Bella: Josh! You've put ketchup all over my ice cream!
Josh: Oh dear! Sorry, Bella!
Zadie: Never mind, Bella. It was an accident!

1 ▶23 🔊 2.32 Watch or listen and read. Where are Josh, Bella and Zadie? What is Josh doing? Why does he apologise to the girls?

2 🔊 2.33 Listen and repeat.

Communication
Making and accepting apologies

Making apologies	Accepting apologies
Sorry!	Never mind.
Oh dear, I'm (really) sorry.	It doesn't matter.
It's all my fault.	Don't worry about it.
I'm sorry, I didn't mean to.	Forget about it.
Don't be mad (at me).	It's OK. It wasn't your fault.
I'm sorry, I made a mistake.	It was an accident.

3 🔊 2.34 Complete the dialogue with one word in each gap.

Girl: Excuse me. I wanted tomato soup, not chicken soup.
Waiter: Oh, sorry! I ¹*made* a mistake.
Girl: It doesn't ² _____ . Don't worry ³ _____ it.
Waiter: Here's your tomato soup.
Girl: Thanks … but there's a fly in it!
Waiter: Oh dear, I didn't ⁴ _____ to give you that!
Girl: ⁵ _____ about it. I'll have a hot dog instead!

4 Read the dialogues and circle the correct answer a, b or c.

1 **Girl:** It's all my fault!
  Boy: a Oh dear. I'm really sorry.
  (b) Relax. It doesn't matter.
  c No, you didn't. Don't worry.

2 **Boy:** I'm sorry I'm late, Mum.
  Mum: a Don't be mad.
  b Don't worry about it.
  c It was a mistake.

3 **Boy:** Oh dear, I've forgotten my homework.
  Teacher: a Don't be mad at me.
  b I'm sorry, I didn't mean that.
  c Never mind. You can bring it tomorrow.

4 **Girl:** Don't be mad at me, but my dog damaged your book.
  Boy: a It's OK. It was an accident.
  b I'm sorry, I've made a mistake.
  c Oh dear, I'm really sorry.

5 **Exam Spot** Work in pairs. Take turns to make and accept apologies.
Student A: Go to page 122.
Student B: Go to page 128.

I can understand a biography. **Reading** 4.5

Don't forget to be awesome!

John Green is a famous American author. Millions of teenagers have read his books, *The Fault in Our Stars* and *Paper Towns*, which are also Hollywood movies.

John was born in 1977 in Indianapolis, but he grew up in Orlando, Florida. He went to school there, but he didn't enjoy it. John was tall, thin and shy, and other students bullied him. Luckily, things changed when he went to college. John studied English and Religious Studies there. After he graduated, he worked at a children's hospital, and then he decided to become a writer.

John moved to Chicago and got a job at a magazine. He wrote book reviews and he also started to work on a novel, *Looking for Alaska*. The book was based on his high school experiences and it was a big success! In Chicago, John also met and fell in love with Sarah, a girl from his old school. They got married and had two children.

Teenagers love John's books because they're different. They aren't about fantasy worlds, they're about real teenagers who live in the real world. *The Fault in Our Stars* is about two teenage cancer patients; *Paper Towns* is about a boy who loves a girl, although he doesn't really know her.

John Green has come a long way from the quiet kid at school. He's written best-selling stories, he's won five awards, and over 30 million people have read his books! So what's his advice for teens? 'Just remember that sometimes, the way you think about a person isn't the way they actually are,' he says. Then he adds: 'And don't forget to be awesome!' What does that mean? Well – do your best!

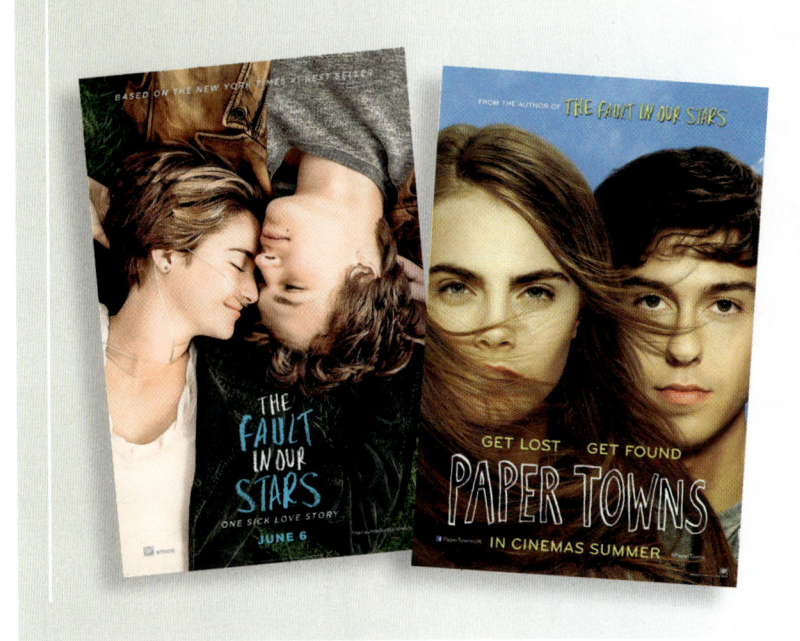

1 Read the text quickly. Which of John Green's books:

1 are also Hollywood movies?
2 was his first novel?
3 is about sick teenagers?

2 🔊 **2.35** Listen and repeat. Then complete the sentences with the correct form of the words in the Vocabulary box.

Vocabulary Life stages

be born   fall in love   get a job   get married
go to school/college   graduate   grow up
have children   retire

1 John Green was _born_ in the United States in 1977. **T** / F
2 He grew _____ in Indianapolis. T / F
3 When John _____ to school, other students didn't like him. T / F
4 After John graduated from college, he _____ a job at a children's hospital. T / F
5 John _____ in love with a girl from Chicago. T / F
6 They _____ married and _____ three children. T / F

3 🔊 **2.36** Read and listen to the text. Read the sentences in Exercise 2 again and circle true (T) or false (F). Correct the false sentences.

4 **Exam Spot** Read the text again and answer the questions.

1 Why didn't John enjoy school?
2 What did John study at college?
3 What three different jobs did John do?
4 What is *Looking for Alaska* about?
5 Why do teenagers like John's books?
6 What advice does John give to teenagers?

5 Do you know John Green's books or the films based on his books? If not, would you like to read or watch them? Why? / Why not? Discuss in pairs.

59

4.6 Listening and Vocabulary

I can understand a listening text about film jobs.

3 **Exam Spot** 🔊 **2.38** Listen to Part 1 of an interview. Complete the sentences.
1 The interviewer is in _London_ .
2 Lara Jackson is an _____ in an action film.
3 It is Lara's _____ job on a film set.
4 She is _____ years old.
5 She's working on the new _____ film.

4 🔊 **2.39** Listen to Part 2. Circle true (T) or false (F). Correct the false sentences.
1 Extras often speak in films. T /(F)
   Extras don't usually speak in films.
2 They never look at the camera. T / F
3 Lara found the extras job online. T / F
4 Extras can read books on the film set. T / F
5 They can take photos of the stars. T / F

1 🔊 **2.37** Listen and repeat. Look at the picture. Match the film jobs to the people (A–G).

Vocabulary Film jobs
actor/actress   cameraman/camerawoman
costume designer   extra   film director
make-up artist   scriptwriter

A *scriptwriter*

2 What film jobs do these people have?
1 I sometimes wear funny costumes!
2 I tell the actors what to do, but I never shout at them!
3 I love telling stories and writing dialogues.
4 It's my dream job – I'm really interested in fashion and film!

5 Would you like to be an extra? Why? / Why not?

6 Read the Vocabulary Builder. Can you think of more verbs that are followed by *for*, *at* and *about*?

Vocabulary Builder
Verbs followed by a preposition

for: apply for, prepare for, wait for, revise for
at: shout at, smile at, laugh at
about: dream about, worry about, complain about

I've applied for jobs in lots of films.
The director shouts at you.
It's a job that I dream about.

7 Read the sentences and circle the correct answer a, b or c.
1 Let's meet at 8 p.m. I'll wait _____ you outside the cinema.
   (a) for   b about   c at
2 I always _____ at Ben Stiller. He's a really funny actor.
   a shout   b laugh   c cry
3 I can't complain _____ the pay. It's the best paid job in Hollywood!
   a to   b for   c about
4 Ready? Great! Now just _____ at the camera. That's perfect!
   a wait   b smile   c dream
5 I'm dreaming _____ being an actress.
   a for   b at   c about

I can write a review. **Writing** 4.7

GUARDIANS OF THE GALAXY 2 REVIEW

1. *Guardians of the Galaxy Volume 2* is an **exciting** science fiction film. I've watched it three times, and I love it! It's **fantastic**!

2. In the film, the main character, Peter Quill, is looking for his father. A group of friends, including Baby Groot and Rocket, help him. They find his father and they also save the galaxy ... for the second time!

3. The film is very **funny**. I laughed at all the jokes, and the music is **great**! Sometimes the story is **silly**, but it's never **boring**. The special effects in the final scene are **amazing**!

4. All in all, *Guardians of the Galaxy* is a **really good** film. I totally recommend it!

1 Read the review of *Guardians of the Galaxy Volume 2*. Is the review positive or negative? Have you seen the film? Do you agree with the opinion?

2 Read the review again. Match a–d to paragraphs 1–4.
- a [4] Recommendation
- b [ ] Title and type of film
- c [ ] What I like / don't like
- d [ ] The story

3 Read the Writing box. Find the expressions in the review.

Writing A review

1 Title and type of film
… is *an exciting science fiction film / an animation.*
It's one of the best *comedies / musicals.*

2 The story
In the film … / The film is about …
The main characters are …

3 What I like/don't like
I didn't really enjoy it. / I love it!
The film is *funny / exciting / boring.*
The story is *amazing / silly.* The music is *fantastic.*
The special effects / characters are *great / not very good.*

4 Recommendation
To sum up, I think the film is …
All in all, *I would / wouldn't* recommend it because …

4 Read the information in the box. Look at the adjectives highlighted in the review. Which are positive and which are negative?

Using a variety of adjectives.
The film is *great*. I laughed at the jokes, and the music is *great*. The special effects are *great*! ✗
The film is *funny*. I laughed at the jokes, and the music is *great*! The special effects are *amazing*! ✓

Positive: exciting, …
Negative: silly, …

5 Circle the correct answer.
1. The film was *exciting /(boring)*. I fell asleep!
2. The ending was *boring / funny*. It was a real surprise!
3. The story was quite *silly / great*. It was difficult to understand.
4. I liked the special effects. They were really *amazing / boring*!

6 🖊 **Writing Time** Write a film review.

❓ **Find ideas**
Think about a film you've watched recently. What do you remember about the story, the characters, the music, the special effects, etc.? Take notes.

✏️ **Draft**
Organise your ideas into paragraphs. Use the Writing box to help you.

👍 **Check and write**
Check that your review has a recommendation. Make sure you have used a variety of adjectives.

4.8 Language Revision

Vocabulary

1 Complete the film festival poster with the correct film types.

Summer Film Festival
Films show every day at 6 p.m. at the Odeon!

- Watch the scariest ¹h<u>orror</u> films and get really frightened on Mondays!
- Watch the most famous ²m_____ and sing along on Tuesdays!
- Watch the best ³r_____ c_____ and get in a romantic mood on Wednesdays!
- Watch the greatest ⁴h_____ films and learn about kings and queens on Thursdays!
- Come with your friends and watch the funniest ⁵c_____ on Fridays!

Click on the day to learn more.

2 Match book titles 1–7 to the book types in the box. Which book would you take to a desert island?

~~adventure novel~~   autobiography   cookbook
fantasy novel   historical novel   romance
science fiction novel

1 'THE WAY TO INDIA'
2 'A DAUGHTER OF THE DRAGON'
3 'THE SINGER: MY LIFE FULL OF MUSIC'
4 'THE BATTLE'
5 'THE KISS ON THE BEACH'
6 'THE ROBOT'
7 '100 EASY STEAK RECIPES'

1 adventure novel

3 Find and circle six film jobs.

4 Circle the correct answer. Are the sentences true or false for you? Discuss in pairs.

1 I often revise *(for)* / *about* exams at night.
2 I think parents should never shout *at* / *to* their kids.
3 I dream *for* / *about* meeting a famous actor.
4 I hate waiting *for* / *to* people.
5 I often laugh *at* / *for* funny actors' jokes.
6 I never complain *about* / *for* homework.

Grammar

5 Write *for* or *since*.

1 _<u>since</u>_ 2015
2 _____ June
3 _____ six months
4 _____ ages
5 _____ five o'clock
6 _____ a hundred years

6 Complete the sentences with the Present Perfect form of the verbs in the box. Circle *for* or *since*.

act   be   collect   live   ~~play~~

Did you know?

1 The actor Johnny Depp <u>has played</u> the guitar *(for)* / *since* more than forty years.
2 The author John Green _____ married *for* / *since* 2006.
3 Zac Efron _____ in TV programmes and films *for* / *since* he was fourteen.
4 The fantasy author J.K. Rowling _____ in Scotland *for* / *since* 1993.
5 The actress Demi Moore _____ dolls *for* / *since* a long time.

7 Complete the fragment of Pops's autobiography with the Present Perfect or the Past Simple form of the verbs.

I ¹ <u>met</u> (meet) Gran when I was twenty-one, and we ² _____ (be) together since then. We ³ _____ (get) married in 1965, and in 1967 we ⁴ _____ (move) to this house. We ⁵ _____ (live) here for more than 50 years. Gran doesn't like travelling, but I ⁶ _____ (travel) to a lot of different places in my life.

8 In your notebook, write questions in the Present Perfect or the Past Simple. Then ask and answer in pairs.

1 you / meet / your friends last weekend?
Did you meet your friends last weekend?
2 you / ever / see / the science fiction film, *Gravity*?
3 What / you / watch / on TV last night?
4 How long / you / be / at this school?
5 you / go / shopping last Saturday?
6 How long / you / know / your best friend?

Round up 4.8

Communication

9 🔊 **2.40** Complete the dialogue with the words in the box. Then listen and check. Act out the dialogue in pairs.

~~sorry~~ don't mad really about

Girl: You're late!
Boy: I'm ¹*sorry*. Don't be ² _____ at me.
Girl: But what happened?
Boy: The bus was late. I waited for ages!
Girl: OK. ³_____ worry about it.
Boy: I'm ⁴_____ sorry.
Girl: Forget ⁵_____ it. Come on! The film is starting!

Dictation

10 **Exam Spot** 🔊 **2.41** Listen to a short text. Then listen again and write down what you hear. Make sure you spell the words correctly.

Pronunciation

11 🔊 **2.42** Listen and repeat /ɔː/.

P**au**l's b**ou**ght his d**au**ghter a n**au**ghty h**o**rse.
Has he t**au**ght her how to ride it?
Yes, of c**ou**rse!

Check yourself! ✓

- I can talk about films, books, film jobs and life stages. ☐
- I can use the Present Perfect with *for* and *since*. ☐
- I can use the Present Perfect and the Past Simple. ☐
- I can make and accept apologies. ☐

12 Read the sentences. Circle the correct answer a, b, or c.

1 I hate watching _____ films like *Star Trek*. I prefer romantic comedies.
 a historical   b horror   **c science fiction**

2 Nelson Mandela wrote about his life in *Long Walk to Freedom*. It's a great _____ .
 a autobiography   b historical novel
 c adventure novel

3 My mum _____ very young. She had two children before she was thirty!
 a retired   b got married   c got a job

4 When I _____ , I want to be an astronaut.
 a get married   b grow up   c fall in love

5 My uncle loves his job. He writes dialogues for films. He's a _____ .
 a film director   b cameraman   c scriptwriter

6 My cousin has applied _____ a job as a film extra!
 a at   b about   c for

7 I've known my best friend _____ we were six years old.
 a since   b for   c already

8 I haven't read a fantasy novel for _____ .
 a a long time   b I was eleven years old
 c the summer holidays

9 _____ have you had piano lessons?
 a How long   b When   c Ever

10 _____ the football match yesterday?
 a Have you watched   b Did you watch
 c Can you watch

11 My grandma _____ writing her autobiography yesterday!
 a finished   b has finished   c finish

12 Colleen Atwood _____ costumes for lots of famous films.
 a designed   b has designed   c designing

13 A: You've broken my pen!
 B: Sorry. I didn't _____ to.
 a mean   b worry   c forget

14 A: Hello. Is that Jess?
 B: No, it isn't. It's John.
 A: Sorry! I made _____ – I've called the wrong number!
 a a fault   b an accident   c a mistake

15 A: Sorry I'm late!
 B: It doesn't _____ . The film hasn't started yet.
 a care   b matter   c mind

63

3 & 4 Skills Revision

Reading and Writing

1 Exam Spot Read the cinema information and Amy's message. Complete the notes.

From: Amy
To: Milly

Hi, Milly!
Would you like to go to the cinema this weekend? I'm busy on Saturday, so how about Sunday? I'd like to see *Two Lions* because I've already seen *The Secret Alien* and *Animal Island*. Is that OK? It's on at 2.15 and 4.15. I'm meeting my cousins for lunch, so the later time is better. Wait for me outside the cinema – there are always a lot of people inside. We're both thirteen, so we can get cheap tickets!
Amy

ABC CINEMA
This week's films

The Secret Alien
Exciting science fiction film with James Merton
6.30 p.m.
8.30 p.m.

Two Lions
Fantasy film with Elsa Brindell as Queen Asanti
2.15 p.m.
4.15 p.m.

Animal Island
Very funny animation with the voice of Natalie Deacon
10.00 a.m.
11.45 a.m.

Tickets: £10
Children under 14: half price

Day: 1 *Sunday*
Name of the film: 2 _____
Type of the film: 3 _____
Time of the film: 4 _____
Place to meet: 5 _____
Cost per person: 6 £ _____

2 Exam Spot Write about a book you've read recently. Say:
- Who are the characters?
- What happens in the story?
- What did you like / didn't you like about it?

I've recently read …
It's a … (novel).
The main characters are …
In the story, …
I liked it because … / I didn't like it because …

Use of English

3 Exam Spot Complete the text with one word in each gap.

Dear Uncle Bob,
How ¹ *are* you? We're ² _____ holiday in New Zealand. I'm sending you some photos. We've been here ³ _____ two weeks, and we're having a fantastic time! It's great for extreme sports. ⁴ _____ week I went snowboarding and bungee jumping. We haven't ⁵ _____ surfing yet, but we all want to try. Have you ⁶ _____ done any extreme sports?
It's nine o'clock ⁷ _____ the morning here, and we ⁸ _____ just had breakfast. Today we're going kayaking. I've ⁹ _____ done it before, but Mum and Dad have, and we're looking forward ¹⁰ _____ it. Mum says you can sometimes see dolphins!
Bye ¹¹ _____ now!
Love, Sophie

64

Skills Revision 3 & 4

Listening

4 **Exam Spot** 🔊 **2.43** Listen to Harry talking to his friend Laura. Circle the correct answer a, b or c.

1 Harry is looking for a birthday present for his
   a dad.   b brother.   (c) uncle.
2 What type of books does this person like?
   a science fiction   b adventure
   c fantasy
3 Which book does Harry buy?
   a *Desert Road*   b *Mystery Beach*
   c *Kangaroo Town*
4 As a child, the author of the book lived in
   a Australia.   b the UK.   c the USA.
5 What type of book has Laura just read?
   a a fantasy novel   b a historical novel
   c an autobiography
6 How much is Harry's book?
   a £10.00   b £8.00   c £2.00

Communication

5 Read the dialogues and circle the correct answer a, b or c.

1 A: Oh, no! You've broken my favourite pen!
   B: a It doesn't matter.   b Never mind.
      (c) Oh, dear! I'm really sorry!
2 A: I'm sorry, I forgot your birthday!
   B: a That's good!   b Don't worry about it.
      c Don't be mad at me!
3 A: First, type in the old password.
   B: a What do I have to do next?
      b Don't type in the password.
      c What happened next?
4 A: How do I make toast?
   B: a Finally, put bread in the toaster.
      b First, switch on the toaster.
      c Remember to switch the toaster off after use.

6 **Exam Spot** Ask and answer the questions in pairs.

1 What's your favourite sport? Why?
2 What exciting experiences would you like to have in your life?
3 What's your favourite film? Why?
4 What type of books do you like reading?

Exam Language Bank

Experiences
do a parachute jump
go scuba diving
have a party
learn to ski
meet a famous person
ride a camel
stay in a castle
win a competition

Types of books
adventure novel
autobiography
cookbook
fantasy novel
historical novel
horror story
romance
science fiction novel

Sports verbs
compete   support
lose   train
score   win

Life stages
be born
fall in love
get a job
get married
go to school / college
graduate
grow up
have children
retire

Sports equipment
boots
gloves
goggles
helmet
hockey stick
ice skates
rollerblades
skateboard
skis
snorkel mask
swimsuit
tennis racket

Film jobs
actor / actress
cameraman / camerawoman
costume designer
extra
film director
make-up artist
scriptwriter

Types of films
action film
adventure film
animation
comedy
fantasy film
historical film
horror film
musical
romantic comedy
science fiction film

Verbs followed by a preposition
apply for   smile at
prepare for   laugh at
wait for   dream about
revise for   worry about
shout at   complain about

Asking for instructions
How do I *put the net on*?   What do I have to do next?
What's the first step?

Giving instructions
Put this post here.   Be careful.
Next, *put the goal upright*.   Don't / Try not to *kick the ball* too hard.

Ordering instructions
Before you begin, …
First, … Then, … Next, … Finally, …

Making apologies
Sorry!
Oh dear, I'm (really) sorry.
It's all my fault.
I'm sorry, I didn't mean to.
Don't be mad (at me).
I'm sorry, I made a mistake.

Accepting apologies
Never mind.
It doesn't matter.
Don't worry about it.
Forget about it.
It's OK. It wasn't your fault.
It was an accident.

5 Don't stop the music!

Vocabulary I can talk about music.

In this unit
Vocabulary
- Music styles and instruments
- Music collocations
- Crime
- Personal qualities
- Adjectives from nouns

Grammar
- *going to* and *will*
- Defining relative clauses with *who*, *which*, *that*, *where*

▶ 24–25
5.2 Grammar video

▶ 26
5.2 Grammar animation

▶ 27
5.3 Grammar animation

▶ 28
5.4 Communication video

▶ 29
BBC Culture video

1 How many music styles do you know? Which is your favourite style?

pop, rock …

I know that!

IRON GUITAR — A, B, C

JUST JAZZ — D, E, F

CLASSIC TRIO — G, H, I

FOLK FRIENDS — J, K

SOUNDS of the SUMMER

St Joseph's School, Highgate
Saturday 10th July from 12 p.m. till 7 p.m.

66

5.1

2 Look at the poster on page 66. When is the concert? Who is playing?

3 🔊 **2.44** Listen and repeat. Which music styles and which instruments can you see in the poster?

Vocabulary
Music styles and instruments

Styles
classical   folk   heavy metal   hip hop   jazz   Latin
pop   punk   rock   techno

Instruments
cello   drums   electric guitar   flute   keyboards
piano   saxophone   trumpet   violin

4 🔊 **2.45** Listen. What instruments are the people playing? Match them to the musicians (A–F) in the poster.

1 *This musician is playing the saxophone. (D)*

5 🔊 **2.46** Listen and repeat. Then cover the Vocabulary box and match the phrase halves.

Vocabulary   Music collocations

give a concert   go on tour   have an audition
join a band   practise an instrument   record an album
sign an autograph   write / compose a song

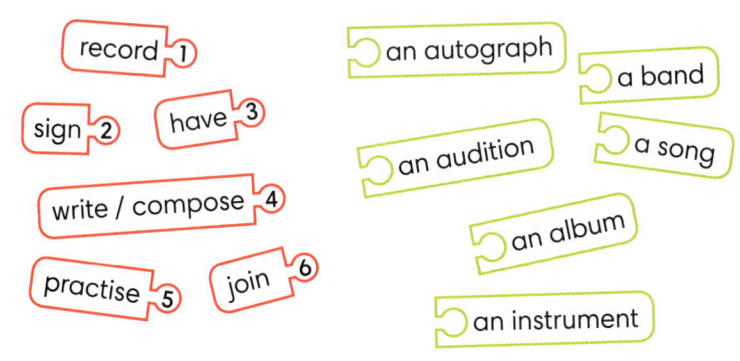

record ① — an autograph — a band
sign ② — have ③ — a song
write / compose ④ — an audition
practise ⑤ — join ⑥ — an album
— an instrument

1 *record an album*

6 **Exam Spot** 🔊 **2.47** Listen to Karl from Classic Trio and complete the sentences.

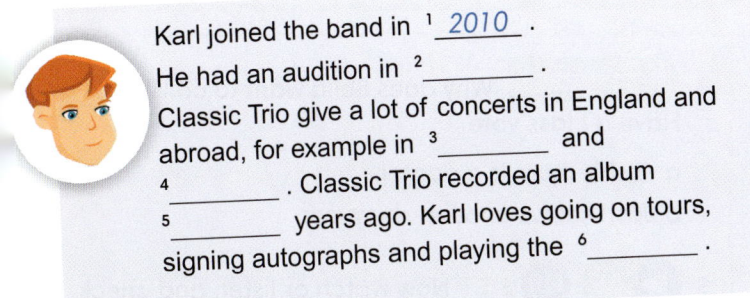

Karl joined the band in ¹ *2010* .
He had an audition in ² _____ .
Classic Trio give a lot of concerts in England and abroad, for example in ³ _____ and ⁴ _____ . Classic Trio recorded an album ⁵ _____ years ago. Karl loves going on tours, signing autographs and playing the ⁶ _____ .

7 🔊 **2.48** Complete the texts with the correct form of the verbs in the Vocabulary box. Then listen and check.

IRON GUITAR
Sam is fifteen and he plays the guitar.

'We always ¹ *write* our own songs! We ² _____ a concert last week and we ³ _____ a lot of autographs!'

JUST JAZZ
Jacob is seventeen and he plays the saxophone.

'I ⁴ _____ the band two years ago. We play jazz and we want to ⁵ _____ an album!'

FOLK FRIENDS
Dora is sixteen and she plays the flute.

'I ⁶ _____ an audition last year and got in! We play in local cafés. We also ⁷ _____ on tour once a year. It's fun!'

8 **Exam Spot** Ask and answer the questions in pairs.

1 What music do you like? What music don't you like?
2 Do you play an instrument? Which instrument would you like to play?
3 Would you like to join a band? What type?
4 Do you like the bands on this page? Which one would you like to see?

9 Think of your own band. Answer the questions. Compare your ideas.

- Think of a name for your band.
- What type of music does it play?
- What instruments are in your band and who plays them?

My band is called Popcorn. We play …

I remember that!

5.2 Grammar   I can use *going to* and *will*.

You'll be great!

Zadie is in a band called Noisy Kids. She plays the guitar and she sings. She's going to take part in the Battle of the Bands competition. This morning she's practising at home. Bella is there too.

Bella: I bet you're excited about the concert tomorrow.
Zadie: I suppose so. But I'm nervous too. It's my first Battle of the Bands.
Bella: Are you going to play any new songs?
Zadie: Yes, we are. We're going to play two: *Big World* and *My Life* …
Bella: What are you going to wear?
Zadie: That's a good question … I don't know.

Zadie: I'm a bit worried. The concert is in the park. Do you think it'll rain?
Bella: I'm sure it won't. The weather forecast says it'll be sunny.
Zadie: That's a relief! But do you think a lot of people will come?
Bella: Yes, Zadie.
Zadie: Hmm … will they like our songs?
Bella: I think people will love your songs.
Zadie: But what if I make a mistake?
Bella: You won't make any mistakes, Zadie. I'm sure you'll be great!

Bella: Oh, look. You've got a message.
Zadie: It's from Elliot, our drummer. Oh, no! He says he's not going to play! He's got a bad cold! What are we going to do?
Bella: Don't panic, Zadie. I have an idea. Let's call Josh.
Zadie: But Josh can't play the drums! What a nightmare!

1 Look at the photos. What is Zadie going to take part in?

2 ▶ 24 🔊 2.49 Watch or listen and read. Answer the questions.
  1 What does Zadie do in the band?
  2 Has she played in the Battle of the Bands before?
  3 What is she worried about?
  4 What has happened to the drummer?

3 🔊 2.50 Listen and repeat. Find these expressions in the story.

I suppose so.   That's a relief.
What a nightmare!

Say it!

4 ▶ **Guess!** Why does Bella want to call Josh? Have a class vote.
  a Josh's mum is a doctor.
  b Josh knows another drummer.

5 ▶ 25 🔊 2.51 Now watch or listen and check.

Grammar *going to* and *will*

going to for future plans and intentions

+	I'm going to take part in the competition.
	We're going to play two new songs.
−	He isn't going to play.
?	Are you going to play new songs? Yes, we are. / No, we aren't.
	What are you going to wear?

will for predictions

+	I think people will love your songs.
−	I'm sure it won't rain.
?	Will people like our songs? Yes, they will. / No, they won't.
	Which songs will they play?

▶ 26 **Get Grammar!**

Max and Fluffy **are going to** play in the park.
Fluffy thinks Max **will** buy her an ice cream!

---

6 Look at Mrs Jones's list of things to do. Say what she is/isn't going to do on Saturday.

1 clean her drum kit ✓
  clean the house ✗

2 practise some songs ✓
  go to the supermarket ✗

1 *She's going to clean her drum kit.*
  She isn't going to clean the house.

3 buy a new T-shirt ✓
  buy some trainers for Josh ✗

4 listen to rock music ✓
  listen to classical music ✗

7 In pairs, ask and answer about your plans for this Saturday.

1 practise an instrument?
  A: *Are you going to practise an instrument on Saturday?*
  B: *No, I'm not. / Yes, I am.*
2 tidy your room?
3 do homework?
4 watch TV?
5 meet friends?

8 Josh and Zadie are talking about Josh's mum. Complete the dialogue with *will* or *won't*.

Zadie: What's the matter, Josh?
Josh: I've got a headache. Mum practises her drums for hours every day!
Zadie: I think she ¹ *will* play really well on Sunday then.
Josh: That's true – she ² _____ make any mistakes! She ³ _____ be the best drummer there!
Zadie: ⁴ _____ your mum join a rock band in the future?
Josh: No, she ⁵ _____ . She ⁶ _____ have time … I hope!
Zadie: Oh, Josh!

9 Ask and answer the questions.

1 Zadie / win / the Battle of the Bands?
  Will Zadie win the Battle of the Bands?
  I think she will. / I'm sure she won't.
2 Mrs Jones / be the best drummer?
3 Zadie / make a mistake?
4 the audience / like the songs?
5 it / rain / at the concert?

10 **Exam Spot** 🔊 2.52 Complete the newspaper extract with one word in each gap. Then listen and check.

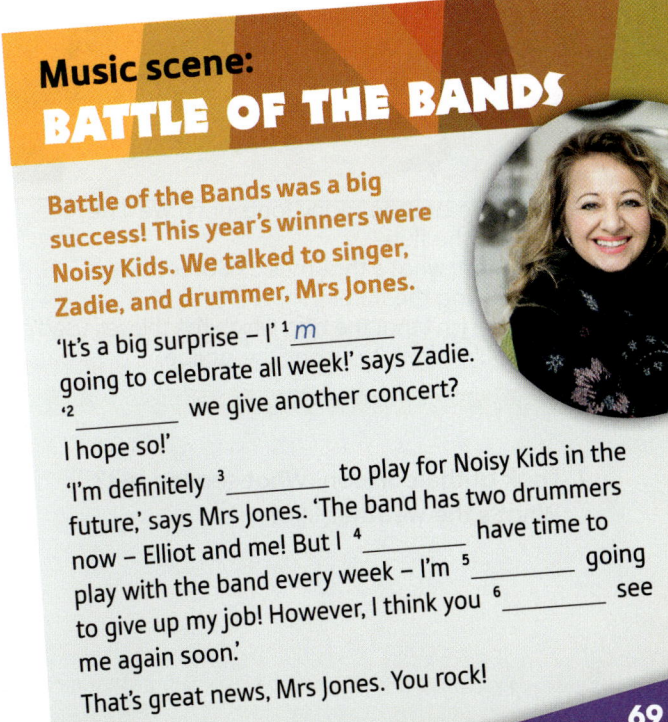

Music scene:
BATTLE OF THE BANDS

Battle of the Bands was a big success! This year's winners were Noisy Kids. We talked to singer, Zadie, and drummer, Mrs Jones.

'It's a big surprise – I' ¹ m_____ going to celebrate all week!' says Zadie. '² _____ we give another concert? I hope so!'

'I'm definitely ³ _____ to play for Noisy Kids in the future,' says Mrs Jones. 'The band has two drummers now – Elliot and me! But I ⁴ _____ have time to play with the band every week – I'm ⁵ _____ going to give up my job! However, I think you ⁶ _____ see me again soon.'

That's great news, Mrs Jones. You rock!

5.3 Grammar
I can use defining relative clauses with *who*, *which*, *that* and *where*.

The Explorers — The silver flute

Museum Robbed!

Yesterday, two criminals stole the famous silver flute from the Museum of Music. A museum guard saw the men who stole the flute. 'One of the men was tall and had a red bag,' he said. The police are still looking for the criminals.

1

Pops: Hey, kids! There was a robbery at the Museum of Music last night!
Mac: Oh, no! Is that the place where we saw the famous silver flute?
Pops: Yes, it is. And someone has stolen it. Come on, kids! We can help!

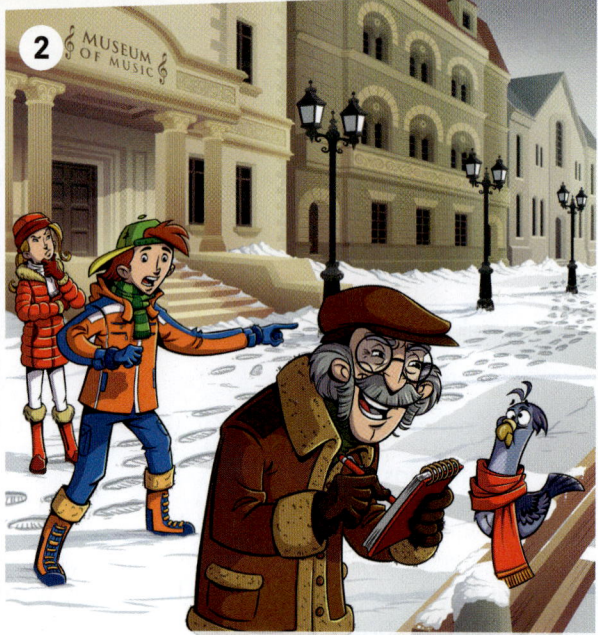

2

Pops: First, we need to interview witnesses.
Eva: Then, we need to find fingerprints.
Mac: Or footprints. Look! Maybe those are the footprints that the thieves left.

3 Later …

Eva: There are too many footprints. We'll never find the flute!
Pops: Hmm, what's that music? Somebody is playing the flute!
Mac: Hey! Isn't that the bag which the thieves used?
Eva: You're right. Let's call the police.

4

Detective: Well done, kids! We've caught the Firenzi brothers, who escaped from prison last year. They are master criminals …
Pops: And master musicians! Erm … can I have your autograph?
Mac, Eva: Oh, Pops!

1 Look at the cartoon. What season is it? What's the weather like?

2 🔊 **2.53** Read and listen. Circle true (T) or false (F).
1 The Explorers have never seen the flute. T / **F**
2 There were fingerprints outside the museum. T / F
3 Mac found the red bag in the street. T / F
4 Pops likes classical music. T / F

5.3

Grammar Defining relative clauses with *who, which, that, where*

Who and *that*

A museum guard saw the men *who / that* stole the flute.
(*who* and *that* refer to people)

Which and *that*

These are the footprints *which / that* the thieves left.
(*which* and *that* refer to objects and things)

Where

That's the place *where* we saw the famous silver flute.
(*where* refers to places)

▶ 27 **Get Grammar!**

This is the thief *who* stole Hammy's blanket!

5 🔊 2.54 Listen and repeat. Which items can you see in the cartoon?

Vocabulary Crime

criminal   detective   fingerprint   footprint   robbery
thief / thieves   witness

3 Circle the correct words. In which sentences can you use *that*?

1. The Museum of Music is the museum *which /* (*where*) the Explorers saw the silver flute.
2. The man *which / who* stole the flute was carrying a red bag.
3. The guard *which / who* saw the criminals couldn't catch them.
4. The bag *which / who* the Explorers saw belonged to the criminals.
5. The criminals *who / where* stole the flute were the Firenzi brothers.
6. The place *who / where* the criminals lived was full of musical instruments.

6 Read the definitions and write the correct words.

1. A person who takes something from someone without their permission.   *thief*
2. When someone's finger leaves a mark.   _____
3. A person who commits a crime.   _____
4. A person who sees a crime.   _____
5. When someone's foot leaves a mark.   _____
6. When you steal money or things from a bank or a shop.   _____
7. Someone who finds out information about a crime.   _____

4 Complete the questions with *who, which* and *where*. Then answer them.

1. Is that the thief *who* had the red bag?
   Yes, it is!

2. Are these the footprints _____ the Explorers followed?

3. Is this the bird _____ Pops interviewed?

4. Is this the house _____ the Explorers saw the brothers?

Fun Spot

7 Work in groups of five. Take turns to copy and complete sentence number 1. Fold the paper and pass it on to your friend. Do the same with the rest of the sentences. Read your story to the class.

1. There was an explorer who …
2. He/She met a monster / alien who …
3. They went to a place where …
4. They found some treasure that …
5. In the end, they …

5.4 Communication I can talk about plans.

What are you up to?

Adam: What are you up to in the holidays, Zadie?
Zadie: I'm going to go to London with my band. We're going to give some concerts.
Adam: That sounds like fun.
Zadie: Yes, my dad's going to drive us, and we're going to go sightseeing too. I can't wait to go on the London Eye! How about you? Have you got any plans?
Adam: I'm going to stay with some friends in Manchester. We've got tickets to see Coldplay.
Zadie: Lucky you! That sounds amazing!
Adam: Yes, I'm really looking forward to it. Hey, can I have a go on your guitar?
Zadie: Sure. Can you play?
Adam: A little bit.
Zadie: Not bad! I know who to call if we need a new guitarist!

1 ▶ 28 🔊 2.55 Watch or listen and read. What are Zadie and Adam going to do in the holidays? Are they excited?

2 🔊 2.56 Listen and repeat.

Communication
Talking about plans

Asking about plans
What are you up to *in the holidays*?
Have you got any plans *for the weekend*?
What are your plans *for Saturday*?

Talking about plans
I'm going to *stay with friends*.
I can't wait to *see my cousins*.
I'm really looking forward to *it / visiting Manchester*.

Reacting
That sounds *amazing / great / like fun*.
Lucky you!

3 🔊 2.57 Put the dialogue in the correct order. Then listen and check. Act out the dialogue in pairs.

☐ **Jack:** I'm going to go to the theatre. My dad's bought tickets to see *School of Rock, the Musical*.
☐ **Beth:** Yes. I'm really looking forward to it. What about you? Have you got any plans?
☐ **Jack:** Yes, I can't wait!
☐ **Beth:** Yes, we're going to have a big family party. It's my great-grandma's ninety-ninth birthday.
[1] **Jack:** Have you got any plans for the weekend, Beth?
☐ **Beth:** That sounds like fun!
☐ **Jack:** That sounds amazing! Wow! Is all your family going to be there?

4 **Exam Spot** Work in pairs. Student A: Ask Student B about his/her plans for the next holidays. Student B: Answer Student A's questions. Then swap roles.

A: *Have you got any plans for the next holidays?*
B: *I'm going to …*

I can understand a text about a musician. **Reading** 5.5

Alma Deutscher – the new Mozart?

Alma Deutscher is like many other girls of her age. She loves reading and spending time with her friends. But Alma has done something that most other thirteen year-olds haven't done: she's written an opera. The opera is based on the story of Cinderella, and Alma started writing it when she was only eight years old! A group of opera singers performed it on stage for the first time just before her twelfth birthday. 'I'm very proud,' says Alma. Now she hopes to take her opera around the world, so that more people will hear it.

Alma has always been interested in music. She started playing the piano when she was two years old, and the violin when she was three. At the age of four, she composed her first tune. Where do her musical ideas come from? Sometimes they come to her in her dreams, and she also has a very special inspiration – her 'magic' purple skipping rope. When she plays with it, music and ideas appear in her head, says Alma.

So what are Alma's plans for the future? At the moment she's writing a book, and then she's going to write the music for a film. A lot of people have called her 'the new Mozart' after the famous Austrian composer. He wrote his first pieces at the age of five. What does Alma think about that? 'I love Mozart,' says Alma, 'but I'm going to be like Alma, not Mozart.'

1 Read the text quickly. Who is the girl in the photo? Why do some people call her 'the new Mozart'?

2 🔊 2.58 Read and listen to the text. Circle the correct answer a, b or c.
   1 Alma doesn't like doing the same things as other teenage girls.
      a Right   (b) Wrong   c Doesn't say
   2 Alma has written a book about Cinderella.
      a Right   b Wrong   c Doesn't say
   3 Her opera is famous around the world.
      a Right   b Wrong   c Doesn't say
   4 Alma is better at playing the piano than the violin.
      a Right   b Wrong   c Doesn't say
   5 Alma sometimes gets ideas for music when she is asleep.
      a Right   b Wrong   c Doesn't say
   6 In the future, Alma is going to visit Austria.
      a Right   b Wrong   c Doesn't say
   7 Alma doesn't like Mozart.
      a Right   b Wrong   c Doesn't say

3 Look up the highlighted words from the text in the dictionary.

4 🔊 2.59 Complete the texts with the words highlighted in the text. Then listen and check.

Paul McCartney ¹composed the famous Beatles song *Yesterday* in less than a minute. He woke up with the ²_____ in his head! It was very successful and Paul McCartney was very ³_____ of it! Today, it's one of the most popular songs of all time.

The Lion King is a famous musical. It is ⁴_____ the animated film of the same name. Actors first ⁵_____ the musical in 1997. Today, more than 90 million people have seen the story of Simba and his horrible uncle, Scar, ⁶_____.

5 Can you think of other young people who became famous when they were children or teenagers? Are they still famous?

Miley Cyrus became famous as an actress. She's still famous, but now she's a singer.

5.6 Vocabulary and Listening

I can understand a listening text about a talent show.

1 Look at the advertisement. What sort of programme is it? Do you have programmes like this in your country? Do you like them? Why? / Why not?

STARS OF TOMORROW — THE FINAL

On TV tonight 7.00 p.m.

It's the final of *Stars of Tomorrow*. On tonight's show, Emily and Sam will perform their favourite songs and the viewers will vote. The winner will receive a recording contract and £50,000, but who will it be? Don't miss tonight's show!

2 🔊 **2.60** Listen and repeat. Which qualities are the most important to be a successful pop star?

Vocabulary Personal qualities

confidence   determination   good looks   hard work
intelligence   style   talent

A: *I think talent is important.*
B: *I agree. / I don't agree. I think …*

3 🔊 **2.61** Listen to the start of the show and answer the questions.
1 Who do the judges, David and Cheryl, think will win?
2 How do Sam and Emily feel?
3 What songs are they going to sing?

4 🔊 **2.61** Listen again. Which qualities do Sam and Emily have? Use the words in the Vocabulary box.
1 Sam: *talent* , _____ , _____
2 Emily: _____ , _____ , _____

5 🔊 **2.62** Who do you think will win? Listen and find out. What is the result?

6 Read the Vocabulary Builder. Then read the text and circle the correct answers.

Vocabulary Builder
Adjectives from nouns

noun	adjective
confidence	confident
determination	determined
good looks	good-looking
hard work	hard-working
intelligence	intelligent
style	stylish
talent	talented

How to be successful in the music business!

1 You won't succeed without a lot of (hard work) / hard-working. You'll need to be very *determination* / *determined*!
2 Are you a singer, a guitarist, or a songwriter? Decide on your *talent* / *talented*, and concentrate on that.
3 You'll need to be *confidence* / *confident* to perform on stage.
4 It isn't important to be *good looks* / *good-looking*, but you must have your own *style* / *stylish* – something that makes you different from other people.
5 Finally, to be successful, you'll probably need a lot of luck!

Fun Spot

7 Work in pairs. Invent your own talent show. Think of:
1 the name of the show,
2 what the contestants have to do,
3 the prizes.

The name of my show is …

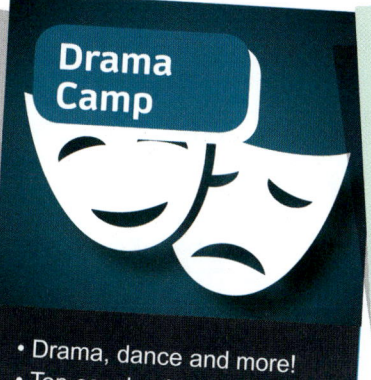

I can write an email asking for information. Writing 5.7

Music Camp UK
Do you love music? Then Music Camp is for you!
- Work with top musicians!
- Learn to write songs!
- Listen to concerts every night!

Drama Camp
- Drama, dance and more!
- Top coaches!
- Build your confidence!

Adventure Camp
- Whitewater rafting, mountain biking, and more…
- Join us this summer!

1 Read the advertisements. Which sounds the most interesting to you? Why?

2 Read Ryan's email. Which advertisement does he respond to?

① Dear Sir/Madam,

② I am thirteen years old and I am writing to find out more about your camp.

I would be grateful if you could answer a few questions. Firstly, how old do you have to be to go to the camp? I am going to be fourteen in July, and my mum and dad are happy for me to go to a camp on my own. Secondly, what will we do at the camp? I sing and play the guitar, and I am interested in learning how to record songs in a studio. Lastly, how much does the camp cost?

I look forward to hearing from you.

③ Yours faithfully,
Ryan Atkins

3 Read the Writing box. How do we begin the email when we write to a man? And how do we begin one to a woman?

Writing
An email asking for information

① **Beginning**
Dear Sir/Madam,
Dear Mr/Mrs/Ms Phillips,

② **Asking for information**
I am writing to find out about …
I would be grateful if you could answer a few questions.

③ **Ending**
I look forward to hearing from you.
Regards,
Yours faithfully, (after Dear Sir/Madam)
Yours sincerely, (after Dear Mr/Mrs/Ms X)

Formal language
When you write to a person that you don't know, use formal language, e.g.
- full forms: *I am writing … , I am going …*
- formal expressions: *I would be grateful … , I look forward to…*
- formal beginnings and endings: *Dear Sir/Madam, Yours faithfully*

4 Read the box above. Copy and complete the table with the phrases in the box below.

Hi, James   Love,   Yours sincerely,   Dear Mr Taylor,
I would be grateful if you could …   Write soon,
Can you …,   Bye for now,   I am interested in …
Regards,   I look forward to hearing from you.

	Formal email	Informal email
Beginning		
Ending		
Other		

5 🖋 **Writing Time** Choose one of the other advertisements in Exercise 1 and write an email asking for more information.

❓ **Find ideas**
Think of questions to ask about the camp.

✏️ **Draft**
Organise your ideas into paragraphs. Use the the Writing box to help you.

👍 **Check and write**
Use the correct beginning and ending for your email. Use polite, formal language.

5.8 Language Revision

Vocabulary

1 Label the instruments in the photos. What type of music uses these instruments?

A *violin, classical music*

2 Complete the facts with the correct verbs.

DID YOU NOW?

Katy Perry sang in a church choir when she was a teenager. The choir ¹ *gave* a lot of concerts!

Christina Aguilera ² _____ an audition for a chidren's TV show before she became famous.

Pink started her career very early. She ³ _____ her first band, Middleground, when she was a teenager. She ⁴ _____ her own songs at that time too!

Adele ⁵ _____ her first album when she was nineteen. It was called *19*! Then she ⁶ _____ on a tour that lasted a year!

3 What can you see in pictures A and B? Use the words in the box.

> thief / criminal   detective   fingerprint
> footprint   robbery   witness

In picture A, there's a criminal.

4 Complete the sentences with the correct form of the words.

1 You should have more *confidence* (confident).
2 She was _____ to win (determination).
3 He always wears _____ clothes (style).
4 Don't do that – use your _____ (intelligent)!
5 My mum is clever and _____ (good looks).

Grammar

5 In your notebook, write what Zadie is going to do next week.

1 MONDAY meet her friends
2 TUESDAY write an essay
3 WEDNESDAY watch a talent show on TV
4 THURSDAY go to basketball practice
5 FRIDAY practise the guitar
6 SATURDAY go shopping with Bella
7 SUNDAY relax!

1 *On Monday, Zadie is going to meet her friends.*

6 Make notes about what you are going to do next week. Then ask and answer in pairs.

A: *What are you going to do on Monday?*
B: *I'm going to buy a new phone.*

7 Complete the sentences with *will* or *won't* and the verbs in brackets.

1 A: Who do you think *will win* (win)?
   B: I'm sure it _____ (be) the girl band. They're terrible!
2 A: _____ you _____ (ask) Adele for her autograph at the concert?
   B: No, I _____ . I'm too shy!
3 I think it _____ (rain) tomorrow, so the band _____ (give) the concert in the park.
4 In the future, robot bands _____ (be) popular! We _____ (listen) to real people.

8 Use *who*, *which*, *where* and match the sentence halves a–f to 1–6.

who   which   where

1 [b] She's the girl   a I bought my trainers.
2 [ ] That's the shop   b won the competition.
3 [ ] That's the song   c invited me to a party
4 [ ] The boy   was called Simon.
5 [ ] The café   d I heard on the radio.
6 [ ] They're the   e I meet my friends is
      jeans   on the High Street.
                               f I wanted to buy.

1 *b – She's the girl who won the competition.*

Communication

9 🔊 **2.63** Complete the dialogue with the words in the box. Then listen and check. Act out the dialogue in pairs. Change the information in blue so that it's true for you.

| forward   fun   lucky   plans   ~~up~~   wait |

Boy: What are you ¹ _up_ to in the summer?
Girl: I'm going to stay with my cousins at their house by the sea. We're going to go surfing and snorkelling.
Boy: That sounds like ² _____ !
Girl: Yes, I can't ³ _____ . What about you? Have you got any ⁴ _____ ?
Boy: Yes, I'm going to go to a music festival. I won tickets in a competition.
Girl: ⁵ _____ you!
Boy: Yes, I'm really looking ⁶ _____ to it.

Dictation

10 **Exam Spot** 🔊 **2.64** Listen to a short text. Then listen again and write down what you hear. Make sure you spell the words correctly.

Pronunciation

11 🔊 **2.65** Listen and repeat: /w/ and /v/.

Watch **W**aldo's hea**v**y metal **v**iolin band in **V**enice, **V**ancouver and **S**witzerland!

Check yourself! ✓
- I can talk about music, crime and personal qualities.
- I can use *going to* and *will*.
- I can use defining relative clauses with *who, which, that, where*.
- I can talk about plans.

Round up 5.8

12 Read the sentences. Circle the correct answer a, b or c.

1 To play in the school orchestra, you have to have _____ .
  (a) an audition   b an autograph   c an album
2 Can you sing and play the guitar? We need you to _____ our band!
  a sign   b join   c practise
3 A _____ took my phone while I was shopping.
  a footprints   b thief   c witness
4 The _____ happened last Tuesday.
  a thieves   b criminal   c robbery
5 This singer is not very pretty, but she is _____ .
  a style   b stylish   c good looks
6 She plays the _____ in the evening.
  a classical   b techno   c cello
7 What _____ to do next weekend?
  a you are going   b you going   c are you going
8 It's time to go home. Mum will _____ worried.
  a be   b being   c to be
9 We _____ understand this film. It's in German!
  a not going   b won't   c aren't
10 The guitarist _____ gave the concert on TV last night is amazing.
  a who   b which   c where
11 The house _____ I lived as a child is in Manchester.
  a who   b which   c where
12 The dog _____ won the talent show was called Max.
  a where   b it   c that
13 I'm really _____ forward to my holiday. I'm going to spend it in Greece!
  a looking   b hoping   c waiting
14 Are you going to a music camp? That sounds _____ fun!
  a like   b as   c how
15 What are you _____ to at the weekend? Would you like to go to the cinema?
  a down   b up   c through

77

Get Culture!

Festivals

Edinburgh: festival city!

Edinburgh is the capital of Scotland, and it's famous for its festivals. There are festivals of music, film, art, science, books, and many more. More than 4.5 million people attend every year. Three Edinburgh teenagers tell us about their favourite festival.

1 ☐ I love the Edinburgh Book Festival. It happens in August, and I go every year to meet my favourite authors and to hear about their latest novels. I always ask them to sign their new books for me. I've got a big collection of autographs! My favourite author is Matt Dickinson, the author of an adventure novel called *Killer Storm*. I hope I'll meet him at the festival this year!

James, 14

2 ☐ My favourite festival is Hogmanay. It's a celebration of the New Year. On the 30th of December, people take part in a parade through the city at night. Then, on New Year's Eve, there's a big street party. You can watch musicians, dancers, acrobats and fire eaters. At midnight, there's an amazing firework show over Edinburgh Castle. This year, I'm going to go with my family and a group of friends – it's going to be awesome!

Evie, 13

3 ☐ I love the Edinburgh Fringe Festival. It takes place in August and it's the biggest cultural festival in the world. You can watch plays, comedy shows, circus acts, music concerts, and lots more. Altogether, there are more than 3,000 shows on hundreds of stages all over the city. Anyone can take part, and this year I'm going to perform with my drama club! We're going to perform the musical, *Oliver*. I can't wait!

Hannah, 14

1 🔊 **2.66** Read and listen to the text about festivals in Edinburgh. Match photos A–C to paragraphs 1–3.

2 Read the text again and complete the table.

	James	Evie	Hannah
Favourite festival?			
When is it?			
What can you do?			

3 🔊 **2.67** Listen to Liam. What's his favourite festival?

4 🔊 **2.67** Listen again and answer the questions.
  1 When is the festival?
  2 What can you do at the festival?
  3 What is Liam going to do this year?

5 Have you ever visited Edinburgh or Scotland? Which of the festivals would you like to go to? Why?

The Notting Hill Carnival

A ▶29 Watch the video and answer the presenter's questions. Where and when does the Notting Hill Carnival take place?

B ▶29 Watch the video again and circle the correct answer a, b or c.

1 When did the Notting Hill Carnival begin?
   a 1966   b 1976   c 1986
2 How many people attend the carnival now?
   a almost 1 million   b over 2 million
   c 3 million
3 What day is Family Day?
   a Saturday   b Sunday   c Monday
4 What type of music is typical of the carnival?
   a pop   b classical   c reggae
5 How long do the people usually work on the carnival costumes?
   a a few days   b many months   c many years
6 How many food stalls are there?
   a 500   b 200   c 300

C What do you like most about the Notting Hill Carnival?

PROJECT

- Work in groups. Prepare a video invitation to a festival at your school.

- Choose a type of festival. Use these ideas to help you.

  | books | films | cartoons | theatre |
  | comedy | street art | music | dance |

- Think of a name and attractions. Then make a video invitation. Use these questions to help you.
  - Where and when is the festival?
  - What can people do there?
  - Why is it special / fun?
  - Can you meet anyone famous?

- The … festival takes place in … (name of place) in … (month).
- You can watch … / listen to … / eat …
- You can meet … at the festival. He / She is a famous …

- Share your videos with the class. Which is the most interesting invitation? Why?

6 Protect the planet

Vocabulary — I can talk about wild animals and the environment.

In this unit

Vocabulary
- Wild animals
- Environment verbs
- Natural events
- Big numbers

Grammar
- First conditional
- Verbs followed by infinitive or -ing

▶ 30–31
6.2 Grammar video

▶ 32
6.2 Grammar animation

▶ 33
6.3 Grammar animation

▶ 34
6.4 Communication video

1 Can you think of an animal for each letter of the alphabet?
ant, bear, …
Which animals:
a live on land / in the sea?   **b** eat meat / plants?

I know that!

Animals in danger

What do you know about these animals? Find out why they are in danger, and how we can help!

Polar bear · Arctic fox · Snow leopard · Giant panda · La Gomera giant lizard · Philippine eagle · Galapagos penguin · Green turtle · Mountain gorilla · Black rhino

Mountain gorilla
Lives in mountain forests in Africa.
Problem: People cut down trees.
Solution: Protect forests.
Wow! Its DNA is 98 percent the same as ours.

Black rhino
Lives in Africa.
Problem: People hunt it for the horn on its head.
Solution: Stop hunters and save this animal.
Wow! It weighs the same as thirty people.

Green turtle
Lives in seas and oceans.
Problem: People throw away rubbish and pollute the sea.
Solution: Look after the sea and recycle your rubbish.
Wow! It can live for a hundred years.

more profiles

2 🔊 **3.1** Listen and repeat. Find the animals in the photos on page 80. Which animals have you seen in the zoo?

Vocabulary Wild animals

eagle   fox   gorilla   leopard   lizard   panda
penguin   polar bear   rhino   turtle

3 Complete the sentences with the names of the animals in the Vocabulary box.

1 A _gorilla_ has long arms.
2 A _____ is a bird, but it doesn't fly.
3 A _____ eats bamboo leaves.
4 A _____ lives at the North Pole.
5 An _____ hunts for small animals.
6 A _____ has spots on its fur.

4 🔊 **3.2** Read and listen to the information on the webpage. What do the animals in the photos have in common?

5 🔊 **3.3** Listen and repeat. Find the verbs in the animal profiles on page 80 and explain their meaning.

Vocabulary Environment verbs

cut down   hunt   look after   pollute   protect
recycle   save   throw away

6 Complete the phrases.

1 c_u_t down trees
2 h___ animals
3 l___ after the sea
4 p_____e the seas
5 p_____t forests
6 r_____ rubbish
7 s___ animals
8 t____ away rubbish

7 **Exam Spot** 🔊 **3.4** Listen about the giant panda and complete the profile.

Giant panda

Lives in forests in the ¹_mountains_ **of** ² _____ .
Problem: People ³ _____ the forests.
Solution: ⁴ _____ the forests and don't cut down trees.
Wow! Pandas have lived on our planet for ⁵ _____ hundred thousand years!

8 Complete the poster with the correct environment verbs. There may be more than one answer.

WHAT DO WE DO TO OUR PLANET?

We ¹ _pollute_ the air in our cities and towns.

We ² _____ rubbish.

We ³ _____ trees.

We still ⁴ _____ animals.

We should plant new trees.

We should ⁵ _____ our cities and rivers.

We should ⁶ _____ animals.

HELP THE ENVIRONMENT! TODAY!

9 Choose to be an animal from page 80. In pairs, guess which animal your partner is. Ask five questions.

A: *Do you live on land?*
B: *Yes, I do.*
A: *Do you live in a cold place?*
B: *No, I don't.*

I remember that!

6.2 Grammar — I can use the first conditional.

The forest clean-up

Volunteers needed for:
The Big Forest Clean-Up!
Saturday 27th March,
10 a.m. – 1 p.m.
Forest Gate, Cherwell Park
Pick up rubbish and make our forest clean!
If you help, you'll protect our local wildlife!
More info:
forestfriends@gmail.com

Last weekend Adam helped to organise a forest clean-up. Bella and Josh joined him and they picked up a lot of rubbish!

Bella: Ugh! Look at all this plastic! It's disgusting!
Adam: People should recycle and reuse plastic bags and bottles. If we throw away plastic, we'll pollute the environment. Hey, don't throw your chewing gum on the ground, Josh!
Josh: Why not? It's only gum.
Adam: It's as bad as plastic! If the animals eat it, they'll get ill.
Josh: Oh, sorry, Adam! I didn't know.
Bella: Let's get started. Who can fill the most bags in an hour?

45 minutes later …

Josh: I'm thirsty.
Bella: Be careful, Josh! Don't waste water!
Josh: Sorry, I'm tired and hungry. Can we have a break?
Adam: No. If we stop now, we won't finish the challenge.
Bella: Relax, Adam. We can have a five-minute break. I've got food in my rucksack. If Josh has a sandwich, he'll work faster. But if he doesn't have a sandwich, he won't stop complaining!
Adam: OK, I give up!

Bella: Hmm, that's weird. Where's my rucksack? It was here a moment ago.
Josh: Oh, what does it look like?
Bella: It's blue. Why?
Josh: Oh dear!

---

1 Look at the advert and photos and answer the questions.

1 What are the friends doing?
2 Have you ever been on a forest clean-up? Do you think it's a good idea? Why? / Why not?

2 ▶30 🔊 3.5 Watch or listen and read. Answer the questions.

1 What do the children find in the forest?
2 Who feels tired?
3 What does Bella suggest?

3 🔊 3.6 Listen and repeat. Find these expressions in the story.

Relax!   That's weird.

Say it!

4 ▶ Guess! What has happened to Bella's rucksack? Have a class vote.

a Josh has put it in a bin bag.
b An animal has taken it.

5 ▶31 🔊 3.7 Now watch or listen and check.

6.2

Grammar First conditional

First conditional

If animals **eat** the gum, they**'ll get** ill.
If we **stop** now, we **won't finish**.
If Josh **has** a sandwich, he**'ll work** faster.
If he **doesn't have** a sandwich, he **won't stop** complaining.

▶ 32 **Get Grammar!**

If Fluffy **has** a bath,
she **will waste** water.

---

6 What does Adam say about the environment? Match sentence halves a–e to 1–5.

1. [c] If I see rubbish in the street,
2. [ ] If we don't recycle paper,
3. [ ] If my parents don't turn off the light,
4. [ ] If we take a quick shower,
5. [ ] If I go shopping with my mum,

a we won't waste a lot of water.
b people will cut down more trees.
c I'll put it in a bin.
d I'll remind them to save energy.
e I'll take a few bags with me.

7 In your notebook, write true sentences. Use the first conditional.

1 If I get up late tomorrow, I …
2 If the weather is good at the weekend, I …
3 If my friends invite me to a party on Sunday, I …
4 If I feel tired after school, I …
5 If I get some extra pocket money, I …

8 🔊 3.8 Complete the chain stories with the correct form of the verbs. Then listen and check.

Chain story 1

If Josh ¹ *finds* (find) a sandwich in Bella's bag, he ² _____ (eat) it. → If he ³ _____ (eat) it, he ⁴ _____ (not be) hungry. → If he ⁵ _____ (not be) hungry, he ⁶ _____ (be happy)!

Chain story 2

If the fox ⁷ _____ (damage) Bella's bag, she ⁸ _____ (need) a new one. → If she ⁹ _____ (need) a new bag, she ¹⁰ _____ (go) shopping on Saturday. → If she ¹¹ _____ (go) shopping on Saturday, she ¹² _____ (not help) her mum at the café.

Fun Spot

9 Write a chain story. Use the first conditional, ideas 1–3 and the prompts in the box to help you.

wear a hat   stay at home   make friends with a kangaroo
go surfing   buy a motorbike   go to a concert

1 You get extra pocket money
2 You have a bad haircut
3 You go to Australia

If I get extra pocket money, I'll go to a concert.
If I go to a concert, I'll see Adele.
If I see Adele, I'll ask for her autograph.

83

6.3 Grammar — I can use verbs followed by infinitive or -ing.

The Explorers — A new friend

The Explorers are in the Himalayas. They're looking for the Yeti!

1

Mac: I hate climbing and I don't like snow.
Eva: I can't stand carrying this backpack. It's heavy! We need to have a break.
Pops: OK, let's go to that cave.

2

Mac: I'm hungry. I'd like to eat something. Let's cook some sausages.
Pops: I'm really looking forward to seeing the Yeti. Let's read about it. I've got a great book. Look!

3

All you need to know about the Yeti

The Yeti …
- enjoys walking in the snow.
- doesn't like running.
- likes sleeping in caves.
- doesn't mind sleeping in the forest.
- can't stand eating sausages without ketchup!

Do you want to find the Yeti? Be prepared!

The Yeti …
- needs to eat a lot.
- always wants to eat more.
- would like to make friends with you!

4

Eva: Hmm … the Yeti likes sleeping in caves. What if this is his cave?
Mac: Look! It's the Yeti!

5

Yeti: Sausages! Yum! I love eating sausages with …
Eva, Mac: Ketchup!
Yeti: How did you know? You are my friends now!

1 Look at the cartoon and answer the questions.
  1 Where are the Explorers?
  2 What's the weather like?
  3 What book is Pops reading?

2 🔊 3.9 Read and listen. Answer the questions.
  1 How do the children feel at the beginning of the story?
  2 Where do they go to have a break?
  3 What does the Yeti want?

6.3

Grammar Verbs followed by infinitive or -ing

Verbs followed by infinitive

We **need / want to have** a break.
I **would like to eat** something.
The Yeti **learned to sleep** in caves.
He **decided to eat** sausages.

Verb followed by -ing

I **hate / can't stand climbing** mountains.
He **doesn't mind sleeping** in the forest.
I**'m looking forward to seeing** the Yeti.
The Yeti **likes / enjoys / loves sleeping** in caves.

▶ 33 **Get Grammar!**

This animal **enjoys eating** fish!

3 Circle the correct answer.
1 Mac can't stand *to walk /(walking)* in the snow.
2 Pops decides *to go / going* to the cave.
3 Eva needs to *take off / taking off* her backpack.
4 Pops is looking forward *to talk / talking* to the Yeti.
5 Mac would like *to run away / running away* from the Yeti.

4 🔊 3.10 Complete Yeti's thoughts with the correct form of the verbs. Then listen and check.

I don't mind ¹ *cooking* (cook) those sausages.

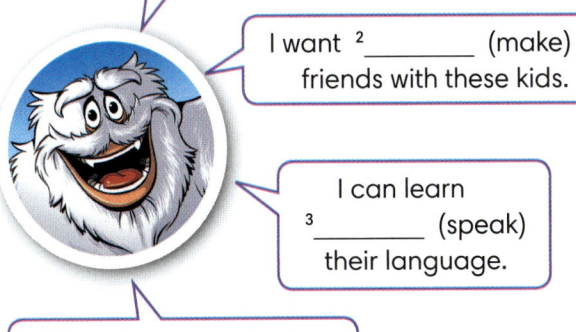

I want ² _____ (make) friends with these kids.

I can learn ³ _____ (speak) their language.

I'd like ⁴ _____ (go) for a walk with them.

I can't stand ⁵ _____ (eat) ice cream.

I'm looking forward to ⁶ _____ (see) my cousin, Bigfoot, in the summer.

5 Read Bigfoot's letter and circle the correct answer a, b or c.

Dear Yeti,

I'm really looking forward to ¹ ___ you this summer. I need ² ___ a holiday! I'd like ³ ___ you in July. Is it warm then? Are there any trees? I always sleep under trees. You know I can't stand ⁴ ___ in caves. And don't worry, I don't mind ⁵ ___ with the housework.
I love ⁶ ___ sausages too!

Your cousin,
Bigfoot

1 a see   (b) seeing   c seen
2 a to have   b have   c having
3 a visiting   b to visit   c visit
4 a sleep   b to sleep   c sleeping
5 a to help   b helping   c help
6 a cooking   b cook   c to cooking

6 In your notebook, write true sentences.
1 I can't stand …
2 My best friend loves …
3 I've decided …
4 My parents want …
5 My class is looking forward to …

6.4 Communication
I can persuade somebody to do something.

It's a deal!

Bella: Hi! What are you guys doing?
Zadie: We're making placards. There's a protest this afternoon against air pollution. Adam and I are going. Do you fancy coming with us?
Bella: I'm not sure. I've got a lot of homework.
Adam: You can do your homework tomorrow – it's Sunday. You really should come – it's important.
Bella: I'll think about it.
Adam: Come on, Bella. The air pollution in the city centre is terrible – we can change that.
We want clean air! We want clean air!
Zadie: If you come, I'll buy you a smoothie afterwards!
Bella: OK, it's a deal! What time does it start?
Zadie: We're meeting outside the town hall at two o'clock. You won't regret it! Now, here's a pen!

20 minutes later ...

Bella: What do you think of my placard?
Zadie: Oh, it's amazing!

1 ▶ 34 🔊 3.11 Watch or listen and read. Where are Zadie and Adam going this afternoon? Does Bella want to go?

2 🔊 3.12 Listen and repeat.

Communication Persuading

Persuading
You really should *come*. / We really should *go*.
Come on, it's important / you'll enjoy it!
You won't regret it!
If you *come*, I'll *buy you a smoothie*.

Responding
I'm not sure.   It's a deal!
I'll think about it.   Maybe you're right.
I suppose so.

3 🔊 3.13 Complete the dialogue with words in the box. Then listen and check.

> about   deal   you'll   regret
> should   suppose   ~~sure~~

Girl: There's a beach clean-up on Saturday. Do you fancy going?
Boy: I'm not ¹*sure* . I'm a bit tired.
Girl: But they need volunteers. We really ² _____ go.
Boy: Hmm, I'll think ³ _____ it.
Girl: Come on, ⁴ _____ enjoy it, and it'll make a big difference to the beach.
Boy: I ⁵ _____ so.
Girl: Leo and Carla are going too.
Boy: OK, it's a ⁶ _____ ! I'll come.
Girl: Great! You won't ⁷ _____ it!

4 **Exam Spot** Work in pairs. Student A: Go to page 122. Student B: Go to page 128.

Message in a bottle

I can understand a text about an environmental issue. **Reading 6.5**

Do you think it's possible to make a boat out of plastic bottles, and then sail it across the Pacific Ocean from California to Australia? No? Well, that's exactly what David de Rothschild did with his boat, Plastiki.

David wanted to use the boat to protest against the pollution of our oceans. Every year about eight million tonnes of plastic gets into the sea. Fish and other sea animals, such as turtles, whales and dolphins eat the plastic and die. Experts say that if we don't do something now, there will soon be more rubbish in the ocean than fish.

To make Plastiki, David collected 12,500 old empty bottles. He used the bottles and other recycled materials to build the 18-metre boat, and he used a special glue made of nuts and sugar! When David and five of his friends left San Francisco at the start of their journey, people thought they were crazy. But four months later, they arrived in Sydney, Australia. The voyage was a big test for Plastiki. It sailed through storms and huge waves, but it survived!

David's message is simple: we have to stop polluting the sea with plastic. But we don't have to build a boat out of bottles to make a difference. If we buy and throw away less plastic, and if we recycle more, we will all help to save our oceans.

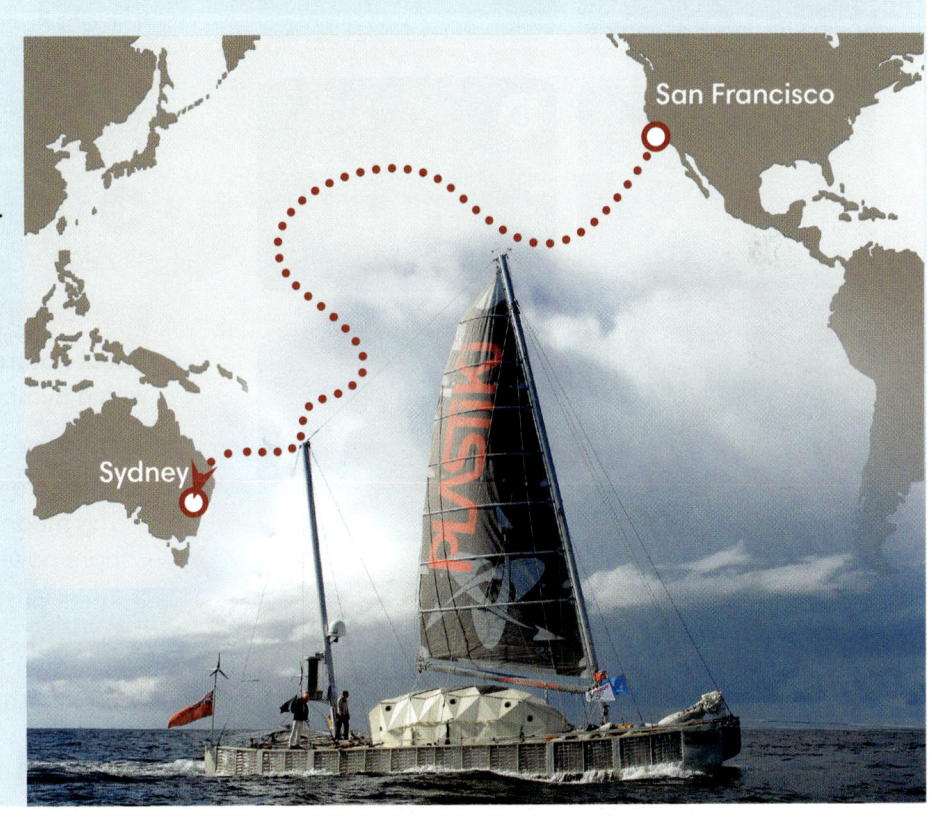

1 Look at the photo of the boat. Why do you think it is called the Plastiki? Read and check.

2 **Exam Spot** 🔊 3.14 Read and listen to the text. Answer the questions.
1 Why did David decide to build a boat out of plastic bottles?
2 How much plastic gets into the sea every year?
3 How many people were there on the journey?
4 Where did Plastiki sail from and to?
5 How long did the journey take?
6 What can we all do to save the oceans?

3 Guess the meaning of the words highlighted in the text. Then look them up in the dictionary.

4 Complete the sentences with words highlighted in the text.
1 The first *voyage* of the Titanic ended dramatically.
2 Monkeys eat fruit, _____ and insects.
3 _____ are the largest animal in the sea.
4 The _____ today are perfect for surfing!
5 You use _____ to join two things together.

5 **Exam Spot** Ask and answer the questions in pairs.
1 Do you and your family recycle?
2 What things do you recycle?
3 When you go shopping, do you take your own bag?

87

6.6 Listening and Vocabulary

I can understand a listening text about natural events.

1 🔊 **3.15** Listen and repeat. Then match the words in the Vocabulary box to photos A–H.

Vocabulary Natural events

drought   earthquake   flood   forest fire   thunderstorm
tornado   tsunami   volcanic eruption

A *drought*

2 Do any of these events happen in your country? Which have you heard about on the news recently?

3 🔊 **3.16** Complete the sentences with the words in the Vocabulary box. Then listen and check.

1 There was a really loud t*hunderstorm* last night with lots of thunder and lightning.
2 Some airports were closed after a v_____ e_____ in Indonesia.
3 The firefighters used 250,000 litres of water to stop the f_____ f_____ .
4 15 million people don't have enough water because of a d_____ .
5 A t_____ with winds of 300 km/h damaged more than 2,000 houses yesterday.

4 Read the Vocabulary Builder. Write the numbers.

Vocabulary Builder
Big numbers

a hundred   a thousand   ten thousand
a hundred thousand   a million

653	= six hundred and fifty-three
5,300	= five thousand three hundred
98,000	= ninety-eight thousand
426,000	= four hundred and twenty-six thousand
3,000,000	= three million

1 eight hundred and seventy-nine *879*
2 fifty-four thousand
3 two hundred and thirty-five thousand
4 seventeen million

5 🔊 **3.17** Listen and write down the numbers.

1 *7,800*

6 **Exam Spot** 🔊 **3.18** Listen to a radio show about natural events. Complete the sentences with a number.

1 There are only about *two* tsunamis every year.
2 There are _____ thunderstorms every year. This means that _____ are happening right now!
3 There are _____ earthquakes every year.

7 **Exam Spot** 🔊 **3.18** Listen again and complete the fact files.

Tsunamis
What to do:
- Move to a ¹ *hill* or a mountain
- Don't stay on the ² _____ !

Thunderstorms
What to do:
- Go home or move inside a ³ _____ .
- Don't stand under a tree or use an ⁴ _____ .

Earthquakes
What to do:
- Move under a table or a ⁵ _____ .
- Don't stand near ⁶ _____ or heavy furniture.

8 In pairs, choose one or two of the other natural events in the Vocabulary box. Complete the table. Compare your ideas in class.

	Do	Don't
Drought	save water collect rainwater	water your garden …

I can write a leaflet with tips or instructions. **Writing** **6.7**

How to save water

We all need water to survive, so it's important that we don't waste it. Here are our top tips for saving water:

Turn off the tap when you clean your teeth. This can save six litres of water per minute.

Don't take a bath, take a shower! A bath uses about eighty litres of water, and a shower about forty-five.

If you spend a minute less in the shower, you'll save another eight litres of water. That's 3,000 litres of water a year!

Don't wash the dishes by hand, use a dishwasher! But remember: the dishwasher must be full.

These are some simple ideas, but in this way, you can help to save water – and that's good for the planet!

1 Look at the pictures. What ideas do they show about saving water? What else can we do?

2 Read the leaflet. Which of your ideas did it mention? Were there any new ideas?

3 Read the Writing box. Find three examples of the imperative.

Writing A leaflet with tips or instructions

1 Introduction
It's very important to *save water*, because …
It's important that we …
We all should …
Here are a few tips / instructions for *saving water*.

2 Tips or instructions
Turn off the tap. Use less *water*.
Don't waste *water*.
This can save *six litres of water per minute*.
If you …, you'll … .

3 Conclusion
These are some ideas …
In this way, you can …

Imperatives for giving tips and instructions

When you give tips and instructions, use the imperative.
Take a shower!   *Don't take* a bath!

4 Read the box above. Complete the sentences below with verbs in the box. Use the imperative.

| not leave | ~~switch off~~ | not switch on |
| not throw away | take | write |

1 *Switch off* your computer and TV at night.
2 _____ paper, plastic and glass – recycle it!
3 _____ your own shopping bag when you go shopping.
4 _____ the fridge door open.
5 _____ on both sides of the paper in your notebooks.
6 _____ lights during the day.

5 Match the ideas in Exercise 4 to the two problems below. Work with a partner and add more ideas.

1 How to save electricity: *Switch off your computer and TV at night, …*
2 How to reduce rubbish: _____

6 🖊 **Writing Time** Write a leaflet about how to reduce rubbish or how to save electricity. Use the ideas in Exercise 5 or your own ideas.

❓ Find ideas
Choose your topic. Think about why the issue is important and what people can do about it. Research facts about the topic on the Internet.

✏️ Draft
Write a draft of your leaflet. Use the ideas in the Writing box. Remember to add a title.

👍 Check and write
Write and design the leaflet. Don't forget to use the imperative to give tips and instructions!

6.8 Language Revision

Vocabulary

1 Label the animals in the photos. Which of these animals can be dangerous?

A _l e o pa r d_
B _h _ _ _
C _u _ _ _ _
D _ _ z _ _ _
E _o _ _ _ _ _ r
F _ _ r _ _ a

2 Complete the sentences with the correct verb.

1 We can s_ave_ animals by supporting wildlife organisations.
2 Bikes are great because they don't p_____ the environment.
3 We have to p_____ animals in danger.
4 If you buy a pet, you'll need to l_____ a_____ it.
5 People h_____ tigers for their fur.
6 We shouldn't c_____ d_____ trees in the rainforest.

3 Match the words in the box to the definitions.

> drought   earthquake   flood   ~~forest fire~~
> thunderstorm   tornado   tsunami

1 a large fire in a forest _forest fire_
2 a strong, dangerous wind _____
3 a period of time without rain _____
4 a storm with thunder, and heavy rain _____
5 when the earth moves violently _____
6 a huge wave _____
7 a lot of water on land _____

4 Complete the numbers with the words in the box.

> hundred   million   thousand

1 9,200 = nine _thousand_ two _hundred_
2 78,500 = seventy-eight _____ five _____
3 300,000 = three _____ _____
4 2,486,000 = two _____ four _____ and eighty-six _____

Grammar

5 In your notebook, write sentences using the first conditional.

1 If / the Yeti / be / hungry / he / eat / all the sausages.
   If the Yeti is hungry, he will eat all the sausages.
2 If / he / eat / everything / Mac / not be / happy.
3 If / Mac / be / still hungry / he / have / an ice cream.
4 If / there / be / a storm / the Explorers / stay / in the cave.
5 If / there / be / more snow / they / build / a snowman.
6 If / the / Explorers / not / stay / in the Himalayas / the / Yeti / be / sad.

6 In your notebook, complete the sentences about yourself.

1 If the weather is good tomorrow,
   I will go jogging in the park.
2 If I find fifty euros in the street, I …
3 If I don't have any homework this evening, I …
4 If there's a party on Saturday, I …
5 If school closes next week, I …
6 If I get a new phone for my birthday, I …
7 If it rains tomorrow, I …

7 Complete the text with the correct forms of the verbs.

Adam likes ¹_learning_ (learn) about the environment. He enjoys ²_____ (help) animals too.

He's looking forward to ³_____ (go) on a beach clean-up next weekend. He can't stand ⁴_____ (see) plastic rubbish in the sea! When he leaves school, Adam would like ⁵_____ (work) with animals. He wants ⁶_____ (be) a vet.

90

Communication

8 🔊 **3.19 Complete the dialogue with the words in the box. Then listen and check. Act out the dialogue in pairs.**

> come   deal   regret   ~~sure~~   think

Boy: There's a talk about the environment at school tomorrow evening. Do you fancy going?
Girl: I'm not ¹sure. I've got a lot of homework this week.
Boy: But it's important. We all need to do more to help the planet.
Girl: I'll ² _____ about it.
Boy: ³ _____ on, it'll be interesting. If you come, I'll help you with your homework afterwards.
Girl: OK, it's a ⁴ _____ .
Boy: Great! You won't ⁵ _____ it.

Dictation

9 **Exam Spot** 🔊 **3.20 Listen to a short text. Then listen again and write down what you hear. Make sure you spell the words correctly.**

Pronunciation

10 🔊 **3.21 Listen and repeat: /θ/ or /f/?**

Theo found three thirsty foxes and four fresh fish in his bathroom!

Check yourself! ✓
- I can talk about wild animals, the environment and natural events. ☐
- I can use the first conditional. ☐
- I can use verbs followed by infinitive or *-ing*. ☐
- I can persuade somebody to do something. ☐

Round up 6.8

11 Read the sentences. Circle the correct answer a, b or c.

1. There are thousands of _____ in London. You often see them in people's gardens.
   a pandas   **(b) foxes**   c gorillas

2. Global warming is a problem for _____ because sea ice is disappearing.
   a pandas   b eagles   c polar bears

3. Don't _____ that plastic bag. Recycle it!
   a pollute   b throw away   c save

4. People shouldn't _____ trees. It's bad for the environment!
   a throw away   b look after   c cut down

5. After a long, hot summer, there was a terrible _____ . There wasn't any rainwater.
   a flood   b drought   c tsunami

6. The _____ damaged roads in the city centre. Luckily, no one was hurt.
   a earthquake   b drought   c forest fire

7. If you see a black cat, you _____ good luck!
   a 'll have   b are having   c will

8. If I _____ a lot of sausages, I'll feel ill.
   a will eat   b eat   c am eating

9. If it snows tomorrow, I _____ to school.
   a don't go   b won't go   c not go

10. I don't mind _____ homework at the weekend.
    a to do   b do   c doing

11. We _____ to go on the beach clean-up.
    a enjoy   b would like   c don't mind

12. We need _____ a solution to plastic in the sea.
    a to find   b finding   c find

13. A: We're protesting against hunting. Do you want to join us?
    B: I'm not sure.
    A: _____ on, it's important!
    a Go   b Come   c Move

14. You should go skateboarding with us! You _____ regret it!
    a will   b don't   c won't

15. OK, I'll go with you. It's a _____ .
    a deal   b regret   c fancy

5 & 6 Skills Revision

Reading and Writing

1 **Exam Spot** Read the texts and the questions. Tick (✔) the correct answers a, b or c.

1 Which picture shows what Ethan needs to bring to the surprise party?

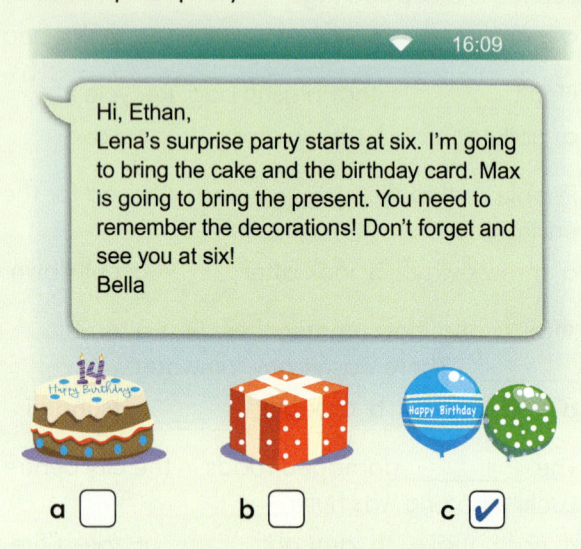

16:09

Hi, Ethan,
Lena's surprise party starts at six. I'm going to bring the cake and the birthday card. Max is going to bring the present. You need to remember the decorations! Don't forget and see you at six!
Bella

a ☐   b ☐   c ✔

2 Which picture shows one of the things that Lily has to do on Saturday?

Saturday
Practise drums
Shopping for trainers!
Lunch with Kate – 2 p.m.

Sunday
Tennis match – 10 a.m.
Revise for music exam
Practise guitar

a ☐   b ☐   c ☐

3 Which picture shows only animals from Episode 2 of *Frozen Planet*?

Frozen Planet
Documentary about climate change and its effect on animal habitats. How can we protect these animals?

Episode 1
Explore Antarctica and learn about the penguins that live there.

Episode 2
Travel to the North Pole and see polar bears and Arctic foxes.

a ☐   b ☐   c ☐

4 What aren't Amy and Elliot going to do in the afternoon?

Hi Amy,
You wanted info about the beach clean-up tomorrow. We're going to meet at the Surf Café at 11 a.m. The plan is to collect rubbish on West Beach first. We'll probably take a break at the Surf Café at 1 p.m., then clean East Beach in the afternoon. We're planning a BBQ for volunteers at the Sailing Club at 5 p.m.! See you soon.
Elliot

a ☐ have a barbecue
b ☐ clean the West Beach
c ☐ clean the East Beach

5 Which film can you only see in the morning?

Palace Cinema
Screen 1 True Love   11:00, 21:00
Screen 2 Space Adventure   18:00, 20:00
Screen 3 Spy Kids Return   9:00, 10:00

a ☐ True Love
b ☐ Space Adventure
c ☐ Spy Kids Return

2 **Exam Spot** Write an email asking for information about an animal charity. Ask:

- how old you have to be to volunteer.
- what activities volunteers can do.
- when volunteers usually help.

I am writing to find out how …
I would be grateful if you could answer a few questions.
Can you tell me what activities …?

Listening

3 **Exam Spot** 🔊 3.22 Listen to an interview and complete the text.

Radio Show: Protect Animal Habitats

- Animal habitats are places where animals live, for example the mountains in Africa for ¹ gorillas , or the ocean for ² _____ .
- We can protect animal habitats by recycling ³ _____ and supporting wildlife ⁴ _____
- We can also help local animals by going on beach or ⁵ _____ clean-ups.

Skills Revision 5 & 6

Use of English

4 Read the sentences about natural events. Circle the correct answer a, b or c.

1 At the moment, there is a _____ in Northern India. There hasn't been any rain for months.
   a tsunami   (b) drought   c flood

2 _____ thousand people don't have enough water to drink.
   a A thousand   b A million   c A hundred

3 The _____ in Bangladesh are destroying lots of cities after the heaviest rainfall in years.
   a floods   b earthquakes   c forest fires

4 Fifty _____ people have lost their homes.
   a thousand   b hundreds   c thousands

5 _____ rescue workers were helping people without homes day and night.
   a Hard work   b Lazy   c Hard-working

6 They are _____ to find people a place to stay.
   a interested   b determined   c surprised

Communication

5 Read the dialogues and circle the correct answer a, b or c.

1 A: What are you up to at the weekend?
   B: a No, thank you.   b I can't wait.
      (c) I'm going to visit my sister.

2 A: I'm going to see a rock musical next Sunday.
   B: a I'm looking forward to it.
      b That sounds amazing!
      c Have you got any plans?

3 A: If you help me with this sofa, I'll buy you lunch!
   B: a It's a deal!   b It doesn't matter.
      c You really should go!

4 A: Please, come to the party. You won't regret it!
   B: a No, I don't, sorry.   b I'll think about it.
      c Come on, it's important!

6 **Exam Spot** Ask and answer the questions in pairs.

1 What's your favourite wild animal? Where does it live? Is it in danger?
2 What can we do to protect the environment?
3 Would you like to play a musical instrument? Which one and why?
4 What personal qualities are the most important to be successful at school?

Exam Language Bank

Music styles
classical	jazz	punk
folk	Latin	rock
heavy metal	pop	techno
hip hop		

Instruments
cello	flute	saxophone
drums	keyboards	trumpet
electric guitar	piano	violin

Music collocations
give a concert	practise an instrument
go on tour	record an album
have an audition	sign an autograph
join a band	write / compose a song

Crime	**Personal qualities**	**Adjectives**
criminal	confidence	confident
detective	determination	determined
fingerprint	good looks	good-looking
footprint	hard work	hard-working
robbery	intelligence	intelligent
thief / thieves	style	stylish
witness	talent	talented

Wild animals	**Environment verbs**	**Natural events**
eagle	cut down	drought
fox	hunt	earthquake
gorilla	look after	flood
leopard	pollute	forest fire
lizard	protect	thunderstorm
panda	recycle	tornado
penguin	save	tsunami
polar bear	throw away	volcanic eruption
rhino		
turtle		

Asking about plans
What are you up to *in the holidays*?
Have you got any plans for *the weekend*?
What are your plans for *Saturday*?

Talking about plans
I'm going to *stay with friends*.
I can't wait to *see my cousins*.
I'm really looking forward to *it / visiting Manchester*.

Reacting
That sounds *amazing / great / like fun*.
Lucky you!

Persuading
You really should *come*. / We really should *go*.
Come on, it's important / you'll enjoy it!
You won't regret it!
If you *come*, I'll *buy you a smoothie*.

Responding
I'm not sure.	It's a deal!
I'll think about it.	Maybe you're right.
I suppose so.	

7 Material world

Vocabulary   I can describe objects.

In this unit
Vocabulary
- Materials
- Adjectives to describe objects
- Verbs of discovery and creativity
- Technology verbs
- Phrasal verbs with *up* and *down*

Grammar
- Present Simple passive
- Past Simple passive

▶ 35–36 7.2 Grammar video
▶ 37 7.2 Grammar animation
▶ 38 7.3 Grammar animation
▶ 39 7.4 Communication video
▶ 40 BBC Culture video

1 Find classroom objects that are made of:
   a paper *notebook*   b plastic   c metal

I know that!

MARVELLOUS MATERIALS QUIZ

1 This old football is made of ^{1}_____. How many pieces are there in this traditional design?

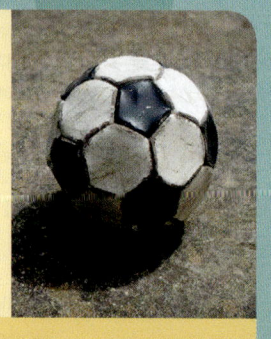

a 20   b 32

2 This pyramid in front of the Louvre Museum is made of ^{2}_____ and metal. Where is the museum?

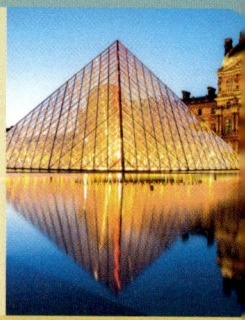

a In Paris   b In Berlin

3 Jeans are made of strong ^{3}_____ called 'denim'. What was the name of the first company that produced jeans?

a Calvin Klein   b Levi Strauss

4 This old doll's house is made of ^{4}_____. When were doll's houses popular?

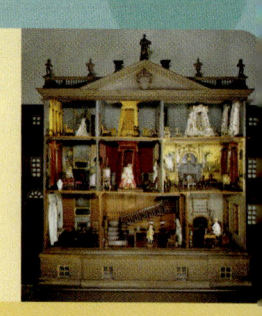

a In the 18th century
b In the 14th century

5 This dessert is made of chocolate, cream and 24-carat ^{5}_____. How much does it cost?

a $15,000   b $25,000

6 These men are wearing kilts – checked skirts made of sheep's ^{6}_____. Where are they from?

a Scotland   b Wales

94

7.1

2 🔊 **3.23** Listen and repeat. Then look at the photos on page 94 and complete the quiz with the words in the Vocabulary box.

Vocabulary Materials

cotton   glass   gold   leather   metal   paper
plastic   silver   wood   wool

3 🔊 **3.24** Do the quiz on page 94. Then listen and check.

4 Decide if the materials in the Vocabulary box are natural or man-made. Compare your answers in pairs.

Natural	Man-made
wood	glass

5 Look at the photos. What objects do they show and what are they made of?

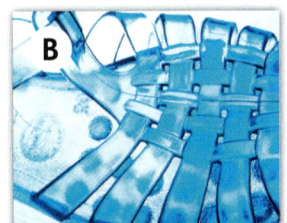

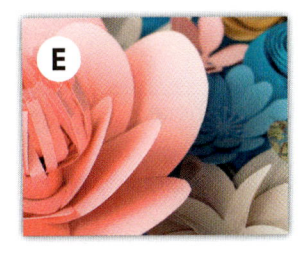

A B
C D
E F
G H

A *It's a clock. It's made of metal, glass and wood.*

6 🔊 **3.25** Listen and repeat. How many objects for each adjective can you think of?

Vocabulary Adjectives to describe objects

hard   heavy   light   shiny   soft   strong
transparent

hard – a mobile phone, a desk, …

7 🔊 **3.26** Listen and complete the descriptions. Which object in Exercise 5 is each person describing?

Ethan: I won this in an ice-skating competition last year. All my family came to watch me, so I was really happy when I came first. It's very ¹*heavy* and ² _____, but it isn't real ³ _____ !

Lucy: I often wear these when I go to the beach. They're made of ⁴ _____ so it's OK to wear them in the water. You can get them in lots of different colours, but mine are ⁵ _____ .

Maddie: When I get home from school, I always take off my school uniform and wear this. It's made of ⁶ _____ and it's really ⁷ _____ . I love it – it's comfortable and it keeps me warm in winter.

8 How many things in your house can you think of that are made of different materials? You have two minutes.

Wool: jumper
Silver: Mum's earrings
Plastic: phone case

I remember that!

95

7.2 Grammar — I can use the Present Simple passive.

They're made of cotton

It's Sports Day at school next week. Josh is in a team with Adam and Zadie. For fun, they've decided to make a team T-shirt.

Josh: Check this out! It's a shop where we can design our own T-shirts.
Zadie: Cool. How are they made?
Josh: Well, first we upload our design to the website. The design is downloaded to the shop's computer, and the T-shirts are printed on a special machine.
Adam: What are the T-shirts made of?
Josh: They're made of cotton.
Zadie: Are they delivered to your door? We need them before Monday.
Josh: Yes, they are. They're delivered in 48 hours, so they should arrive on Sunday.

Zadie: We need a team name.
Adam: What about 'Shooting Stars'?
Josh: I like it. We can have a picture of three gold stars!
Zadie: You're kidding me! Three gold stars?
Josh: Trust me, it'll look great. Right, here's a picture of some stars. OK, I'm sending our design now.

48 hours later a parcel arrived.

Adam: Wow, these are amazing. And they aren't sold in shops, so they're completely original!
Josh: Let's try them on. What do you think, Zadie?
Zadie: Erm, I don't know what to say …

---

1 ▶35 🔊 3.27 Watch or listen and read. Why do the friends order some T-shirts?

2 ▶35 🔊 3.27 Watch or listen again. Complete the summary.

Josh, Adam and Zadie design a ¹ _T-shirt_ for Sports Day. The name of their ² _____ is 'Shooting Stars'. ³ _____ hours later the T-shirts arrive. Adam thinks that they look ⁴ _____, but Zadie isn't sure.

3 🔊 3.28 Listen and repeat. Find these expressions in the story.

Check this out!   You're kidding me!
Trust me!

Say it!

4 ▶ **Guess!** Why does Zadie say 'I don't know what to say'? Have a class vote.
  a There's a spelling mistake in one of the words.
  b The stars are the wrong colour.

5 ▶36 🔊 3.29 Now watch or listen and check.

7.2

Grammar Present Simple passive

+	The design **is downloaded** to our computer.
	The T-shirts **are printed** on a special machine.
–	The word **isn't spelt** correctly.
	The T-shirts **aren't sold** in shops.
?	**Is** the design **sent** to the shop? Yes, it **is**. / No, it **isn't**.
	Are the T-shirts **delivered**? Yes, they **are**. / No, they **aren't**.
	What **are** the T-shirts **made** of?

Active: They **download** the design to their computer.
Passive: The design **is downloaded** to their computer.

▶ 37 **Get Grammar!**

This jewellery **is made** of silver and gold. The necklaces **are designed** by famous artists.

Necklace £10,000
Earrings £5,000

---

6 Read the sentences and circle the correct answer.

Your T-shirt in easy steps
- Your design ¹(is)/ are sent to our shop.
- The design is ²download / downloaded to our computer.
- The T-shirts ³is / are printed with your design.
- Dangerous chemicals ⁴aren't / haven't used.
- The environment isn't ⁵polluted / polluting.
- Our T-shirts are ⁶wear / worn by sports teams, dance clubs, and more!

7 🔊 3.30 Complete the description about how chocolate is made with the the Present Simple passive form of the verbs. Then listen and check.

How is chocolate made?

1. Chocolate _is made_ (make) from cocoa beans. They come from the fruit of the cocoa tree.
2. The beans _____ (dry) in the sun.
3. Then they _____ (take) by train or lorry to a factory.
4. In the factory, the beans _____ (cook) in a special oven.
5. Milk and sugar _____ (add).
6. Finally, the mixture _____ (cool down) to make chocolate!

8 In your notebook, write the sentences in the Present Simple passive. Begin with the underlined words.

1 They grow <u>cotton</u> in China and India.
   Cotton is grown in China and India.
2 They make <u>glass</u> from sand.
3 They don't grow <u>rice</u> in the UK.
4 They eat <u>spiders</u> in Cambodia.
5 They don't keep <u>blue whales</u> in zoos.
6 They use <u>leather</u> to make shoes.

9 🔊 3.31 Put the words in the correct order to make questions. Ask and answer in pairs. Then listen and check.

1 played What sport at Wimbledon is ?
   What sport is played at Wimbledon?
2 saris are worn Where ?
3 is in a florist's shop sold What ?
4 baby cats are What called ?
5 the boat, Plastiki is made of What ?
6 is celebrated St Patrick's Day In which month ?
7 found Where polar bears are ?

Fun Spot

10 In pairs, write similar quiz questions as in Exercise 9. Then ask and answer with another pair.

Where is tea grown?
What is sold in …
In which month …

97

7.3 Grammar   I can use the Past Simple passive.

The Explorers   The emperor's vase

1

The Explorers are at a museum in London.

Eva: Look at this vase. It's beautiful. When was it made, Pops? Do you know?
Pops: Yes, I do! It was made 700 years ago for the emperor of China. It was painted by a famous Chinese artist. It's very valuable. The emperor had lots of treasures. After he died, all the treasures were lost. This vase was discovered a few years ago.
Mac: Were the other treasures found?
Pops: No, they weren't. Now let's go downstairs.

2

Pops: And give me that selfie stick, Mac, before you have an accident! Ouch!

3

Mac: I'm sorry, Pops. Are you OK?
Pops: Yes, I'm fine, but the vase …
Eva: Look, I've found a piece of paper inside the vase.
Mac: Perhaps it's a map of the emperor's treasures.
Eva: No, it says: 'Made in England in 2014.' This vase wasn't made for the emperor, and it wasn't painted by a famous Chinese artist! It's just a cheap copy!
Pops: Phew! That's lucky for me!

---

1 Look at the cartoon. Find objects that are made of the materials in the box.

| cotton | glass | gold | leather | metal |
| paper | plastic | silver | wood | wool |

cotton – Pops's T-shirt

2 🔊 **3.32** Read and listen. Match a–e to 1–5.

1. [e] The emperor
2. [ ] Mac
3. [ ] Pops
4. [ ] Eva
5. [ ] The vase

a found a piece of paper.
b broke the vase.
c was a cheap copy.
d took a selfie.
e was very rich.

7.3

Grammar Past Simple passive

+	The vase **was painted by** a Chinese artist.
	The Emperor's treasures **were lost**.
−	The vase **wasn't made** for the Emperor.
	His other treasures **weren't found**.
?	**Was** the vase **made** for the Emperor? Yes, it **was**. / No, it **wasn't**.
	Were the other treasures **found**? Yes, they **were**. / No, they **weren't**.
	Who **was** the vase **painted by**?

Active: A famous Chinese artist **decorated** the vase.
Passive: The vase **was decorated by** a famous Chinese artist.

▶ 38 **Get Grammar!**
There was a big storm last night. Hammy's cage **was damaged by** the storm.

---

3 Complete the sentences with the Past Simple passive.

1. _Was_ the vase _made_ (make) in China? No, it wasn't. It _____ (make) in England.
2. _____ the vase _____ (create) 700 years ago? No, it wasn't. It _____ (create) in 2014.
3. _____ the emperor's treasures _____ (lose)? Yes, they were. They _____ (not discover).
4. _____ the vase _____ (break)? Yes, it was, but luckily Pops _____ (not hurt).

LOOK! Pops broke the vase.
The vase was broken **by** Pops.
Who was the vase broken **by**?

4 In your notebook, write the sentences in the Past Simple passive. Use *by*.

1. Mac took the photo. The photo … *was taken by Mac.*
2. Eva found the piece of paper. The piece of paper …
3. An English factory produced the vase. The vase …
4. A Chinese artist didn't paint it. It …
5. Luckily, the guard didn't arrest the Explorers. Luckily, the Explorers …

5 🔊 3.33 Listen and repeat. Circle the correct answer.

Vocabulary
Verbs of discovery and creativity

compose   design   discover   invent   paint   produce

1. Scientists (invent) / *paint* new technologies.
2. Architects *compose* / *design* buildings.
3. Astronomers *discover* / *produce* new planets.
4. Musicians *invent* / *compose* songs.
5. Factories *produce* / *invent* cars.
6. Artists *compose* / *paint* pictures.

6 🔊 3.34 Complete the questions and choose the correct answer. Then listen and check. Write similar questions and ask and answer in pairs.

The History of Objects

1. Who _was_ the *Mona Lisa* _painted_ (paint) by?
   a. Vincent van Gogh
   b. Leonardo da Vinci

2. When _____ the first video games consoles _____ (produce)?
   a. In the 1970s   b. In the 2000s

3. Who _____ Barcelona's *Sagrada Familia* _____ (design) by?
   a. Salvador Dalí   b. Antoni Gaudí

4. When _____ America _____ (discover)?
   a. In 1492   b. In 1592

7.4 Communication

I can ask for clarification and check understanding.

Are you following me?

Dad: What are you doing, Josh?
Josh: I'm making a drone for my school project.
Dad: That's interesting. How do you do that?
Josh: I have to connect these parts and … Dad, are you following me?
Dad: Sorry, Josh. Can you say that again?
Josh: I have to connect these parts and then it's ready to fly. I need to do a video on my phone now. Can you help me?
Dad: Sure. What's your password?
Josh: 3-4-1-6-9-7. Did you get that, Dad?
Dad: No, can you repeat it?
Josh: 3-4-1-6-9-7.
Dad: Got it. Now, where's the camera app?
Josh: It's at the top of the screen, Dad.
Dad: OK, I'm recording now. Smile!
Josh: Introducing my drone … It can pick up objects and …
Dad: Hang on, Josh! There isn't any battery left in your phone.
Josh: Watch out, Dad! The drone!

1 ▶ 39 🔊 3.35 Watch or listen and read. What are Josh and his dad doing?

2 🔊 3.36 Listen and repeat.

Communication Asking for clarification and checking understanding

Asking for clarification
Sorry, can you say that again?
Can you repeat that, please?
Could you explain, please?
What do you mean?

Checking understanding
Did you understand that?
Did you get that?
Are you following me?

3 🔊 3.37 Complete the dialogue with one word in each gap. Then listen and check.

Mum: Have you seen my phone, Matt?
Boy: Sorry, Mum, I haven't. Use the *Find My Phone* app.
Mum: ¹Could you explain, please? I can't use an app when I haven't got my phone.
Boy: The app is on the computer too. Open the app, then enter your phone number. ² _____ you following me, Mum?
Mum: Yes, I'm just looking under the sofa. Can you say that ³ _____ ?
Boy: Enter your number, then … ⁴ _____ you get that, Mum?
Mum: Yes, but what's that noise?
Boy: It's your phone! It's there, in the fruit bowl!

4 Read the dialogues and circle the correct answer a, b or c.

1 **Girl:** Is Oak Road near here?
   Boy: Yes, it's the second road on the left.
   Girl: a Sorry, can you say that again?
   b Are you following me?
   c Did you understand that?

2 **Boy:** How do you spell your name?
   Girl: H-a-n-n-a-h.
   Boy: a Can you explain?
   b Could you repeat that, please?
   c Am I speaking too quickly?

3 **Boy:** My phone number is 600875681.
   a Did you get that?
   b Are you following me?
   c Can you repeat that?
   Girl: Yes, I did. Thanks.

4 **Girl:** If you want to send a photo, click on 'share'.
   a Did you understand that?
   b Can you explain?
   c Are you following me?
   Boy: Yes, I am. Look! I've done it!

5 **Exam Spot** Work in pairs. Take turns to ask for clarification and check understanding. Student A: Go to page 122. Student B: Go to page 128.

7.5 Reading
I can understand a text about everyday objects.

What's it made of?

We use paper to make books, leather to make shoes and wool to make jumpers. However, sometimes these everyday materials are used in unusual ways!

Funky furniture

We read newspapers all the time and then we throw them away. In the UK, 12.5 million tonnes of paper is thrown away every year! One day designer Yasmin Sethi had an idea. She started to create chairs and tables from old newspapers. The paper is made into rolls and glued together – the furniture is light, but it is also very strong. It looks colourful and it's good for the environment too!

Chic car

Is it a car? Or a shoe on wheels? Cars sometimes have leather on the inside, but the Velorex Oskar had leather on the outside! This three-wheeled car was invented in the 1950s. It was designed by two brothers, who worked in a bike shop. Old leather clothes were used to build it. The car was a bit slow and it wasn't great in the rain, but people loved the Velorex Oskar because it was cheap and it looked very different!

Wool wonderland

This tiny village is called Mersham. It's got a school, a shop and lots of little cottages ... all made of wool! Thirty years ago, a group of people from the real Mersham village in England started to knit little houses in their free time, and over 100 buildings were made. Everything looked the same as buildings in the real village, with the same gardens, flowers and cars. The village was made to raise money for charity, and every year there was an exhibition of the tiny buildings. The exhibitions were very popular and raised 10,000 pounds!

1 What objects can you see in the photos? What do you think they are made of?

2 **Exam Spot** 🔊 3.38 Read and listen to the text. Circle the correct answer a, b or c.

1 Yasmin Sethi uses
   a different kinds of paper.
   b only old newspapers.
   c) old newspapers and glue.

2 Yasmin Sethi's furniture
   a isn't really strong.   b is white.
   c protects the environment.

3 The Velorex Oskar was invented
   a in a bike shop.   b by three brothers.
   c in a clothes shop.

4 People liked the car because it
   a was fast.   b wasn't expensive.
   c was good for all kinds of weather.

5 The knitted Mersham village
   a is very similar to the real village.
   b is completly different to the real village.
   c has only some houses similar to the real ones.

6 People made the village
   a for one special exhibition.
   b to raise money for charity.
   c because it was a hobby.

3 Guess the meaning of the words higlighted in the text. Then look them up in the dictionary.

4 Complete the text with the words highlighted in the text above.

Kniffiti 
- Urban knitting, also called 'kniffiti', is ¹ *knitting* covers for different objects in the city.
- People ² _____ covers for ³ _____ objects like street signs, bins, trees and bikes!
- The covers are usually ⁴ _____ and bright.
- There are ⁵ _____ of urban knitting in galleries.
- Kniffiti is used to ⁶ _____ money for charity too.

5 Discuss the questions as a class.

1 Which object in this lesson do you like best? Why?
2 Do you think it's a good idea to use materials in unusual ways? Why? / Why not?

7.6 Listening and Vocabulary

I can understand a listening text about gadgets.

1 🔊 **3.39** Listen and repeat. Complete the sentences.

> **Vocabulary** Technology verbs
>
> charge   click on   connect   download
> switch off   switch on   turn down
> turn up   upload

¹ <u>Switch off</u> the TV, Milo. Action films are boring!

You have to ² _____ the phone if you want to use it.

³ _____ the music! It's too loud!

Let's ⁴ _____ this app.

You have to ⁵ _____ the mouse, Mia.

Let's ⁶ _____ the phone to my computer …

2 🔊 **3.40** Match the nouns in the box to verbs 1–6. There may be more than one noun for each verb. Listen and check.

> a radio   a mouse   a battery
> a computer   an app   the Internet
> the volume   a TV   a photo   a phone

1 switch on / off *a radio* …
2 download / upload
3 connect to
4 turn up / down
5 charge
6 click on

3 **I know that!** What gadgets can you name in English?

mobile phone, toaster …

4 🔊 **3.41** Read the extract from a webpage. Then listen to an interview. Cross out one thing each gadget can't do.

> **Your favourite gadgets**
>
> **Personal assistant**
> It can …
> • play music
> • take photos
> • help with homework
> • wake me up
>
> **Smart watch**
> It can …
> • give directions
> • take photos
> • cool down food
> • control the TV
>
> Send us a short description of what your gadget can do!

5 🔊 **3.41** Listen again and circle true (T) or false (F).

1 Alice is woken up by her mum.   T /(F)
2 Her gadget is connected to the Internet.   T / F
3 It was invented a long time ago.   T / F
4 James's gadget is a new invention.   T / F
5 It's very expensive.   T / F
6 It's made of metal.   T / F

6 **Exam Spot** Do you have a favourite gadget? What is it? What can it do? Discuss in pairs.

7 Read the Vocabulary Builder. Then complete the sentences with *up* or *down*.

> **Vocabulary Builder**
> **Phrasal verbs with *up* and *down***
>
> Phrasal verbs with *up* often mean 'more'.
> *speed up* = go faster   *turn up* = make louder
> *warm up* = be/make warmer
>
> Phrasal verbs with *down* often mean 'less'.
> *slow down* = go more slowly   *turn down* = make quieter
> *cool down* = make cooler

1 Don't ride your bike so fast. Slow <u>down</u>!
2 Can you turn _____ the music? It's too loud!
3 The heating is on. You'll warm _____ soon.
4 I can't hear it. Turn _____ the volume, please!
5 Remember to cool _____ after jogging.
6 We haven't got much time! We need to speed _____.

I can write a text about a popular product. Writing 7.7

Shoe story

1. I love my sports shoes. I wear them every day. So when were sports shoes first invented? And where?

2. The first sports shoes were produced in England in the 18th century. They were used to play tennis, but soon shoes were designed for other sports too.

3. Sports shoes became popular as street fashion in the 1950s. They were worn by American teenagers every day. By the 1980s, everyone had a pair. Sports shoes were produced in different styles and colours, and were often made of hi-tech materials. Designer shoes were expensive and cost more than 100 euros!

4. Today most people own a pair of sports shoes. Last year, more than a billion people bought them – and that's just in the United States!

1 What do you know about sports shoes? Do the quiz.

What do you know about … sports shoes

1. Sports shoes were first made in *America / (England).*
2. They were used to play *tennis / basketball.*
3. Sports shoes became popular street fashion in the *1950s / 1970s.*
4. In the 1980s, designer sports shoes were *very cheap / expensive.*
5. In the United States more than a *million / billion* people buy sports shoes every year.

2 Read the text 'Shoe story' and check your answers.

3 Read the Writing box. Which expressions can you find in the text 'Shoe story'?

Writing
Describing a popular product

1 Introduction
I love / like / often use *my sports shoes.*
I use them for *running.* I wear them to *school.*
So when were they first invented / used?

2 When it was first made and why
The first *sports shoes* were produced in *the 18th century.*
They were used to *play tennis.*

3 How the product developed
They became popular in *the 1950s.*
They were worn by *teenagers.*
They were produced in different styles.
They were often made of *hi-tech materials.*

4 Conclusion
Today most people *own a pair.*
More than a billion people bought them last year.
That's why *sports shoes* are so popular.

Using the passive
You can use the Present Simple and the Past Simple passive when you describe a product.
Sports shoes **are used** to play basketball.
They **were invented** in England.

4 Read the box above. Complete the information with the correct passive forms of the verbs in the box.

| bake   design   ~~eat~~   invent   slice   write |

1. **Cornflakes** <u>are eaten</u> for breakfast in most homes in the UK. They _____ in the 1900s.
2. **Crisps** are very thin slices of potato. They _____ or fried, then salted. The first recipes for home crisps _____ in the 19th century.
3. Do you like **toast**? Bread _____ and then put into a toaster! The first toaster _____ in Scotland, in 1893.

5 🟢 **Writing Time** Choose one of the products in Exercise 4 and write about it.

❓ Find ideas
1. When was it invented and where?
2. How has it developed and changed?
3. How popular is it today?

✏️ Draft
Organise your ideas into paragraphs. Use the ideas in the Writing box to help you.

👍 Check and write
Check that you have used the passive and write the final version of your text.

103

7.8 Language Revision

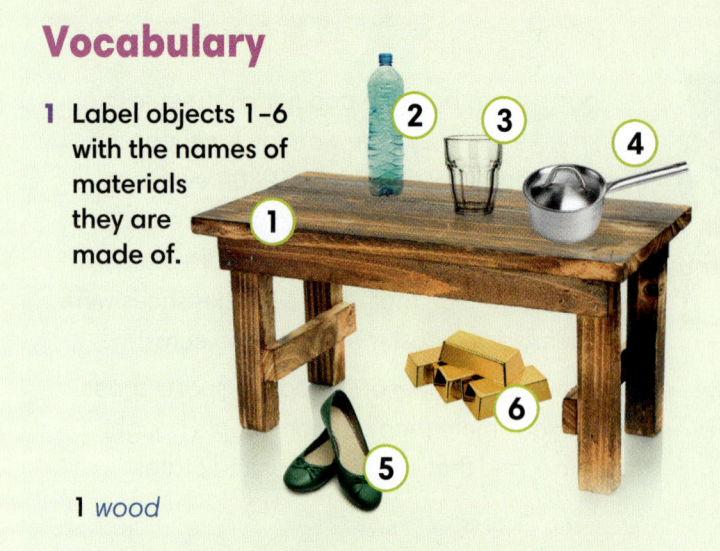

Vocabulary

1 Label objects 1–6 with the names of materials they are made of.

1 *wood*

2 Cross out the adjective that <u>doesn't</u> describe the objects in Exercise 1.

1 a hard	b strong	c soft
2 a transparent	b light	c heavy
3 a soft	b hard	c transparent
4 a transparent	b shiny	c hard
5 a hard	b soft	c light
6 a heavy	b light	c shiny

3 Read and circle the correct verb.

Did you know …?

- Christopher Columbus ¹(discovered)/ *invented* America in 1492.
- Van Gogh ²*invented* / *painted* a lot of pictures of flowers.
- John Logie Baird ³*composed* / *invented* the television.
- Coco Chanel ⁴*designed* / *discovered* dresses and suits.
- Bruno Mars ⁵*designs* / *composes* a lot of songs for other singers.

4 Complete the text with correct verbs. Are you good or bad at technology?

Technology? I'm really bad at it!

I often can't ¹c*onnect* to the Internet. I find it really difficult to ²d_____ songs or to ³u_____ photos onto Instagram. I do it too quickly – I just ⁴c_____ on everything! My laptop is very old – it often ⁵w_____ up and then it ⁶s_____ down! Sometimes I have to ⁷s_____ it off so it can ⁸c_____ down!
I often forget to ⁹c_____ my phone! But when the battery is full, I forget to ¹⁰s_____ it off at school. Then it rings in the middle of the lesson. Disaster!

Grammar

5 In your notebook, complete the sentences with the Present Simple passive form of the verbs.

1 What *is* pasta *made* of? ✔
  It *is made* of flour and eggs. ✔
  It *isn't made* of chocolate. (make) ✘

2 Where _____ coffee _____?
  It _____ in Brazil. ✔
  It _____ in Russia. (produce) ✘

3 Where _____ oranges _____?
  They _____ in the Arctic. ✘
  They _____ in Spain. (grow) ✔

6 In your notebook, write sentences in the Past Simple passive.

1 Pop's house / build
  ✘ in the 20th century ✔ in the 19th century
  Pops's house wasn't built in the 20th century.
  It was built in the 19th century.

2 Mac's T-shirt / produce
  ✘ in China ✔ in the UK

3 The emperor's vase / paint
  ✘ by a French artist ✔ by a Chinese artist

4 The Firenzi brothers / arrest
  ✘ in the street ✔ in their house

5 The Golden Boomerang / find
  ✘ by Mac ✔ by Eva

7 In your notebook, write sentences in the Past Simple passive. Use *by*. Begin with the underlined words.

1 My mum wrote <u>this book</u>.
  This book was written by my mum.

2 My sister bought <u>these jeans</u>.

3 Ed Sheeran sang <u>this song</u>.

4 My brother ate <u>the biscuits</u>.

5 Mrs Jones took <u>Charlie</u> to school.

6 My grandad made <u>this cake</u>.

Round up 7.8

Communication

8 🔊 **3.42** Complete the dialogue with the words in the box. Then listen and check. Act out the dialogue in pairs.

> sorry   ~~following~~   again
> mean   get   repeat

Girl: Look, Gran! I've got a new selfie stick for my phone. Now we can take a photo together.
Gran: A selfie stick? How do you use it?
Girl: Well, the phone goes here … are you ¹*following* me, Gran?
Gran: ² ____ , Eva, I'm putting on my glasses. Can you say that ³ ____ ?
Girl: Sure. The phone goes here …
Gran: Oh, I see! Can I take a photo now?
Girl: Yes, of course, Gran. Put in my password.
Gran: What do you ⁴ ____ ?
Girl: The password for my phone – it's 4-0-3-2-7-9. Did you ⁵ ____ that, Gran?
Gran: No, can you ⁶ ____ it?
Girl: 4-0-3-2-7-9. Now you can take a picture.
Gran: OK, smile!

Dictation

9 **Exam Spot** 🔊 **3.43** Listen to a short text. Then listen again and write down what you hear. Make sure you spell the words correctly.

Pronunciation

10 🔊 **3.44** Listen and repeat: **voiced** or **voiceless** endings.

Fre**d** go**t** up and ma**de** his be**d**,
downloade**d** a game and texte**d** Te**d**.
They lo**ve** to play and lo**ve** to lau**gh**,
I be**t** they'll play all day – that's ba**d**!

Check yourself! ✓

- I can talk about objects, materials and technology. ☐
- I can use the Present Simple passive. ☐
- I can use the Past Simple passive. ☐
- I can ask for clarification and check understanding. ☐

---

11 Read the sentences. Circle the correct answer a, b or c.

1. For my birthday, my grandma gave me a jumper. It's made of ____ , and it's very soft.
   a wood   b gold   **c wool**

2. Can you help me to move this table? It's really ____ .
   a light   b heavy   c strong

3. The planet Uranus was ____ in 1781.
   a designed   b invented   c discovered

4. ____ that music! It's too loud!
   a Turn down   b Turn up   c Switch on

5. I forgot to ____ my phone, so I can't call my mum.
   a click   b charge   c upload

6. The floor of the boat was ____ , so we could see the fish in the sea below.
   a light   b shiny   c transparent

7. Tea is ____ in India.
   a grow   b grew   c grown

8. ____ cars produced in Brazil?
   a Are   b Did   c Have

9. My shoes aren't ____ of leather – they're plastic.
   a make   b made   c making

10. ____ invited to her party?
    a Were you   b You were   c Have you

11. That building was built ____ my grandad.
    a of   b by   c from

12. These books ____ in China in 2017.
    a were printed   b was printed   c are printed

13. A: You've broken my phone!
    B: What do you ____ ?
    a get   b mean   c follow

14. Did you ____ that? Or should I repeat it?
    a get   b mean   c repeat

15. Are you ____ me, or am I speaking too quickly?
    a explaining   b switching   c following

105

Get Culture!

American cities

1 What are these American cities famous for? Match landmarks A–C to cities 1–3.

1. ☐ New York
2. ☐ Los Angeles
3. ☐ Washington

2 🔊 **3.45** Listen to two friends, Kelly and Peter, who are doing a quiz about American landmarks. Check your ideas in Exercise 1.

3 🔊 **3.45** Listen again. Circle true (T) or false (F).
1. Kelly has got family in America. **(T)** / F
2. The White House has got 123 rooms. T / F
3. It's also got a cinema. T / F
4. The Statue of Liberty is 19 metres tall. T / F
5. Kelly and Peter learnt about the statue at school. T / F
6. The famous sign originally read 'Hollywoodland'. T / F

4 🔊 **3.46** Read and listen to the text about another American city and landmark. What do these numbers refer to?

1933   100,000   35 million   1937   870,000   2,737

1933 – the year work started on the bridge

5 **Exam Spot** Read the text again and answer the questions.
1. What is San Francisco famous for?
2. Why was it difficult for boats to cross the bay?
3. Why was there a safety net under the bridge?
4. What did people do in Fiesta Week?
5. What tried to destroy the bridge in a film?
6. Why is the bridge painted 'international orange'?

6 Think about a town or city in your country. What important places or buildings can people see there?

The Golden Gate Bridge

San Francisco is situated on the West Coast of America on San Francisco Bay. It's a big city with over 870,000 people! It's famous for its earthquakes, Alcatraz prison and Chinatown, but most of all it's famous for the Golden Gate Bridge. The Golden Gate Bridge is the most photographed bridge in the world and over 100,000 cars use it every day! So what's the story behind this famous landmark?

A hundred years ago, San Francisco was growing fast. Many people came in and out of the city across the bay. Ferries and boats were used to cross the water, but there was often thick fog and strong winds. As a result, in 1933, work started on a new bridge.

The Golden Gate Bridge was built by hundreds of construction workers. It was a dangerous job and there was a huge safety net under it. In June 1935, there was an earthquake while men were working on the bridge. The bridge towers moved four metres each way. Luckily, nobody fell.

The bridge was finished in 1937 and it cost 35 million dollars. When it was opened, people celebrated with a Fiesta Week. There were parades, competitions and firework displays for seven days!

Today the bridge is open every day, even in strong winds and fog … A giant octopus tried to destroy it once, but that was in a film!

Did you know?

The Golden Gate Bridge:
- is 2,737 metres long – that's longer than 220 buses!
- is painted 'international orange' because this colour is easy to see in the fog.
- has two cafés! They serve drinks, hot dogs and American apple pie!
- has appeared in films such as X-Men 3, Star Trek and James Bond!

New York City

A ▶ 40 Watch the video and answer the presenter's questions. Which three famous places can you see in the video?

B ▶ 40 Watch the video again and circle true (T) or false (F).

1. There are more than eight million people in New York City.   T / F
2. Most people get around the city by taxi.   T / F
3. There are over 500 steps to the top of the Statue of Liberty.   T / F
4. The Empire State Building was completed in 1940.   T / F
5. The building has appeared in many Hollywood films.   T / F
6. Central Park has got special lampposts.   T / F

C Would you like to visit New York? Which places would you like to see? Discuss your ideas as a class.

PROJECT

- Work in groups. Make a digital presentation about an important or interesting place, or building in your town or city.

- Write about this place or building. Do research on the Internet. Use these questions to help you.
    - When was it built and why?
    - How long did it take to build?
    - Why is it important or interesting?
    - What is it used for today?

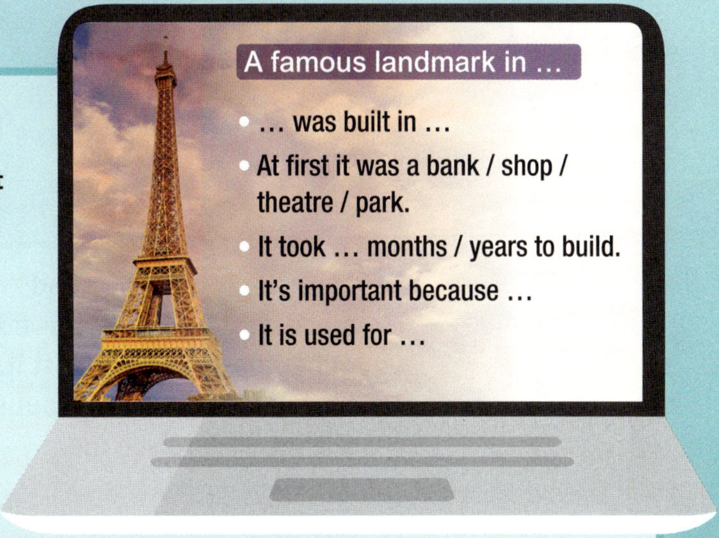

- Plan your presentation. Find photographs to illustrate each part. Try to include one surprising fact.

- Share your presentation with the class. Which is the most interesting place or building? Why?

A famous landmark in …
- … was built in …
- At first it was a bank / shop / theatre / park.
- It took … months / years to build.
- It's important because …
- It is used for …

8 That's life

Vocabulary I can talk about relationships.

In this unit

Vocabulary
- Relationships and conflicts
- Feelings
- Extreme adjectives

Grammar
- be allowed to, let
- Revision of tenses

▶ 41–42 
8.2 Grammar video

▶ 43 
8.2 Grammar animation

▶ 44 
8.3 Grammar animation

▶ 45 
8.4 Communication video

1 How many relatives in English can you name?
uncle, cousin ...
a Which of your relatives is the oldest, which is the youngest?
b Which is the funniest, the wisest, the most annoying?

I know that!

Amy's blog

Hi, I'm Amy. I live with my mum, dad, sister and little brother. I usually get on with my family, but not always ...

My dad is quite strict. He sometimes gets angry with me, especially if I get up late at the weekend.

My mum and I don't often argue, but if my room is untidy, she sometimes shouts at me!

My sister is often in a bad mood. Last week, I borrowed one of her tops and then I lost it. I bought her a new top, but she still hasn't forgiven me.

My little brother is sometimes really rude! He says sorry, but later he does the same thing again!

? What about you? Do you get on with your family?

8.1

2 🔊 **3.47** Read and listen to Amy's blog. Which relatives does she mention?

3 🔊 **3.48** Listen and repeat. Find the verbs in Amy's blog. Then answer the questions.

Vocabulary
Relationships and conflicts

argue (with someone / about something)
forgive (someone)   shout (at someone)
say sorry (to someone)
be   in a bad / good mood
     rude / nice (to someone)
     friends (with someone)
get on (with someone)
     angry (with someone)

1 Does Amy usually get on with her family?
  Yes, she does.
2 Who is often in a bad mood?
3 Who sometimes gets angry with her? Why?
4 Who is sometimes rude?
5 Do Amy and her mum often argue?
6 What happens when Amy's room is untidy?

4 Write the phrases from the Vocabulary box into the correct column.

Positive	Negative
forgive (someone)	*shout (at someone)*

5 Complete the sentences with the correct words in the Vocabulary box.

1 When people don't agree about something, they sometimes a <u>r g u e</u>.
2 When people are angry, they sometimes s _ _ _ _ or talk in a loud voice.
3 If you're friends with someone, you g _ _ on well with them.
4 When you're angry and don't want to talk to people, you're in a bad m _ _ _ _.
5 If you're rude to someone, you should say s _ _ _ _ _ afterwards.
6 When you stop being angry with someone, you f _ _ _ _ _ _ _ them.

6 **Exam Spot** 🔊 **3.49** Complete Amy's blog with one word in each gap. Then listen and check.

Amy's blog, Part 2

Is it really so bad with my family? No, of course not! When my dad's ¹ *in* a good mood, he never ² _____ angry with me. We often play games, or go ice-skating together. I'm good friends ³ _____ my mum. She's the nicest person in the world and I can talk to her about anything. Most of the time, I get ⁴ _____ well with my sister. We love watching videos, and she often helps me with my homework. My little brother is usually really nice ⁵ _____ me, and he's so cute that I forgive ⁶ _____ almost anything!

7 Do the questionnaire. Choose answers a, b or c. Then check your score on page 128. Compare your answers with a partner.

How well do you get on with your family?

1 I _____ get on well with my family.
  a always   b usually   c never
2 My parents _____ get angry with me or shout at me.
  a never   b sometimes   c often
3 We _____ argue about things like household chores.
  a never   b sometimes   c always
4 I'm _____ in a good mood at home.
  a always   b usually   c never
5 If I'm rude or do something bad, I _____ say sorry afterwards.
  a always   b usually   c never

8 🔊 **3.50** Listen to three of Amy's friends. Who do they argue with? Why do they argue?

1 Liv: argues with _____ ; they argue because _____
2 Matt: argues with _____ ; they argue because _____
3 Jess: argues with _____ ; they argue because _____

9 Write sentences about your relationships. Use the phrases in the Vocabulary box.

often	sometimes	never
I'm often in a bad mood.	*My brother and I sometimes argue.*	*My dad never shouts at me.*

I remember that!

8.2

Grammar I can use *be allowed to* and *let*.

You don't let me go out

1

— Hi, Bella. The Kites are playing a concert tomorrow night. Do you fancy going?

— I'd love to, but I'm not allowed to stay out after 9 p.m. My mum treats me like a child sometimes.

— Don't get angry! You should try talking to her. What about cooking her dinner first?

— Mmm, that's an idea …

2

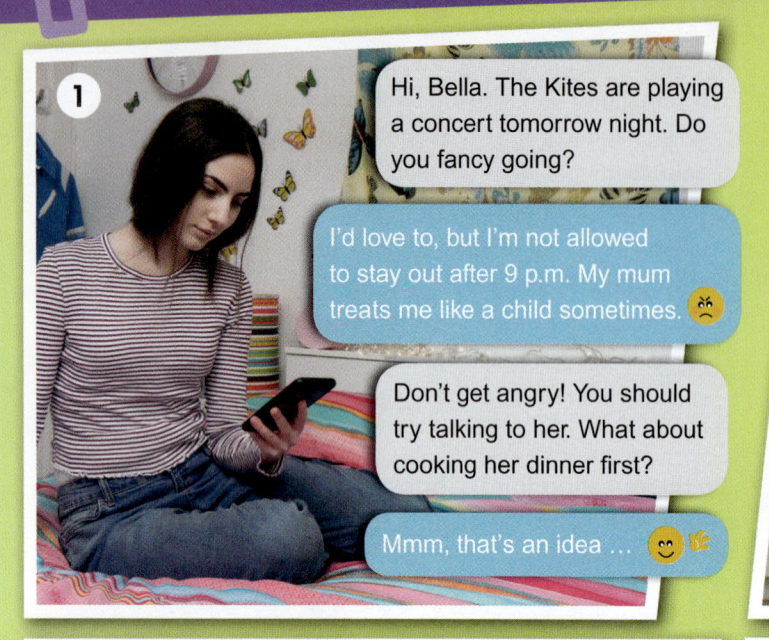

Mum: Something smells good!
Bella: I've made pancakes. Do you want some?
Mum: Yes, please. Ooh, strawberries too!

3

Bella: So … there's a concert on in town tomorrow night. Can I go? It's at the Northgate Arena and it finishes at eleven.
Mum: I'm sorry, but you know you're not allowed to be out that late.
Bella: But I'll be with Zadie. Her parents let her go to concerts. And it's the weekend.
Mum: I'm sorry, but you're too young.

4

Bella: It's so unfair! You don't let me go out with my friends. You don't let me stay out late! I'm not allowed to do anything!
Mum: Calm down, Bella! You don't have to shout.
Bella: I'm going to my room.
Mum: Come back, Bella. We haven't finished talking.
Bella: What's the point? You aren't going to change your mind.

1 ▶41 ◉ 3.51 Watch or listen and read. Why are Bella and her mum arguing?

2 ▶41 ◉ 3.51 Watch or listen again. Answer the questions.
1 Where is the concert?
2 What time does it finish?
3 What is Zadie's idea?
4 Does Zadie's idea work?

3 ◉ 3.52 Listen and repeat. Find these expressions in the story.

Say it!

It's so unfair!   Calm down!   What's the point?

4 ▶ **Guess!** What happens next? Have a class vote.
a Bella's mum changes her mind.
b Bella and Zadie change their plans.

5 ▶42 ◉ 3.53 Now watch or listen and check.

8.2

Grammar be allowed to, let

be allowed to

+	We're allowed to stay out late.
–	I'm not allowed to do anything.
?	Is she allowed to do it? Yes, she is. / No, she isn't. What are you allowed to do?

let

+	Zadie's mum lets her go out at night.
–	You don't let me go out with my friends.
?	Do your parents let you stay out late? Yes, they do. / No, they don't. When does Bella's mum let her go out?

Zadie's parents let her go out with friends.
(= Zadie is allowed to go out with friends.)
My parents don't let me have a social media account.
(= I'm not allowed to have a social media account.)

▶ 43 **Get Grammar!**

Hammy isn't allowed to go out at night.

9 Match notices in Bella's school A–H to sentences 1–6. There are two extra notices.

1 [G] You aren't allowed to talk.
2 [ ] Teachers don't let you use your phone during lessons.
3 [ ] Students are allowed to leave school early.
4 [ ] Students aren't allowed in here.
5 [ ] The school doesn't let you wear your own clothes.
6 [ ] You aren't allowed to wear boots in here.

6 What are you (not) allowed to do? Put a tick (✔) or a cross (✘) next to the activities. Then write sentences.

1 [ ] invite friends home
2 [ ] stay out after midnight
3 [ ] go to concerts on my own
4 [ ] get up late at the weekend
5 [ ] walk home on my own at night
6 [ ] have a social media account

1 *I'm allowed to invite friends home.*
2 *I'm not allowed to stay out after midnight.*

7 **Exam Spot** In pairs, ask and answer about the activities in Exercise 6.

A: *Are you allowed to invite friends home?*
B: *Yes, I am. / No, I'm not.*

8 Write sentences with the correct form of *let*.

1 Adam's mum / let / him / watch TV in the evening. ✔
   Adam's mum lets him watch TV in the evening.
2 Josh's sister / not let / Josh / use her computer. ✘
3 Adam's teacher / not let / him watch videos in class. ✘
4 Josh's dad / let / Josh / borrow his bike. ✔
5 Adam's parents / let / him / have a social media account. ✔
6 Josh's mum / not let / him / go out very late. ✘

A **DON'T RUN IN THE CORRIDORS!**

B **TRAINERS ONLY IN THE GYM**

C **STUDENTS MUST HAVE THE CORRECT UNIFORM AT ALL TIMES.**

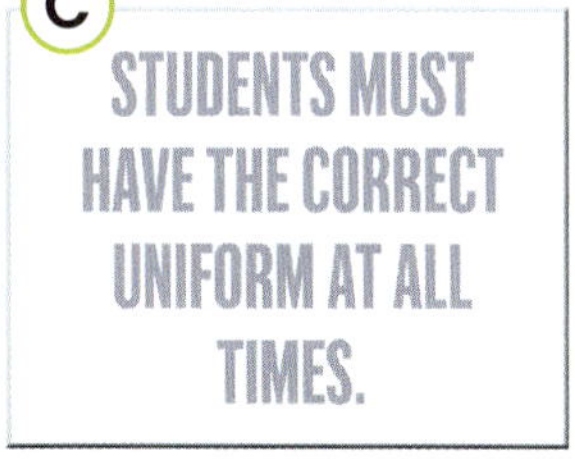

D **NO MOBILES IN CLASS!**

E **STAFF ROOM ENTRY FOR TEACHERS ONLY**

F To: Class 13NL
No lessons this afternoon.
You can go home.
Mr Nelson

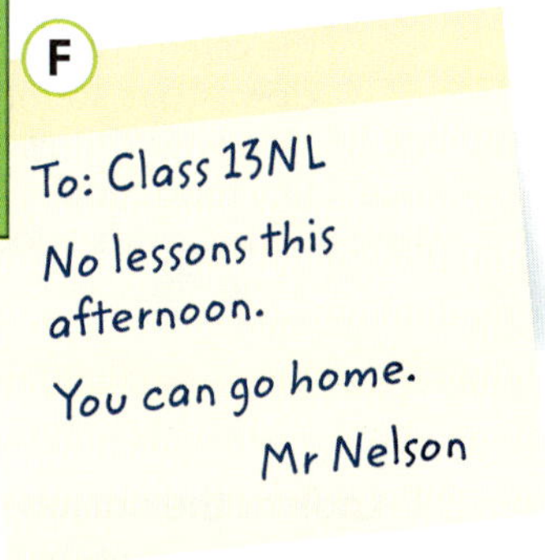

G **QUIET PLEASE. EXAM IN PROGRESS.**

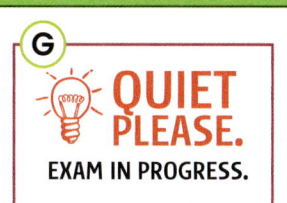

H **NO FOOD OR DRINK IN THE LIBRARY**

8.3 Grammar — I can use present, past and future tenses.

The Explorers — A surprise visitor

It's Pops's birthday. Gran, Mac and Eva are planning a small party.

1

Eva: Who's coming to the party, Gran?
Gran: It's just us. Oh, and I've invited Monty, one of Pops's old friends, but I don't think he'll come. Pops and Monty haven't spoken for twenty years.
Mac: Why's that?
Gran: Oh, it's a long story …

2

Gran: It was during a trip to Peru. Pops and Monty were exploring the rainforest when they got lost. Pops had to eat insects to survive. But Monty didn't eat insects. When Pops woke up one night, Monty was secretly eating sausages! He had food in his backpack! Pops has never forgiven Monty! And Monty has never said sorry!

3

Eva: Where is Pops?
Gran: He always relaxes in his room in the afternoon, but I'm sure he'll be downstairs soon. Ah, here he is.
All: Happy birthday, Pops!
Pops: Oh, thank you!
Mac: Somebody's knocking at the door! Pops, we've got guests!

4

Pops: Wow, is that you, Monty? What a surprise!
Monty: I've come to say sorry. I behaved badly all those years ago.
Pops: Don't worry! I forgive you.
Monty: By the way, I'm going to organise another trip to Peru. Would you like to join me?
Pops: I'd love to! Now, what's that noise?
Monty: Oh, I hope you don't mind – I've invited some of your friends to the party.
Pops: Wow! This is going to be a great party!

---

1 Look at the cartoon. Whose birthday is it? Which characters from Episodes 1–7 can you see?

2 🔊 3.54 Read and listen. Circle true (T) or false (F).
1. Gran is planning a big party for Pops. T / **F**
2. Pops and Monty often speak to each other. T / F
3. Monty wasn't kind to Pops in the rainforest. T / F
4. At the party, Pops doesn't forgive Monty. T / F

8.3

Grammar Revision of tenses

the present
Present Simple: He always relaxes in the afternoon.
Present Continuous: Somebody's knocking at the door!

the past
Past Simple: Pops and Monty got lost in Peru.
Past Continuous: They were exploring the rainforest.

the present and the past
Present Perfect: They haven't spoken for twenty years.

the future
will: I'm sure he'll be downstairs soon.
going to: I'm going to organise a trip to Peru!
Present Continuous: Who's coming to the party?

▶ 44 Get Grammar!
While Hammy was waiting for the bus, it started to rain.

3 Complete the sentences with the Present Simple or the Present Continuous form of the verbs.

1 At the moment, Gran, Mac and Eva _are preparing_ (prepare) a party for Pops.
2 Gran is in the kitchen. She _____ (make) a cake.
3 Gran often _____ (make) cakes for parties.
4 Pops always _____ (go) to sleep in the afternoon.
5 Hurry up! The guests _____ (come).
6 Pops _____ (love) parties!

4 🔊 3.55 Read Pops's old diary. Circle the correct answer. Then listen and check.

Peru, Day 7
A terrible thing ¹(happened)/ was happening yesterday. We ²walked / were walking in the rainforest when Monty ³lost / was losing the map. While we ⁴looked / were looking for it, he also ⁵dropped / was dropping our sandwiches in the river. So now we're completely lost, and we've got no food. Monty ⁶caught / was catching some insects last night and he ⁷gave / was giving me some for breakfast. They were horrible!

5 🔊 3.56 Complete the next part of Pops's diary with the Present Perfect or Past Simple form of the verbs. Then listen and check.

Peru, Day 8
I ¹'ve known (know) Monty for years! We ² _____ (have) lots of adventures together! We ³ _____ (be) to jungles and deserts, to Africa and Australia. Yesterday I ⁴ _____ (eat) some insects. 'There's no other food,' Monty ⁵ _____ (say). But last night I ⁶ _____ (sleep) badly. I ⁷ _____ (wake up) at midnight and I ⁸ _____ (see) Monty ... with a backpack full of sausages!

6 Write about Pops's plans, predictions and arrangements. Use *be going to*, *will* and the Present Continuous.

Plans (*be going to*)
1 (I / return) to Peru.
  I'm going to return to Peru.
2 (Monty / come) with me.
3 (I / carry) the food this time!

Predictions (*will*)
4 I hope (the weather / be) good.
  I hope the weather will be good.
5 I think (we / have) a good trip.
6 I'm sure (Monty / not lose) the map again!

Arrangements (Present Continuous)
7 On Monday, (I / have) a haircut.
  On Monday, I'm having a haircut.
8 On Tuesday, (Gran and I / go) to the dentist.
9 On Wednesday, (I / meet) Monty for lunch.

7 **Exam Spot** In pairs, ask and answer the questions.

1 How long have you known your best friend?
2 Did you see him / her last weekend?
3 What do you usually do together?

8.4 Communication — I can sympathise and encourage.

What's the matter?

It's Saturday. Josh and Adam are at the local sports centre.

Adam: What's the matter, Josh? You look angry.
Josh: They haven't chosen me for the school team! And I played really well last year!
Adam: That's a shame. That's really disappointing.
Josh: And I practised every weekend!
Adam: Cheer up, Josh. We all know you're a good player.
Coach: Morning, Josh. That was really good! Why weren't you at the training on Saturday?
Josh: On Saturday?
Coach: Yes, Saturday. Didn't you get my email? We were choosing players for the team, but you were absent so …
Josh: Erm … my computer was broken. Sorry.
Coach: OK … but I think you can still be in the team. You're a really good player, Josh!
Adam: You see? Well done!

1 ▶ 45 🔊 3.57 Watch or listen and read. Answer the questions.
1 Where are Josh and Adam?
2 How does Josh feel at the start of the video? Why?
3 How does Josh feel at the end? Why?

2 🔊 3.58 Listen and repeat.

Communication
Sympathising and encouraging

Asking questions
What's the matter?
What's up? / What's wrong?

Sympathising
I'm (so) sorry.
That's a pity! / That's a shame!
What a pity! / What a shame!
Poor you! That's disappointing.

Encouraging
Cheer up!   Well done!

3 🔊 3.59 Complete the dialogue with one word in each gap. Then listen and check.

Ella: Hi, Lara. Are you coming to the cinema tonight?
Lara: No, I can't.
Ella: Why? ¹*What's* up?
Lara: I have to babysit my little sister.
Ella: Oh, what ² _____ pity!
Lara: I know. I was really looking forward to it.
Ella: ³ _____ you! That's ⁴ _____ . But cheer ⁵ _____ ! We can go again next weekend.

4 Exam Spot In pairs, act out two dialogues. Use the expressions in the Communication box.

Student A:
1 You didn't get an invitation to a friend's party.
2 Your pet cat or dog is ill.

Student B:
1 Your exam results were disappointing.
2 You can't go on a school trip because you're not well.

I can understand a text about family conflicts. **Reading** **8.5**

Bedroom battles

Is your bedroom like this? Are your parents angry? Don't worry – you're not alone! Daniel, 16, and his dad, Steve, talk about bedroom battles!

Daniel's father's story

Daniel's bedroom is a nightmare! I'm not usually allowed to go in. He's got a 'Do not enter' sign on his door. There are clothes on the floor, and a mess under his bed. He's not allowed to take food into his room, but last week I found a pizza box there … with some pizza inside!

Daniel never tidies his desk. There are old magazines on it, so there's no space to do his homework. Two weeks ago, he had exams. He did OK, but I know he can do better. He needs to organise his study space. There are house rules, but not in Daniel's room.

Daniel's story

My room is messy, but there is a system: important things are on the bed, unimportant things are on the floor. It's no big deal, so why is dad in a bad mood about it? I always help with the chores around the house, so dad can't get angry about that. And no one else uses my room, so dad should let me do what I want. I don't share my room with anyone – it's my space so it's up to me.

Comments:

[Jade106] I feel sorry for your dad! You should keep your room clean – it's part of the house. Pizza boxes under the bed? Yuk!

[Lucas09] It's your space! Your dad should let you have a messy room. Tidy rooms are boring.

---

1 Look at the photo. Which words describe the room? How is it different from your room? How is it similar? Compare answers in pairs.

> interesting   original   horrible   normal
> unusual   dirty   clean   tidy   untidy   messy

I think this room is horrible. It's really …

2 🔊 3.60 Read and listen to the text. Circle the correct answer.
1 Daniel *lets* / (*doesn't let*) his father go into his bedroom.
2 Daniel's father *lets* / *doesn't let* Daniel eat in his bedroom.
3 Daniel *passed* / *failed* his exams.
4 He *understands* / *doesn't understand* why his dad is angry.
5 Daniel *helps* / *doesn't help* with the housework.

3 Match the expressions highlighted in the text to explanations 1–4.
1 It's my decision. *It's up to me.*
2 I sympathise with your dad.
3 It's like a bad dream.
4 It's not a problem, it's not important.

4 **Exam Spot** Discuss the questions in pairs.
1 Is a tidy room important to you? Why? / Why not?
2 Who do you agree with – Daniel or Daniel's dad?
3 What do you have to do at home?
4 What are you allowed to do at home?

Fun Spot

5 Design a funny 'House Rules' poster.

House rules
- Always put rubbish on the floor. Never in the bin.
- Never put your clothes in the wardrobe.
- You're allowed to eat pizza anywhere (but NOT in the kitchen).
- You're allowed to wear trainers when you lie on the sofa.

8.6 Listening and Vocabulary

I can understand a listening text about bullying.

DIFFICULT MOMENTS AT SCHOOL

I'm often disappointed with my test results. I revise a lot and I'm **exhausted**, so when I get bad marks I feel **depressed** and my parents are **furious**.

I'm really **upset** about school. Some boys call me bad names because I'm short and not very slim. They hurt me too – I'm **terrified** of them!

Some girls at school laugh at my clothes. They are rich! At first I was **jealous** and **embarrassed**. Now I'm just **annoyed**!

1 🔊 **3.61** Listen and repeat. Find the adjectives in the speech bubbles and explain their meaning.

Vocabulary Feelings

annoyed   depressed   disappointed   embarrassed
exhausted   furious   jealous   terrified   upset

2 I know that! Complete the adjectives.

1 s_a_d   2 sc_r_d   3 b_r_d
4 w_rr__d   5 h_pp_   6 _ngr_
7 t_r_d

3 Circle the correct answer.

1 My best friend can't come to my pizza party. I'm *disappointed* / *terrified*.
2 When my bike was stolen, I was *furious* / *embarassed*.
3 My brother was *jealous* / *exhausted* when I got my expensive, new trainers.
4 I always feel *annoyed* / *terrified* when I watch horror films!
5 I was *jealous* / *embarrassed* when my mum picked me up from the rock concert.
6 My friend is *exhausted* / *upset* about her exam results. She worked really hard, but she still failed!

4 Read the Vocabulary Builder. Describe how you would feel in these situations. Use the adjectives from the Vocabulary Builder.

Vocabulary Builder
Extreme adjectives

Some adjectives in English are called extreme adjectives. We don't use 'very' with them.
furious = very angry   exhausted = very tired
terrified = very scared
My mum was ~~very~~ furious when I lost my mobile phone.

1 It's ten o'clock at night and I'm still doing my homework. *I'm exhausted*.
2 A big dog runs up to me in the park. It's angry and it's barking.
3 My sister has borrowed my favourite scarf and she has lost it.

5 Read the definitions. Which situations in the cartoon are examples of bullying?

to bully (v) to hurt or frighten someone, and make them do things they don't want to do → **bullying** (n)
a bully (n) someone who hurts other people, and makes them feel bad.

6 🔊 **3.62** Listen to a radio interview. What's the connection between Spiderman and Lady Gaga?

7 Exam Spot 🔊 **3.62** Listen again and circle the correct answer a, b or c.

1 Superheroes were bullied at school because they
 a wore different clothes.   b had super powers.
 c weren't 'cool'.
2 Superhero stories tell us that
 a you should be rude to bullies.
 b bullies are the 'winners'.
 c kids who are bullied can become 'winners'.
3 Lady Gaga was bullied because of her
 a name.   b nose.   c ears.
4 When you or your friends are bullied, you
 a should talk to teachers and parents.
 b shouldn't do anything.
 c should talk to the bullies.

8 Choose three adjectives in the Vocabulary box or the Vocabulary Builder. When did you last feel this way? Why?

I can reply to a letter and give advice. **Writing**

8.7

NEED ADVICE? ASK SALLY!

Dear Sally,
I've started a new school and I'm really upset. I'm shy, so it's difficult to make new friends. What can I do to make friends more easily?
Karl

Dear Karl,

1 *Thank you for your letter. Don't worry! It's normal to feel like this when you start a new school.*

2 *First, you should smile and look friendly. If you look friendly, people will talk to you. Then, when you talk to people, listen to what they say. Perhaps you could ask questions too. It shows you're interested and want to make friends. Finally, it's a good idea to join after-school clubs, and meet people with the same interests as you. Try to relax and enjoy your time at school.*

3 *Good luck!*
Sally

1 Read the problem and the reply on a magazine problem page. Do you agree with the advice? Can you think of any other advice?

2 Read the Writing box. Which expressions can you find in the letter from Sally?

Writing
Replying to a problem page letter

❶ **Introduction**
Thank you for your letter. Don't worry.
It's normal to feel like this.
Lots of people have this problem.

❷ **Advice and suggestions**
Try to *relax*.
You should *smile*.
Perhaps you could *ask questions*.
It's a good idea to *join after-school clubs*.
What about *joining a club*?

❸ **Ending**
I hope next time you will feel better. Good luck!

Giving advice and suggestions
Use various structures to give advice and suggestions.
You *should* smile. You *shouldn't* look unfriendly.
Try to relax. *Perhaps you could* invite them home.
What about talking to your teacher?
It's a good idea to ask questions.

3 Read the information in the box 'Giving advice and suggestions'. Then complete the sentences.

1 'You *should* talk to your teachers about the sports you practise.'
2 '_____ to help your friend, but don't give her your work!'
3 'You _____ give your friend the wrong answers!'
4 'Perhaps you _____ stop sports practice for a few months.'

4 Read the two letters below. Match the advice in Exercise 3 to them.

Dear Sally,
My best friend is lazy and she copies my homework. I've tried to talk to her about it, but she gets annoyed. What should I do?
Daisy

Dear Sally,
I love sports, but I don't have time for my exams, homework and sports practice. I'm exhausted and my exams results were bad this year! How can I do both – school and sports?
Max

5 **Writing Time** Choose one of the letters in Exercise 4 and write a reply.

Find ideas
Choose a problem and brainstorm solutions.

Draft
Organise your ideas into paragraphs. Use the Writing box to help you.

Check and write
Check that you have used expressions for giving advice and suggestions.

8.8 Language Revision

Vocabulary

1 Complete the quiz questions with the words in the box. Then ask and answer in pairs.

> rude   angry   ~~argue~~   shout   mood

Do you get on well with people?

1 How often do you _argue_ with your friends?
2 Are you often in a bad _____ at school?
3 If you're _____ to people, do you say sorry later?
4 Do you get _____ easily?
5 Do you _____ at people when you're angry?

2 Circle the correct answer.
1 Elliot was really *jealous / (upset)* when his pet dog was ill.
2 Lola was very popular and pretty. A lot of girls were *jealous / disappointed* of her.
3 Daniel was *exhausted / embarrassed* when he fell over in the school canteen.
4 My mum gets *terrified / angry* when I spend a long time on my phone.
5 Monty's parents were *disappointed / jealous* with his poor exam results.

3 Complete the sentences with the words in the box. Then say what you do in these situations.

> furious   terrified   exhausted

- When you feel ¹_____ (very tired), always go to bed.
- When you're ²_____ (very angry) with a friend, try to calm down. Then talk to them.
- When you're ³_____ (very scared) of exams, remember you can always do them again. Don't panic!

When I am exhausted, I take a hot shower.

Grammar

4 Complete the sentences with the words in the box.

> are allowed   ~~aren't allowed~~
> doesn't let   is allowed   lets

1 We _aren't allowed_ to use our phones in class. We have to give them to the teacher.
2 Our teacher sometimes _____ us have lessons outside. It's great on a sunny day!
3 We don't have a school uniform, so we _____ to wear our own clothes.
4 My teacher _____ me sit next to my best friend. She says we talk too much!
5 My brother is seventeen and he _____ to leave school at lunch time. He's so lucky!

5 Read Pops's letter from Peru. Circle the correct answer.

> Dear Gran, Mac and Eva,
> It's beautiful here in Peru. Monty and I ¹*have /*(*are having*) a great time. We ²*stay / 're staying* in a small village in the forest. Every morning, we ³*get up / 're getting up* early and we ⁴*walk / 're walking* down to the river. I ⁵*already saw / 've already seen* monkeys and snakes, but I ⁶*didn't see / haven't seen* any crocodiles yet. Yesterday, while we ⁷*had / were having* breakfast, we ⁸*saw / were seeing* a jaguar!
> Monty ⁹*sleeps / is sleeping* now and I ¹⁰*write / 'm writing* this letter.
> Bye for now!
> Pops

6 In your notebook, write the questions in the correct form. Then ask and answer in pairs.

Plans (*going to*)
1 What (you / do) in the summer?
   What are you going to do in the summer?
2 Where (you / stay)?

Predictions (*will*)
3 (the weather / be) hot there?
4 (you / have) a good time?

Arrangements (Present Continuous)
5 What (you / do) this weekend?
6 (you / see) your friends on Sunday?

Round up 8.8

Communication

7 🔊 **3.63** Complete the dialogue with the words in the box. Then listen and check. Act out the dialogue in pairs.

> Poor   cheer   That's   shame   ~~matter~~

Boy: What's the ¹_matter_ ?
Girl: I can't go to Matt's birthday party this weekend.
Boy: ² ____ you! That's a ³ ____ . Why not?
Girl: I've got to go to my Gran's.
Boy: ⁴ ____ disappointing, but ⁵ ____ up! They'll be other parties.
Girl: I know. It's my Gran's birthday as well – she's seventy on Saturday.
Boy: Saturday? But Matt's party is on Friday.
Girl: Great! I can go then!

Dictation

8 **Exam Spot** 🔊 **3.64** Listen to a short text. Then listen again and write down what you hear. Make sure you spell the words correctly.

Pronunciation

9 🔊 **3.65** Listen and repeat: /aʊ/ or /əʊ/.

> Are we all**ow**ed to go into t**ow**n on our **ow**n, do you kn**ow**?

Check yourself! ✓
- I can talk about relationships and feelings.
- I can use *let* and *be allowed to*.
- I can talk about events in the present, past and future.
- I can sympathise and encourage.

---

10 Read the sentences. Circle the correct answer a, b or c.

1. I _____ with my brother. We like the same things.
   a argue   **(b) get on well**   c get angry

2. My cousin is often rude _____ me.
   a at   b with   c to

3. I've got a new computer. My best friend is _____ . She wants one too!
   a jealous   b embarrassed   c terrified

4. My mum was _____ when I broke her new teapot.
   a furious   b terrified   c exhausted

5. Kate was very _____ because people were bullying her.
   a terrified   b exhausted   c scared

6. Our teacher gets angry and _____ us when we send text messages in class.
   a forgives   b shouts at   c gets on with

7. My dad doesn't let _____ to parties! It's really unfair!
   a me to go   b me go   c go

8. We aren't _____ our mobile phones in school.
   a allowed use   b allow to use   c allowed to use

9. Are you _____ stay up late on weekdays?
   a allowed   b let   c allowed to

10. At the moment, I _____ a computer game with my friend.
    a 'm playing   b play   c will play

11. Yesterday I was walking to school when it _____ to snow.
    a was starting   b started   c has started

12. I _____ to England, but I'd love to go!
    a never went   b am going to go   c have never been

13. A: I can't go swimming this afternoon. I've got a cold.
    B: That's a _____ ! I hope you feel better soon.
    a pity   b matter   c disappointing

14. A: What's _____ ?
    B: I've forgotten my P.E. kit – again!
    a matter   b up   c a shame

15. A: Hey, look! I got an 'A' in my History exam!
    B: Wow! _____ !
    a Poor you   b Well done   c What a shame

119

7 & 8 Skills Revision

Our designers:

Chris Warren
Chris produces beautiful silver necklaces, gold bracelets and glass rings.
Prices from £10 to £130.

Celia Jones
Celia designs and makes fashionable jumpers and hats, using wool or cotton.
Prices from £15 to £40.

Jim Edison
We love Jim's phone covers. They're made of strong plastic and they come in lots of different designs and colours.
Prices from £10 to £20.

Welcome to Perfect Presents

Are you looking for a special and unusual present? Then why not visit our shop? Perfect Presents is full of beautiful objects, and they are all produced by local designers. We are located on Ship Street, near the market square.

Opening times
We are open from 10 a.m. to 5.30 p.m., Mondays to Saturdays. We are closed on Sundays.
Sorry, but dogs are not allowed in the shop.

Reading and Writing

1 Exam Spot Read the advertisement above and complete the information with one, two or three words in each gap.

1 The name of the shop is *Perfect Presents*.
2 The shop is not far from _____.
3 The necklaces are made of _____.
4 The jumpers are designed by _____.
5 Jim makes _____.
6 The most expensive object costs _____.
7 The shop closes at _____.
8 If you visit the shop, you can't take _____.

2 Exam Spot Write about your favourite gadget. Say:

- What is it made of? Where was it made?
- When did you get it or buy it?
- What do you use it for?

My favourite gadget is …
It's made of … It was made in …
I bought it … months ago. /
I've had it for … months.
I use it to …

Use of English

3 Exam Spot Read the article and circle the correct answer a, b or c.

Brothers and sisters

Do you sometimes ¹_____ with your brothers or sisters? Do you get angry ²_____ them? Well, don't be ³_____. A report says that it can be good for you! You learn how to solve problems, and it prepares you for life as an adult. Write and tell us about your brothers or sisters. Do you get ⁴_____ with them? ⁵_____ you ever argued with them?

Dan, 14:
My brother is so annoying. Yesterday I was playing a computer game when he suddenly ⁶_____ the games console. I was furious! He often takes my things too. Right now he ⁷_____ my favourite hoodie.

Kelly, 15:
My parents let my sister ⁸_____ out late at the weekend, but I ⁹_____ to be out after nine o'clock. She's only two years older than me, so it's really unfair.

	a	b	c
1	forgive	shout	**(c) argue**
2	with	to	of
3	terrified	jealous	upset
4	in	on	up
5	Did	Have	Were
6	cooled down	switched on	switched off
7	wears	is wearing	has worn
8	stay	to stay	staying
9	'm not allowed	don't allow	didn't allow

Skills Revision 7 & 8

Listening

4 Exam Spot 🔊 **3.66** What do they most often do with their phones? Listen and match activities a–h to people 1–6. There are two extra activities.

1. [g] Dad
2. [ ] Grandma
3. [ ] Anna
4. [ ] Grandpa
5. [ ] Sam
6. [ ] Mum

a play music
b download recipes
c get directions
d use social media
e watch videos
f take photos
g send emails
h make phone calls

Communication

5 Read the dialogues and circle the correct answer a, b or c.

1. A: I live in Tottenham Court Road.
   B: a Are you following me?
      b Could you explain, please?
      (c) Can you repeat that, please?

2. A: It's the second turning on the left. Did you get that?
   B: a Yes, I do.
      b Yes, I did, thank you.
      c It's a deal!

3. A: What's the matter? You look sad.
   B: a That's disappointing.
      b Someone has stolen my bike.
      c I've won a gold medal!

4. A: My hamster is very ill.
   B: a Well done!
      b I'm so sorry.
      c Never mind.

6 Exam Spot Ask and answer the questions in pairs.

1. What clothes and accessories are you wearing? What are they made of?
2. How do you and the people in your family use your mobile phones?
3. Are your parents strict? What do they let you do? What don't they let you do?
4. Do you sometimes argue with your friends? What do you argue about?

Exam Language Bank

Materials
cotton   metal   wood
glass   paper   wool
gold   plastic
leather   silver

Adjectives to describe objects
hard   shiny   transparent
heavy   soft
light   strong

Verbs of discovery and creativity
compose   discover   paint
design   invent   produce

Technology verbs
charge   download   turn down
click on   switch off   turn up
connect   switch on   upload

Phrasal verbs with *up* and *down*
speed up   warm up   slow down
turn up   cool down   turn down

Relationships and conflicts
argue (with someone / about something)
forgive (someone)
shout (at someone)
say sorry (to someone)
be in a bad mood / good mood
be rude / nice (to someone)
be friends (with someone)
get on (with someone)
get angry (with someone)

Feelings
annoyed   embarrassed   jealous
depressed   exhausted   terrified
disappointed   furious   upset

Asking for clarification   **Checking understanding**
Sorry, can you say that again?   Did you understand that?
Can you repeat that, please?   Did you get that?
Could you explain, please?   Are you following me?
What do you mean?

Sympathising – asking questions   **Encouraging**
What's the matter?   Cheer up!
What's up?   Well done!
What's wrong?

Sympathising
I'm (so) sorry.
That's a pity! / That's a shame!
What a pity! / What a shame!
Poor you! That's disappointing.

121

Extra reference

Student A activities

Unit 3 Lesson 3.4, Page 44, Exercise 5

1. You want to know how to send a text message. Ask Student B for instructions.

   How do I send a text message?
   What's the first step?   What do I have to do next?

2. Student B asks you how to print a document. Give Student B instructions. Use the phrases below in the correct order.

   > switch on the printer   click 'print'
   > choose how many copies you want to print
   > open the document you want to print
   > connect the printer to your computer

   First, open … Then, … Next, … Finally, …

3. You want to know how to make a pizza. Ask Student B for instructions.

   How do I make a pizza? What do I have to buy?
   What's the first step? What do I have to do next?

4. Student B wants to know how to make a smoothie. Give Student B instructions. Use the phrases below in the correct order.

   > add fruit   blend everything together
   > put some milk or yoghurt in a blender
   > buy some fruit   add some honey or sugar

   Before you begin, buy … Then, … Next, … Finally, …

Unit 4 Lesson 4.4, Page 58, Exercise 5

1. You are a student and Student B is your teacher. You are thirty minutes late for school and it's the day of an exam. Apologise to Student B.

   I'm really sorry I'm … I forgot to set my alarm clock. /
   My bus was late … I really couldn't …

2. Student B is your friend. He/She forgot about your birthday and about your birthday party and he/she apologises. Accept Student B's apologies.

   It's OK. Never mind. Forget about it. We can …

3. Student B is your mum/dad. You haven't made your bed or tidied your room. Apologise to Student B.

   I'm sorry, Mum/Dad I haven't … I just …
   Don't be mad at me …

4. You are Student B's aunt/uncle. He/She borrowed a book from you, but his/her dog ate it. He/She apologises. Accept Student B's apologies.

   It's OK. It wasn't your fault. It was an accident.

Unit 6 Lesson 6.4, Page 86, Exercise 4

1. There's a film about mountain gorillas at your school tomorrow. It's important because people are cutting down the forests and mountain gorillas are in danger. Persuade Student B to go with you. Promise to help him/her with the essay after the film.

   There is … Do you fancy coming with me?
   You really should … It's important, because …
   You won't regret it! If you come, I'll …

2. Student B suggests making and selling cakes to collect money for your local hospital. You're not sure because you want to go shopping. You really need a new hoodie!

   I'm not sure. I have to … I suppose so, but
   I really need … It's a deal!

Unit 7 Lesson 7.4, Page 100, Exercise 5

1. Student B is your mum/dad. He/She wants to download an app but needs some help. Listen and answer their questions. Check that they understand.

   First, you look for an app you want to download in your mobile phone store.
   Next, you check if it's free …. Then, you download it.
   Are you following me?

2. You are Student B's grandparent and you want to send him/her an email. Ask Student B for his/her email address. Ask him/her to repeat it, so that you can check you have written it correctly.

   I'd like to send you an email …
   What's your email address?
   Can you say that again?

Word list

Unit 0
Get started!

0.2
Vocabulary
Free-time activities
go cycling /ˌgəʊ ˈsaɪklɪŋ/
go ice-skating /ˌgəʊ ˈaɪs ˌskeɪtɪŋ/
go shopping /ˌgəʊ ˈʃɒpɪŋ/
go to a concert /ˌgəʊ tə ə ˈkɒnsət/
go to a museum /ˌgəʊ tə ə mjuːˈziəm/
go to the cinema /ˌgəʊ tə ðə ˈsɪnəmə/
help your parents /ˌhelp jə ˈpeərənts/
play sport /ˌpleɪ ˈspɔːt/
stay at home /ˌsteɪ ət ˈhəʊm/
visit your grandparents /ˌvɪzət jə ˈgrænd,peərənts/

0.3
Vocabulary
Adjectives
awful /ˈɔːfəl/
boring /ˈbɔːrɪŋ/
cheap /tʃiːp/
cold /kəʊld/
delicious /dɪˈlɪʃəs/
difficult /ˈdɪfɪkəlt/
easy /ˈiːzi/
exciting /ɪkˈsaɪtɪŋ/
expensive /ɪkˈspensɪv/
fast /fɑːst/
hot /hɒt/
slow /sləʊ/
Other
heat up /ˌhiːt ˈʌp/
roller coaster /ˈrəʊlə ˌkəʊstə/

0.4
Other
adventurous /ədˈventʃərəs/
archaeologist /ˌɑːkiˈɒlədʒɪst/
mark /mɑːk/
mountain climber /ˈmaʊntən ˌklaɪmə/
pyramid /ˈpɪrəmɪd/
treasure /ˈtreʒə/

0.5
Vocabulary
Weather
cloudy /ˈklaʊdi/
cold /kəʊld/
hot /hɒt/
rainy /ˈreɪni/
snowy /ˈsnəʊi/
sunny /ˈsʌni/
warm /wɔːm/
windy /ˈwɪndi/
Other
helpful /ˈhelpfəl/
jungle /ˈdʒʌŋgəl/
penguin /ˈpeŋgwɪn/

Unit 1
Who we are

1.1
Vocabulary
Clothes and accessories
belt /belt/
boots /buːts/
bracelet /ˈbreɪslɪt/
cardigan /ˈkɑːdɪgən/
coat /kəʊt/
dress /dres/
earrings /ˈɪərɪŋz/
handbag /ˈhændbæg/
hat /hæt/
hoodie /ˈhʊdi/
jacket /ˈdʒækɪt/
leggings /ˈlegɪŋz/
ring /rɪŋ/
sandals /ˈsændlz/
scarf /skɑːf/
shirt /ʃɜːt/
shorts /ʃɔːts/
skirt /skɜːt/
socks /sɒks/
tie /taɪ/
tights /taɪts/
top /tɒp/
trainers /ˈtreɪnəz/
Describing clothes
Patterns
checked /tʃekt/
floral /ˈflɔːrəl/
plain /pleɪn/
spotted /ˈspɒtɪd/
striped /straɪpt/
Style
baggy /ˈbægi/
casual /ˈkæʒuəl/
smart /smɑːt/
tight /taɪt/
Other
design (n) /dɪˈzaɪn/

1.2
Say it!
That's gross! /ˌðæts ˈgrəʊs/
This is the worst day of my life! /ˌðɪs ɪz ðə wɜːst deɪ əv maɪ ˈlaɪf/
Other
Cornish pasty /ˌkɔːnɪʃ ˈpæsti/
kilt /kɪlt/
meat pie /ˌmiːt ˈpaɪ/
set an alarm /ˌset ən əˈlɑːm/
surfboard /ˈsɜːfbɔːd/
teapot /ˈtiːpɒt/
washing machine /ˈwɒʃɪŋ məˌʃiːn/

1.3
Other
awful /ˈɔːfəl/
disappear /ˌdɪsəˈpɪə/
fall into /ˌfɔːl ˈɪntə/
hieroglyphics /ˌhaɪrəˈglɪfɪks/
necklace /ˈnekləs/
princess /ˌprɪnˈses/
put on /ˌpʊt ˈɒn/
scream /skriːm/
tomb /tuːm/
trip on something /ˈtrɪp ɒn ˌsʌmθɪŋ/

1.4
Communication
Telling a story
Guess what happened on Saturday!
First, we went to Lacey's.
Then, we went to Bramley's.
Finally, she found a pair she liked.
Reacting
How funny / embarrassing / strange!
Lucky him!
No way!
Poor Zadie!
So what did he do?
So what happened next?
Then what?
Other
embarrassing /ɪmˈbærəsɪŋ/
football kit /ˈfʊtbɔːl kɪt/
security guard /sɪˈkjʊərəti gɑːd/
try on /ˌtraɪ ˈɒn/

1.5
Vocabulary
Hairstyles
bald /bɔːld/
beard /bɪəd/
curly hair /ˈkɜːli heə/
dyed hair /ˈdaɪd heə/
moustache /məˈstɑːʃ/
shaved hair /ˈʃeɪvd heə/
spiky hair /ˈspaɪki heə/
straight hair /ˈstreɪt heə/
wavy hair /ˈweɪvi heə/
Other
embarrassed /ɪmˈbærəst/
freedom /ˈfriːdəm/
hole /həʊl/
hurt /hɜːt/
leather jacket /ˌleðə ˈdʒækɪt/
loud /laʊd/
peace /piːs/
safety pins /ˈseɪfti pɪnz/
trick /trɪk/

1.6
Vocabulary
Personality adjectives
friendly /ˈfrendli/
generous /ˈdʒenərəs/
hard-working /ˌhɑːd ˈwɜːkɪŋ/
honest /ˈɒnɪst/
kind /kaɪnd/
lazy /ˈleɪzi/
organised /ˈɔːgənaɪzd/
patient /ˈpeɪʃənt/
polite /pəˈlaɪt/
rude /ruːd/
selfish /ˈselfɪʃ/
serious /ˈsɪəriəs/
shy /ʃaɪ/
talkative /ˈtɔːkətɪv/
Vocabulary Builder
Negative adjectives
dishonest /dɪsˈɒnɪst/
disorganised /dɪsˈɔːgənaɪzd/
impatient /ɪmˈpeɪʃənt/
impolite /ˌɪmpəˈlaɪt/
unfriendly /ʌnˈfrendli/
unkind /ʌnˈkaɪnd/
Other
admire /ədˈmaɪə/
first impression /ˌfɜːst ɪmˈpreʃən/
realise /ˈrɪəlaɪz/
scientist /ˈsaɪəntɪst/

1.7
Other
get on well straight away /ˌget ɒn ˈwel ˌstreɪt əˈweɪ/
secondary school /ˈsekəndəri skuːl/

Get Culture
Clothes for special occasions
bagpipes /ˈbægpaɪps/
bright /braɪt/
celebrate /ˈseləbreɪt/
come over /ˌkʌm ˈəʊvə/
dress up /ˌdres ˈʌp/
haggis /ˈhægɪs/
high-heeled shoes /ˌhaɪ hiːəld ˈʃuːz/
occasion /əˈkeɪʒən/
poetry /ˈpəʊətri/
school prom /ˈskuːl prɒm/
tweed /twiːd/
wedding /ˈwedɪŋ/

Unit 2
Working hard

2.1
Vocabulary
Jobs
architect /ˈɑːkɪtekt/
cleaner /ˈkliːnə/
computer programmer /kəmˈpjuːtə ˌprəʊgræmə/
dentist /ˈdentɪst/
engineer /ˌendʒəˈnɪə/
factory worker /ˈfæktəri ˌwɜːkə/
firefighter /ˈfaɪəˌfaɪtə/
hairdresser /ˈheəˌdresə/
journalist /ˈdʒɜːnəl-ɪst/
secretary /ˈsekrətəri/
tour guide /ˈtʊə ˌgaɪd/
Describing jobs
badly paid /ˌbædli ˈpeɪd/
boring /ˈbɔːrɪŋ/
challenging /ˈtʃælǝndʒɪŋ/
dangerous /ˈdeɪndʒərəs/
easy /ˈiːzi/
exciting /ɪkˈsaɪtɪŋ/
safe /seɪf/
well-paid /ˌwel ˈpeɪd /
Other
after that /ˌɑːftə ˈðæt/
bridge /brɪdʒ/
customer /ˈkʌstəmə/
earn money /ˌɜːn ˈmʌni/
office /ˈɒfɪs/
road /rəʊd/
toy factory /ˈtɔɪ ˌfæktəri/

2.2
Say it!
She's super busy. /ʃiz ˌsuːpə ˈbɪzi/
I can manage. /ˌaɪ kən ˈmænɪdʒ/
Vocabulary
Make and do
do my homework /ˌduː maɪ ˈhəʊmwɜːk/
do the dishes /ˌduː ðə ˈdɪʃɪz/
do the shopping /ˌduː ðə ˈʃɒpɪŋ/
do your best /ˌduː jə ˈbest/
make a mess /ˌmeɪk ə ˈmes/
make breakfast / lunch / dinner /ˌmeɪk ˈbrekfəst / ˈlʌntʃ / ˈdɪnə/
make your bed /ˌmeɪk jə ˈbed/
Other
apron /ˈeɪprən/
chillies /ˈtʃɪliz/
come round /ˌkʌm ˈraʊnd/
dream come true /ˌdriːm kʌm ˈtruː/
gentleman /ˈdʒentlmən/
gloves /glʌvz/
mix up /ˌmɪks ˈʌp/
peppers /ˈpepəz/
spicy /ˈspaɪsi/
waitress /ˈweɪtrɪs/

2.3
Other
canoe /kəˈnuː/
dictionary /ˈdɪkʃənəri/
give up /ˌgɪv ˈʌp/
in my day /ˌɪn ˈmaɪ deɪ/
lost tribe /ˌlɒst ˈtraɪb/
motorboat /ˈməʊtəbəʊt/
out of battery /ˌaʊt əv ˈbætəri/
paddle /ˈpædl/
translate app /trænsˈleɪt æp/

2.4
Communication
Asking for advice
Can I ask your advice?
I need your advice.
What should I wear?

123

Word list

Giving advice
In my opinion, you shouldn't wear trainers.
What about wearing a white shirt?
Why don't you put on a tie?
You should look smart.
You shouldn't wear trainers.
Other
animal rescue centre /ˌænəməl ˈreskjuː ˌsentə/
by the way /ˌbaɪ ðə ˈweɪ/
clean the cages /ˌkliːn ðə ˈkeɪdʒɪz/
volunteer /ˌvɒlənˈtɪə/

2.5
Other
bitter /ˈbɪtə/
circus performer /ˈsɜːkəs pəˌfɔːmə/
circus school /ˈsɜːkəs skuːl/
creamy /ˈkriːmi/
disadvantage /ˌdɪsədˈvɑːntɪdʒ/
expert /ˈekspɜːt/
juggle /ˈdʒʌɡəl/
knives /naɪvz/
practise /ˈpræktɪs/
score /skɔː/
take a look at /ˌteɪk ə ˈlʊk æt/
taste /teɪst/
train /treɪn/

2.6
Vocabulary
Learning and exams
copy someone's work /ˌkɒpi ˌsʌmwʌnz ˈwɜːk/
do well / badly /ˌduː ˈwel / ˈbædli/
got a good / bad mark /ˌɡet ə ɡʊd / bæd ˈmɑːk/
hand in your homework /ˌhænd ɪn jə ˈhəʊmwɜːk/
pass / fail an exam /ˌpɑːs / ˌfeɪl ən ɪɡˈzæm/
revise for a test /rɪˈvaɪz fər ə ˈtest/
take an exam /ˌteɪk ən ɪɡˈzæm/
take notes /ˌteɪk ˈnəʊts/
Vocabulary Builder
Expressions with take
take a photo /ˌteɪk ə ˈfəʊtəʊ/
take an exam /ˌteɪk ən ɪɡˈzæm/
take medicine /ˌteɪk ˈmedsən/
take notes /ˌteɪk ˈnəʊts/
take the bus /ˌteɪk ðə ˈbʌs/
Other
enough /ɪˈnʌf/
successful /səkˈsesfəl/

2.7
Other
atmosphere /ˈætməsfɪə/
countryside /ˈkʌntrisaɪd/
funfair /ˈfʌnfeə/
playground /ˈpleɪɡraʊnd/
school club /ˈskuːl klʌb/
school trip /ˈskuːl trɪp/
trampoline /ˈtræmpəliːn/

Unit 3
That's exciting!

3.1
Vocabulary
Experiences
do a parachute jump /ˌduː ə ˈpærəʃuːt dʒʌmp/
go scuba diving /ˌɡəʊ ˈskuːbə ˌdaɪvɪŋ/
have a party /ˌhæv ə ˈpɑːti/
learn to ski /ˌlɜːn tə ˈskiː/
meet a famous person /ˌmiːt ə ˌfeɪməs ˈpɜːsən/
ride a camel /ˌraɪd ə ˈkæməl/
stay in a castle /ˌsteɪ ɪn ə ˈkɑːsəl/
win a competition /ˌwɪn ə ˌkɒmpəˈtɪʃən/
Other
go bungee jumping /ˌɡəʊ ˈbʌndʒi ˌdʒʌmpɪŋ/
look down at /ˌlʊk ˈdaʊn æt/
probably /ˈprɒbəbli/
ride in a hot-air balloon /ˌraɪd ɪn ə ˌhɒt ˈeə bəˌluːn/
win a prize /ˌwɪn ə ˈpraɪz/

3.2
Say it!
Follow me! /ˈfɒləʊ mi/
High five! /ˌhaɪ ˈfaɪv/
That's not fair. /ˌðæts nɒt ˈfeə/
Other
crash /kræʃ/
drive a go-kart /ˌdraɪv ə ˈɡəʊkɑːt/
extreme sports /ɪkˌstriːm ˈspɔːts/
go-karting track /ˈɡəʊ kɑːtɪŋ træk/
have an accident /ˌhæv ən ˈæksədənt/
helmet /ˈhelmɪt/
lap /læp/
loser /ˈluːzə/
skydiving /ˈskaɪˌdaɪvɪŋ/
race /reɪs/
terrified /ˈterɪfaɪd/

3.3
Other
ancient treasure /ˌeɪnʃənt ˈtreʒə/
break down /ˌbreɪk ˈdaʊn/
cave /keɪv/
desert /ˈdezət/
discover /dɪsˈkʌvə/
fill something with /ˈfɪl ˌsʌmθɪŋ wɪð/
put up a tent /ˌpʊt ʌp ə ˈtent/
weather forecast /ˈweðə ˌfɔːkɑːst/

3.4
Communication
Asking for instructions
How do I put the net on?
What do I have to do next?
What's the first step?
Giving instructions
Be careful.
Don't / Try not to kick the ball too hard.
Next put the goal upright.
Put this post here.
Ordering instructions
Before you begin, …
First, … Then, … Next, … Finally, …
Other
button /ˈbʌtn/
goal /ɡəʊl/

3.5
Vocabulary
Sports verbs
compete /kəmˈpiːt/
lose /luːz/
score /skɔː/
support /səˈpɔːt/
train /treɪn/
win /wɪn/
Other
at break time(s) /ət ˈbreɪk taɪmz/
however /haʊˈevə/
score a goal /ˌskɔːr ə ˈɡəʊl/

3.6
Vocabulary
Sports equipment
boots /buːts/
gloves /ɡlʌvz/
goggles /ˈɡɒɡəlz/
helmet /ˈhelmɪt/
hockey stick /ˈhɒki stɪk/
ice skates /ˈaɪs skeɪts/
rollerblades /ˈrəʊləbleɪdz/
skateboard /ˈskeɪtbɔːd/
skis /skiːz/
snorkel mask /ˈsnɔːkəl mɑːsk/
swimsuit /ˈswɪmsuːt/
tennis racket /ˈtenəs ˌrækət/
Other
ice rink /ˈaɪs rɪŋk/
mention /ˈmenʃən/
parachute /ˈpærəʃuːt/
skydive /ˈskaɪˌdaɪv/
speed /spiːd/

3.7
Other
be off to /ˌbi ˈɒf tə/
cable car /ˈkeɪbəl kɑː/
loads of things /ˌləʊdz əv ˈθɪŋz/
theme park /ˈθiːm pɑːk/

Get Culture
Extreme sports
athlete /ˈæθliːt/
champion /ˈtʃæmpiən/
connection /kəˈnekʃən/
destination /ˌdestəˈneɪʃən/
go climbing /ˌɡəʊ ˈklaɪmɪŋ/
hills /hɪlz/
on your own /ˌɒn jər ˈəʊn/
rowing /ˈrəʊɪŋ/
sailing /ˈseɪlɪŋ/
wetsuit /ˈwetsuːt/

Unit 4
A good story

4.1
Vocabulary
Types of films
action film /ˈækʃən fɪlm/
adventure film /ədˈventʃə fɪlm/
animation /ˌænəˈmeɪʃən/
comedy /ˈkɒmədi/
fantasy film /ˈfæntəsi fɪlm/
historical film /hɪˈstɒrɪkəl fɪlm/
horror film /ˈhɒrə fɪlm/
musical /ˈmjuːzɪkəl/
romantic comedy /rəʊˌmæntɪk ˈkɒmədi/
science fiction film /ˌsaɪəns ˈfɪkʃən fɪlm/
Types of books
adventure novel /ədˈventʃə ˌnɒvəl/
autobiography /ˌɔːtəbaɪˈɒɡrəfi/
cookbook /ˈkʊkbʊk/
fantasy novel /ˈfæntəsi ˌnɒvəl/
historical novel /hɪˈstɒrɪkəl ˌnɒvəl/
horror story /ˈhɒrə ˌstɔːri/
romance /rəʊˈmæns/
science fiction novel /ˌsaɪəns ˈfɪkʃən ˌnɒvəl/
Other
costumes /ˈkɒstʃuːmz/
donkey /ˈdɒŋki/
drawing /ˈdrɔːɪŋ/
dream of /ˈdriːm əv/
evil /ˈiːvəl/
fall in love with /ˌfɔːl ɪn ˈlʌv wɪð/
fight for / against /ˌfaɪt fɔː / əˈɡenst/
magic /ˈmædʒɪk/
monster /ˈmɒnstə/
recently /ˈriːsəntli/
rescue /ˈreskjuː/
soldier /ˈsəʊldʒə/
special effects /ˌspeʃəl ɪˈfekts/
story /ˈstɔːri/

4.2
Say it!
I don't think so. /ˌaɪ ˌdəʊnt ˈθɪŋk səʊ/
It's tricky! /ˌɪts ˈtrɪki/
Just looking. /ˌdʒəst ˈlʊkɪŋ/
What shall we get? /ˌwɒt ʃəl wi ˈɡet/
Other
for ages /fər ˈeɪdʒɪz/
have an argument /ˌhæv ən ˈɑːɡjəmənt/
lovely /ˈlʌvli/
primary school /ˈpraɪməri skuːl/
recipe /ˈresɪpi/
suggest /səˈdʒest/
vegetarian /ˌvedʒəˈteəriən/

4.3
Other
bone /bəʊn/
dinosaur /ˈdaɪnəsɔː/
discover /dɪˈskʌvə/
discovery /dɪsˈkʌvəri/
insect /ˈɪnsekt/
jeep /dʒiːp/
memory /ˈmeməri/
newspaper /ˈnjuːsˌpeɪpə/
page /peɪdʒ/
prehistoric /ˌpriːhɪˈstɒrɪk/
silver /ˈsɪlvə/
skeletons /ˈskelətənz/

4.4
Communication
Making apologies
Don't be mad (at me).
I'm sorry, I didn't mean to.
I'm sorry, I made a mistake.
It's all my fault.
Oh dear, I'm (really) sorry.
Sorry!
Accepting apologies
Don't worry about it.
Forget about it.
It doesn't matter.
It was an accident.
It's OK. It wasn't your fault.
Never mind.
Other
apologise /əˈpɒlədʒaɪz/
calm down /ˌkɑːm ˈdaʊn/
damage /ˈdæmɪdʒ/
do a puzzle /ˌduː ə ˈpʌzəl/
fly (n) /flaɪ/
instead /ɪnˈsted/

4.5
Vocabulary
Life stages
be born /ˌbi ˈbɔːn/
fall in love /ˌfɔːl ɪn ˈlʌv/
get a job /ˌɡet ə ˈdʒɒb/
get married /ˌɡet ˈmærid/
go to school/college /ˌɡəʊ tə ˈskuːl / ˈkɒlɪdʒ/
graduate (v) /ˈɡrædʒueɪt/
grow up /ˌɡrəʊ ˈʌp/
have children /ˌhæv ˈtʃɪldrən/
retire /rɪˈtaɪə/
Other
actually /ˈæktʃuəli/
adult /ˈædʌlt/
although /ɔːlˈðəʊ/
author /ˈɔːθə/
award /əˈwɔːd/
awesome /ˈɔːsəm/
bully (v) /ˈbʊli/

Word list

be based on /ˌbi ˈbeɪst ɒn/
best-selling /ˌbest ˈselɪŋ/
book review /ˈbʊk rɪˌvjuː/
cancer patient /ˈkænsə ˌpeɪʃənt/
luckily /ˈlʌkəli/
magazine /ˌmæɡəˈziːn/
teenager /ˈtiːneɪdʒə/
writer /ˈraɪtə/

4.6
Vocabulary
Film jobs
actor /ˈæktə/
actress /ˈæktrɪs/
cameraman /ˈkæmərəmən/
camerawoman /ˈkæmrəˌwʊmən/
costume designer /ˈkɒstjʊm dɪˌzaɪnə/
extra /ˈekstrə/
film director /ˈfɪlm dəˌrektə/
make-up artist /ˈmeɪkʌp ˌɑːtɪst/
scriptwriter /ˈskrɪptˌraɪtə/

Vocabulary Builder
Verbs followed by a preposition
apply for /əˈplaɪ fə/
complain about /kəmˈpleɪn əˌbaʊt/
dream about /ˈdriːm əˌbaʊt/
laugh at /ˈlɑːf ət/
prepare for /prɪˈpeə fə/
revise for /rɪˈvaɪz fə/
shout at /ˈʃaʊt ət/
smile at /ˈsmaɪl ət/
wait for /ˈweɪt fə/
worry about /ˈwʌri əˌbaʊt/

Other
appearance /əˈpɪərəns/
film set /ˈfɪlm set/
make-up /ˈmeɪkʌp/
take care of /ˌteɪk ˈkeə əv/

4.7
Other
amazing /əˈmeɪzɪŋ/
boring /ˈbɔːrɪŋ/
character /ˈkærəktə/
exciting /ɪkˈsaɪtɪŋ/
fantastic /fænˈtæstɪk/
funny /ˈfʌni/
great /ɡreɪt/
joke /dʒəʊk/
recommend /ˌrekəˈmend/
silly /ˈsɪli/

Unit 5
Don't stop the music!

5.1
Vocabulary
Music styles
classical /ˈklæsɪkəl/
folk /fəʊk/
heavy metal /ˌhevi ˈmetl/
hip hop /ˈhɪp hɒp/
jazz /dʒæz/
Latin /ˈlætɪn/
pop /pɒp/
punk /pʌŋk/
rock /rɒk/
techno /ˈteknəʊ/

Instruments
cello /ˈtʃeləʊ/
drums /drʌmz/
electric guitar /ɪˌlektrɪk ɡɪˈtɑː/
flute /fluːt/
keyboards /ˈkiːbɔːdz/
piano /piˈænəʊ/
saxophone /ˈsæksəfəʊn/
trumpet /ˈtrʌmpɪt/
violin /ˌvaɪəˈlɪn/

Music collocations
give a concert /ˌɡɪv ə ˈkɒnsət/
go on tour /ˌɡəʊ ɒn ˈtʊə/
have an audition /ˌhæv ən ɔːˈdɪʃən/
join a band /ˌdʒɔɪn ə ˈbænd/
practise an instrument /ˌpræktəs ən ˈɪnstrəmənt/
record an album /ˌreˌkɔːd ən ˈælbəm/
sign an autograph /ˌsaɪn ən ˈɔːtəɡrɑːf/
write / compose a song /ˌraɪt / kəmˌpəʊz ə ˈsɒŋ/

Other
abroad /əˈbrɔːd/

5.2
Say it!
I suppose so. /aɪ səˈpəʊz səʊ/
That's a relief. /ˌðæts ə rɪˈliːf/
What a nightmare! /ˌwɒt ə ˈnaɪtmeə/

Other
audience /ˈɔːdiəns/
definitely /ˈdefɪnətli/
drum kit /ˈdrʌm kɪt/
drummer /ˈdrʌmə/
headache /ˈhedeɪk/
I bet… /aɪ ˈbet/
I have an idea. /aɪ həv ən aɪˈdɪə/
nervous /ˈnɜːvəs/
take part /ˌteɪk ˈpɑːt/
winner /ˈwɪnə/
You rock! /juː ˈrɒk/

5.3
Vocabulary
Crime
criminal /ˈkrɪmɪnəl/
detective /dɪˈtektɪv/
fingerprint /ˈfɪŋɡəˌprɪnt/
footprint /ˈfʊtˌprɪnt/
robbery /ˈrɒbəri/
thief /θiːf/
thieves /θiːvz/
witness /ˈwɪtnəs/

Other
belong /bɪˈlɒŋ/
commit a crime /kəˌmɪt ə ˈkraɪm/
escape from /ɪˈskeɪp frəm/
leave a mark /ˌliːv ə ˈmɑːk/
master /ˈmɑːstə/
prison /ˈprɪzən/
steal /stiːl/

5.4
Communication
Asking about plans
Have you got any plans for the weekend?
What are you up to in the holidays?
What are your plans for Saturday?

Talking about plans
I can't wait to see my cousins.
I'm going to stay with friends.
I'm really looking forward to it / visiting Manchester.

Reacting
Lucky you!
That sounds amazing / great / like fun.

Other
Can I have a go? /ˌkæn aɪ həv ə ˈɡəʊ/
great-grandma /ˌɡreɪt ˈɡrænmɑː/

5.5
Other
appear /əˈpɪə/
based on /ˈbeɪst ɒn/
Cinderella /ˌsɪndəˈrelə/
compose /kəmˈpəʊz/
on stage /ɒn ˈsteɪdʒ/
opera /ˈɒprə/
perform /pəˈfɔːm/
piece /piːs/
proud of /ˈpraʊd əv/
skipping rope /ˈskɪpɪŋ rəʊp/
tune /tjuːn/

5.6
Vocabulary
Personal qualities
confidence /ˈkɒnfɪdəns/
determination /dɪˌtɜːməˈneɪʃən/
good looks /ˌɡʊd ˈlʊks/
hard work /ˌhɑːd ˈwɜːk/
intelligence /ɪnˈtelɪdʒəns/
style /staɪl/
talent /ˈtælənt/

Vocabulary Builder
Adjectives from nouns
confident /ˈkɒnfɪdənt/
determined /dɪˈtɜːmɪnd/
good-looking /ˌɡʊd ˈlʊkɪŋ/
hard-working /ˌhɑːd ˈwɜːkɪŋ/
intelligent /ɪnˈtelɪdʒənt/
stylish /ˈstaɪlɪʃ/
talented /ˈtæləntɪd/

Other
contestant /kənˈtestənt/
Don't miss tonight's show! /ˌdəʊnt ˌmɪs təˌnaɪts ˈʃəʊ/
judge /dʒʌdʒ/
receive a recording contract /rɪˌsiːv ə rɪˌkɔːdɪŋ ˈkɒntrækt/
succeed /səkˈsiːd/
viewer /ˈvjuːə/
vote /vəʊt/

5.7
Other
coach /kəʊtʃ/
find out /ˌfaɪnd ˈaʊt/
I would be grateful. /ˌaɪ wəd bi ˈɡreɪtfəl/
whitewater rafting /ˌwaɪtwɔːtə ˈrɑːftɪŋ/

Get Culture
Festivals
attend /əˈtend/
capital /ˈkæpɪtəl/
carnival /ˈkɑːnəvəl/
collection /kəˈlekʃən/
fire eaters /ˈfaɪə ˌiːtəz/
firework show /ˈfaɪəwɜːk ʃəʊ/
latest /ˈleɪtɪst/
parade /pəˈreɪd/

Unit 6
Protect the planet

6.1
Vocabulary
Wild animals
eagle /ˈiːɡəl/
fox /fɒks/
gorilla /ɡəˈrɪlə/
leopard /ˈlepəd/
lizard /ˈlɪzəd/
panda /ˈpændə/
penguin /ˈpeŋɡwɪn/
polar bear /ˈpəʊlə beə/
rhino /ˈraɪnəʊ/
turtle /ˈtɜːtl/

Environment verbs
cut down /ˌkʌt ˈdaʊn/
hunt /hʌnt/
look after /ˌlʊk ˈɑːftə/
pollute /pəˈluːt/
protect /prəˈtekt/
recycle /ˌriːˈsaɪkəl/
save /seɪv/
throw away /ˌθrəʊ əˈweɪ/

Other
fly (v) /flaɪ/
horn /hɔːn/
hunter /ˈhʌntə/
percent /pəˈsent/
solution /səˈluːʃən/
spot /spɒt/
the North Pole /ðə ˌnɔːθ ˈpəʊl/
weigh /weɪ/

6.2
Say it!
Relax! /rɪˈlæks/
That's weird. /ˌðæts ˈwɪəd/

Other
bin /bɪn/
bag /bæɡ/
challenge /ˈtʃæləndʒ/
chewing gum /ˈtʃuːɪŋ ɡʌm/
clean-up /ˈkliːnʌp/
complain /kəmˈpleɪn/
disgusting /dɪsˈɡʌstɪŋ/
energy /ˈenədʒi/
haircut /ˈheəkʌt/
pick up /ˌpɪk ˈʌp/
reuse /ˌriːˈjuːz/
rucksack /ˈrʌksæk/
waste /weɪst/
wildlife /ˈwaɪldlaɪf/

6.3
Other
cave /keɪv/
the Himalayas /ðə ˌhɪməˈleɪəz/
sausage /ˈsɒsɪdʒ/
run away /ˌrʌn əˈweɪ/
Yeti /ˈjeti/

6.4
Communication
Persuading
Come on, it's important / you'll enjoy it!
If you come, I'll buy you a smoothie.
You really should come. / We really should go.
You won't regret it!

Responding
I suppose so.
I'll think about it.
I'm not sure.
It's a deal.
Maybe you're right.

Other
afterwards /ˈɑːftəwədz/
air pollution /ˈeə pəˌluːʃən/
Do you fancy coming with us? /ˌduː jə ˌfænsi ˈkʌmɪŋ wɪð əs/
make a difference /ˌmeɪk ə ˈdɪfərəns/
placard /ˈplækɑːd/
protest (n) /ˈprəʊtest/
town hall /ˌtaʊn ˈhɔːl/

6.5
Other
arrive /əˈraɪv/
boat /bəʊt/
empty /ˈempti/
exactly /ɪɡˈzæktli/
glue /ɡluː/
huge /hjuːdʒ/
nuts /nʌts/

Word list

sail through /ˌseɪl ˈθruː/
survive /səˈvaɪv/
tonne /tʌn/
voyage /ˈvɔɪ-ɪdʒ/
wave /weɪv/
whale /weɪl/

6.6
Vocabulary
Natural events
drought /draʊt/
earthquake /ˈɜːθkweɪk/
flood /flʌd/
forest fire /ˈfɒrəst ˌfaɪə/
thunderstorm /ˈθʌndəstɔːm/
tornado /tɔːˈneɪdəʊ/
tsunami /tsʊˈnɑːmi/
volcanic eruption /vɒlˌkænɪk ɪˈrʌpʃən/

Vocabulary Builder
Big numbers
hundred /ˈhʌndrəd/
thousand /ˈθaʊzənd/
million /ˈmɪljən/

Other
damage /ˈdæmɪdʒ/
furniture /ˈfɜːnɪtʃə/
lightning /ˈlaɪtnɪŋ/
thunder /ˈθʌndə/

6.7
Other
less /les/
reduce /rɪˈdʒuːs/
tap /tæp/
tip /tɪp/
turn off /ˌtɜːn ˈɒf/

Unit 7
Material world

7.1
Vocabulary
Materials
cotton /ˈkɒtn/
glass /glɑːs/
gold /ɡəʊld/
leather /ˈleðə/
metal /ˈmetl/
paper /ˈpeɪpə/
plastic /ˈplæstɪk/
silver /ˈsɪlvə/
wood /wʊd/
wool /wʊl/

Vocabulary
Adjectives to describe objects
hard /hɑːd/
heavy /ˈhevi/
light /laɪt/
shiny /ˈʃaɪni/
soft /sɒft/
strong /strɒŋ/
transparent /trænˈspærənt/

Other
company /ˈkʌmpəni/
doll's house /ˈdɒlz haʊs/
phone case /ˈfəʊn keɪs/

7.2
Say it!
Check this out! /ˌtʃek ðɪs ˈaʊt/
You're kidding me! /jə ˈkɪdɪŋ mi/
Trust me! /ˈtrʌst mi/

Other
chemicals /ˈkemɪkəlz/
cocoa beans /ˈkəʊkəʊ biːnz/
deliver /dɪˈlɪvə/
design (v) /dɪˈzaɪn/
download /ˌdaʊnˈləʊd/
dry (v) /draɪ/
florist's shop /ˈflɒrɪsts ʃɒp/
machine /məˈʃiːn/
original /əˈrɪdʒənəl/
oven /ˈʌvən/
parcel /ˈpɑːsəl/
sand /sænd/
shooting star /ˈʃuːtɪŋ stɑː/
spelling mistake /ˈspelɪŋ məˌsteɪk/
upload /ʌpˈləʊd/

7.3
Vocabulary
Verbs of discovery and creativity
compose /kəmˈpəʊz/
design /dɪˈzaɪn/
discover /dɪsˈkʌvə/
invent /ɪnˈvent/
paint /peɪnt/
produce /prəˈdjuːs/

Other
astronomer /əˈstrɒnəmə/
copy /ˈkɒpi/
emperor /ˈempərə/
musician /mjuːˈzɪʃən/
selfie stick /ˈselfi stɪk/
take a selfie /ˌteɪk ə ˈselfi/
valuable /ˈvæljuəbəl/
vase /vɑːz/

7.4
Communication
Asking for clarification
Can you repeat that, please?
Could you explain, please?
Sorry, can you say that again?
What do you mean?

Checking understanding
Are you following me?
Did you get that?
Did you understand that?

Other
at the top of /ət ðə ˈtɒp əv/
camera app /ˈkæmərə æp/
connect /kəˈnekt/
drone /drəʊn/
enter /ˈentə/
fruit bowl /ˈfruːt bəʊl/
introduce /ˌɪntrəˈdjuːs/
password /ˈpɑːswɜːd/
watch out /ˌwɒtʃ ˈaʊt/

7.5
Other
all the time /ˌɔːl ðə ˈtaɪm/
charity /ˈtʃærəti/
colourful /ˈkʌləfəl/
cover /ˈkʌvə/
create /kriˈeɪt/
exhibition /ˌeksəˈbɪʃən/
everyday (adj) /ˈevrideɪ/
funky /ˈfʌŋki/
glue together /ˌɡluː təˈɡeðə/
knit /nɪt/
on wheels /ˌɒn ˈwiːəlz/
raise money /ˌreɪz ˈmʌni/
street sign /ˈstriːt saɪn/
tiny /ˈtaɪni/
unusual /ʌnˈjuːʒəl/
village /ˈvɪlɪdʒ/
wonderland /ˈwʌndəlænd/

7.6
Vocabulary
Technology verbs
charge /tʃɑːdʒ/
click on /ˌklɪk ˈɒn/
connect /kəˈnekt/
download /ˌdaʊnˈləʊd/
switch off /ˌswɪtʃ ˈɒf/
switch on /ˌswɪtʃ ˈɒn/
turn down /ˌtɜːn ˈdaʊn/
turn up /ˌtɜːn ˈʌp/
upload /ʌpˈləʊd/

Vocabulary Builder
Phrasal verbs with *up* and *down*
cool down /ˌkuːl ˈdaʊn/
slow down /ˌsləʊ ˈdaʊn/
speed up /ˌspiːd ˈʌp/
turn down /ˌtɜːn ˈdaʊn/
turn up /ˌtɜːn ˈʌp/
warm up /ˌwɔːm ˈʌp/

Other
give directions /ˌɡɪv daɪˈrekʃənz/
heating /ˈhiːtɪŋ/
volume /ˈvɒljuːm/

7.7
Other
high-tech materials /ˌhaɪtek məˈtɪərɪəlz/
popular /ˈpɒpjələ/
slice /slaɪs/

Get Culture
American cities
apple pie /ˈæpəl paɪ/
as a result /ˌəz ə rɪˈzʌlt/
bay /beɪ/
cross /krɒs/
construction worker /kənˈstrʌkʃən ˌwɜːkə/
destroy /dɪˈstrɔɪ/
ferry /ˈferi/
firework displays /ˈfaɪəwɜːk dɪˌspleɪz/
gate /ɡeɪt/
lamppost /ˈlæmp-pəʊst/
landmark /ˈlændmɑːk/
octopus /ˈɒktəpəs/
safety net /ˈseɪfti net/
situated /ˈsɪtjueɪtɪd/
the Statue of Liberty /ðə ˌstætʃuː əv ˈlɪbəti/
thick fog /ˌθɪk ˈfɒɡ/
tower /ˈtaʊə/

Unit 8
That's life

8.1
Vocabulary
Relationships and conflicts
argue about something /ˈɑːɡjuː əˌbaʊt ˌsʌmθɪŋ/
argue with someone /ˈɑːɡjuː wɪð ˌsʌmwʌn/
be friends with someone /ˌbi ˈfrendz wɪð ˌsʌmwʌn/
be in a bad / good mood /ˌbi ɪn ə bæd / ɡʊd ˈmuːd/
be rude / nice to someone /ˌbi ˈruːd / ˈnaɪs tə ˌsʌmwʌn/
forgive someone /fəˈɡɪv ˌsʌmwʌn/
get angry with someone /ˌɡet ˈæŋɡri wɪð ˌsʌmwʌn/
get on with someone /ˌɡet ˈɒn wɪð ˌsʌmwʌn/
say sorry to someone /ˌseɪ ˈsɒri tə ˌsʌmwʌn/
shout at someone /ˈʃaʊt ət ˌsʌmwʌn/

Other
borrow /ˈbɒrəʊ/
household chores /ˌhaʊshəʊld ˈtʃɔːz/
relatives /ˈrelətɪvz/
strict /strɪkt/
untidy /ʌnˈtaɪdi/
voice /vɔɪs/

8.2
Say it!
Calm down! /ˌkɑːm ˈdaʊn/
It's so unfair! /ˌɪts səʊ ʌnˈfeə/
What's the point? /ˌwɒts ðə ˈpɔɪnt/

Other
change your mind /ˌtʃeɪndʒ jə ˈmaɪnd/
in progress /ˌɪn ˈprəʊɡres/
social media account /ˌsəʊʃəl ˈmiːdiə əˌkaʊnt/
staff room /ˈstɑːf ruːm/
strawberries /ˈstrɔːbəriz/
treat /triːt/

8.3
Other
behave badly /bɪˌheɪv ˈbædli/
downstairs /ˌdaʊnˈsteəz/
drop /drɒp/
explore /ɪkˈsplɔː/
knock at the door /ˌnɒk ət ðə ˈdɔː/
relax /rɪˈlæks/
secretly /ˈsiːkrətli/

8.4
Communication
Asking questions
What's the matter?
What's up?
What's wrong?

Sympathising
I'm so sorry.
Poor you!
That's a pity!
That's a shame!
That's disappointing.
What a pity!
What a shame!

Encouraging
Cheer up!
Well done!

Other
absent /ˈæbsənt/
exam results /ɪɡˈzæm rɪˌzʌlts/

8.5
Other
feel sorry for someone /ˌfiːl ˈsɒri fə ˌsʌmwʌn/
messy /ˈmesi/
nightmare /ˈnaɪtmeə/
It's no big deal! /ˌɪts nəʊ ˌbɪɡ ˈdiːl/
It's up to me. /ˌɪts ʌp tə ˈmiː/
share /ʃeə/
study space /ˈstʌdi speɪs/
wardrobe /ˈwɔːdrəʊb/

8.6
Vocabulary
Feelings
annoyed /əˈnɔɪd/
depressed /dɪˈprest/
disappointed /ˌdɪsəˈpɔɪntɪd/
embarrassed /ɪmˈbærəst/
exhausted /ɪɡˈzɔːstɪd/
furious /ˈfjʊəriəs/
jealous /ˈdʒeləs/
terrified /ˈterɪfaɪd/
upset /ʌpˈset/

Other
bark /bɑːk/
bully (v, n) /ˈbʊli/
call someone bad names /ˌkɔːl ˌsʌmwʌn ˌbæd ˈneɪmz/

Irregular verbs

Infinitive	Past Simple	Past Participle
be /bɪ:/	was/were /wɒz/wɜ:/	been /bɪ:n/
become /bɪˈkʌm/	became /bɪˈkeɪm/	become /bɪˈkʌm/
break /breɪk/	broke /brəʊk/	broken /ˈbrəʊkən/
bring /brɪŋ/	brought /brɔ:t/	brought /brɔ:t/
build /bɪld/	built /bɪlt/	built /bɪlt/
buy /baɪ/	bought /bɔ:t/	bought /bɔ:t/
catch /kætʃ/	caught /kɔ:t/	caught /kɔ:t/
choose /tʃu:z/	chose /tʃəʊz/	chosen /ˈtʃəʊzn/
come /kʌm/	came /keɪm/	come /kʌm/
cost /kɒst/	cost /kɒst/	cost /kɒst/
cut /kʌt/	cut /kʌt/	cut /kʌt/
do /du:/	did /dɪd/	done /dʌn/
draw /drɔ:/	drew /dru:/	drawn /drɔ:n/
dream /drɪ:m/	dreamt /dremt/	dreamt /dremt/
	dreamed /drɪ:md/	dreamed /drɪ:md/
drink /drɪŋk/	drank /dræŋk/	drunk /drʌŋk/
drive /draɪv/	drove /drəʊv/	driven /ˈdrɪvn/
eat /ɪ:t/	ate /et, eɪt/	eaten /ˈɪ:tn/
fall /fɔ:l/	fell /fel/	fallen /ˈfɔ:ln/
feed /fɪ:d/	fed /fed/	fed /fed/
feel /fɪ:l/	felt /felt/	felt /felt/
fight /faɪt/	fought /fɔ:t/	fought /fɔ:t/
find /faɪnd/	found /faʊnd/	found /faʊnd/
fly /flaɪ/	flew /flu:/	flown /fləʊn/
forget /fəˈget/	forgot /fəˈgɒt/	forgotten /fəˈgɒtn/
forgive /fəˈgɪv/	forgave /fəˈgeɪv/	forgiven /fəˈgɪvn/
get /get/	got /gɒt/	got /gɒt/
give /gɪv/	gave /geɪv/	given /ˈgɪvn/
go /gəʊ/	went /went/	gone /gɒn/
grow /grəʊ/	grew /gru:/	grown /grəʊn/
hang /hæŋ/	hung /hʌŋ/	hung /hʌŋ/
have /hæv/	had /hæd/	had /hæd/
hear /hɪə/	heard /hɜ:d/	heard /hɜ:d/
hurt /hɜ:t/	hurt /hɜ:t/	hurt /hɜ:t/
keep /kɪ:p/	kept /kept/	kept /kept/
know /nəʊ/	knew /nju:/	known /nəʊn/
learn /lɜ:n/	learnt /lɜ:nt/	learnt /lɜ:nt/
	learned /lɜ:nd/	learned /lɜ:nd/
leave /lɪ:v/	left /left/	left /left/
lend /lend/	lent /lent/	lent /lent/
lie /laɪ/	lay /leɪ/	lain /leɪn/
lose /lu:z/	lost /lɒst/	lost /lɒst/
make /meɪk/	made /meɪd/	made /meɪd/
mean /mɪ:n/	meant /ment/	meant /ment/
meet /mɪ:t/	met /met/	met /met/
pay /peɪ/	paid /peɪd/	paid /peɪd/
put /pʊt/	put /pʊt/	put /pʊt/
read /rɪ:d/	read /red/	read /red/
ride /raɪd/	rode /rəʊd/	ridden /ˈrɪdn/
run /rʌn/	ran /ræn/	run /rʌn/
say /seɪ/	said /sed/	said /sed/
see /sɪ:/	saw /sɔ:/	seen /sɪ:n/
sell /sel/	sold /səʊld/	sold /səʊld/
send /send/	sent /sent/	sent /sent/
set /set/	set /set/	set /set/
sing /sɪŋ/	sang /sæŋ/	sung /sʌŋ/
sit /sɪt/	sat /sæt/	sat /sæt/
sleep /slɪ:p/	slept /slept/	slept /slept/
speak /spɪ:k/	spoke /spəʊk/	spoken /ˈspəʊkən/
spend /spend/	spent /spent/	spent /spent/
spell /spel/	spelt /spelt/	spelt /spelt/
	spelled /speld/	spelled /speld/
stand /stænd/	stood /stʊd/	stood /stʊd/
steal /stɪ:l/	stole /stəʊl/	stolen /ˈstəʊlən/
swim /swɪm/	swam /swæm/	swum /swʌm/
take /teɪk/	took /tʊk/	taken /ˈteɪkən/
teach /tɪ:tʃ/	taught /tɔ:t/	taught /tɔ:t/
tell /tel/	told /təʊld/	told /təʊld/
think /θɪŋk/	thought /θɔ:t/	thought /θɔ:t/
throw /θrəʊ/	threw /θru:/	thrown /θrəʊn/
understand /ˌʌndəˈstænd/	understood /ˌʌndəˈstʊd/	understood /ˌʌndəˈstʊd/
wake /weɪk/	woke /wəʊk/	woken /ˈwəʊkən/
wear /weə/	wore /wɔ:/	worn /wɔ:n/
win /wɪn/	won /wʌn/	won /wʌn/
write /raɪt/	wrote /rəʊt/	written /ˈrɪtn/

Extra reference

Student B activities

Unit 3 Lesson 3.4, Page 44, Exercise 5

1. Student A wants to know how to send a text message. Give Student A instructions. Use the phrases below in the correct order.

   > click on 'send'   write a message
   > open a messaging app on your phone
   > select a contact from your contacts list

   First, open … . Then, … Next, … Finally, …

2. You want to know how to print a document. Ask Student A for instructions.

   How do I print a document? What's the first step? What do I have to do next?

3. Student A wants to know how to make a pizza. Give Student A instructions. Use the phrases below in the correct order.

   > serve your pizza   add cheese and ham
   > put your pizza in the hot oven for twenty minutes
   > put tomato sauce on the pizza base
   > buy pizza base, tomato sauce, cheese and ham

   Before you begin, buy … Then, … Next, … Finally, …

4. You want to know how to make a smoothie. Ask Student A for instructions.

   How do I make a smoothie? What do I have to buy? What's the first step? What do I have to do next?

Unit 4 Lesson 4.4, Page 58, Exercise 5

1. You are a teacher and Student A is your student. He/She is thirty minutes late for school and it's the day of an exam. He/She apologises for being late. Accept Student A's apologies.

   It's OK. It wasn't your fault. Now, please hurry up.

2. Student A is your friend. You've forgotten about his/her birthday and about the party too! Apologise to Student A.

   *Oh dear! I'm really sorry … I forgot about …
   I didn't mean to … Now I would like to invite you …*

3. Student A is your daughter/son. He/She hasn't made his/her bed or tidied his/her room and now he/she apologises. Accept Student A's apologies.

   It's OK … Never mind … You can do it now …

4. Student A is your aunt/uncle. You borrowed a book from him/her and your dog ate it. Apologise to Student A.

   I'm really sorry … My dog … I'll buy you a new one …

Unit 6 Lesson 6.4, Page 86, Exercise 4

1. Student A suggests watching a film about mountain gorillas. You're not sure because you have to write an English essay.

   I'm not sure. I have to … Maybe you're right, but I really should … It's a deal!

2. You're going to make and sell cakes tomorrow to collect money for your local hospital. It's important because the hospital needs new equipment and the money can help to save lives. Suggest that Student A should help you. Promise him/her to go shopping with him/her later.

   *We're going to … Could you help me?
   You really should … It's important, because …
   You won't regret it! If you come, I'll …*

Unit 7 Lesson 7.4, Page 100, Exercise 5

1. Student A is your son/daughter. You want to download an app but you need some help.

   *How do you download an app?
   What do you mean?
   Could you explain, please?*

2. Student A is your grandparent and he/she wants to send you an email. He asks you for your email address. Make sure he/she has written it correctly.

   *My email address is … Are you following me?
   Did you get that?*

Answers

Unit 8 Lesson 8.1, Page 109, Exercise 7

How well do you get on with your family?

Mostly as: You get on really well with your family. You're never rude, you don't argue about household chores and you are always in a good mood. But remember, sometimes you can argue with your parents or your brother or sister – if there is a good reason!

Mostly bs: You get on quite well with your family. You are usually in a good mood, but it depends on the situation. You argue if you feel you're right!

Mostly cs: You don't really get on well with your family. You often get angry, you're often in a bad mood and you never say sorry. Try to find things you like doing together and try to be nicer!